SCRIPTURE IN THE THOUGHT OF SØREN KIERKEGAARD

L. JOSEPH ROSAS, III

BROADMAN & HOLMAN PUBLISHERS

Nashville, Tennessee

4216-24
0-8054-1624-2

Dewey Decimal Classification: 220.6
Subject Heading: BIBLE / / CRITICISM,
INTERPRETATION, ETC.
Library of Congress Card Catalog Number: 93-15865
Printed in the United States of America

Library of Congress Cataloging-in-Publication Data
Rosas, L. Joseph, 1953—
    Scripture in the thought of Søren Kierkegaard / L. Joseph
Rosas III
        p. cm.
    Includes bibliographical references.
    ISBN 0-8054-1624-2
    1. Kierkegaard, Søren, 1813-1855. 2. Bible—Philosophy—
History—19th century. 3. Hermeneutics—History—19th
century. 4.Bible—Inspiration—History of doctrines—19th
century. I. Title.

B4378.B52R67   1994
198'.9—dc20   93-15865
                                                         CIP

Contents

1

Kierkegaard in Context

Søren Kierkegaard is one of the most enigmatic philosophers and religious thinkers of the modern era. His ideas have greatly influenced philosophy of religion and Christian theology. Pelikan called him the "first Christian philosopher to develop a critical philosophy in the truest sense of the word."[1] Barth appreciated his attack upon "all speculation which blurred the infinite qualitative difference between God and man."[2] Brunner praised Kierkegaard as "the greatest Christian thinker of modern times."[3]

Kierkegaard has influenced twentieth-century theology, and as a philosopher he is regarded as the father of both Christian and non-Christian philosophical existentialism. He influenced non-Christians like Heidegger and Sartre, and many of his concerns are indirectly echoed in Nietzsche, Feuerbach, and Marx. Psychology, literature, and the arts have also felt his influence. Yet Brita Stendahl has observed that no discipline fully claims him as its own.[4] Indeed, Kierkegaard remains as controversial today as he was during his lifetime.[5]

Kierkegaard's name is almost a synonym for *existentialism*, but his concerns were not limited to philosophical issues. The later Kierkegaard was a self-consciously Christian writer. He sought to protest against and correct both the "disarray and confusion which was plaguing the discourse of Christians."[6] He also sought to "edify" true Christianity and to oppose Christendom.[7]

Kierkegaard's Four Crises

A complete Kierkegaard biography is beyond the scope of this study. Almost every introduction to Kierkegaard's works contains a biographical sketch. Radically divergent biographical interpretations of his life are available.[8] John William Angell observed:

> Many have pointed out the outward facts of his life can be briefly told and that they contain little that is unusual or indicative of special importance. However, there can be no doubt that those seemingly insignificant events were decisive for him.[9]

Stendahl agreed, noting that "[Kierkegaard] cleverly organized his material so that it came to look that way."[10] Kierkegaard himself highlighted four significant crises of his life and repeatedly returned to these in his personal writings. These are more important in understanding his thought than is normally the case with the autobiographical statements of most philosophers. Yet even the *Journals and Papers* cannot simply be interpreted as the "real Kierkegaard." Rather, Kierkegaard skillfully "uses" his own life as a creative paradigm for understanding the nature of personal existence.[11] Indeed, S.K., via his *persona*, became a "witness to the truth."[12]

Relationship to Father

Michael Pedersen Kierkegaard was born December 12, 1756, the youngest child of a poverty-stricken family living in the West Jutland heaths, a remote region of Denmark. The family had been tenant farmers of Church-owned property, hence the surname "Kierkegaard" (then written "Kirkegaard" and "Kjerkegaard"), which means "church yard" or "grave yard." As a boy he cursed God, an experience that provoked great guilt and a religious preoccupation that colored the rest of his life. In 1846, years after his father's death, Kierkegaard observed:

> How appalling for the man who, as a lad watching sheep in the Jutland heath, suffering painfully, hungry and exhausted,

once stood on a hill and cursed God—and the man was unable to forget it when he was eighty-two years old.[13]

In the fall of 1768, at the age of 11, M. P. Kierkegaard was rescued from this life of hardship by an uncle, Neils Anderson Seding. Seding, a licensed hosier, was a traveling salesman of woolen goods who later opened his own shop. By 1780 Michael Pedersen Kierkegaard had acquired his own license as a hosier. He eventually built a large clothing and dry goods business. Through the development of foreign trade, as a wholesale grocer, and through numerous successful investments, he became very wealthy and retired at age forty to devote the rest of his life to study, religion, and family.

In 1794 M. P. Kierkegaard married a Jutland native, Kristine Nielsdatter Royen. She died childless of pneumonia two years later. The widower married his household servant, also a Jutlander, Ane Sorendatter Lund (1768-1834) and in less than five months their first child was born. This event, coupled with his childhood cursing of God, intensified the morbid religious guilt and melancholy of the elder Kierkegaard. There were seven children born to the Kierkegaard family, the last of whom was Søren Aabye.

Søren A. Kierkegaard was born in Copenhagen, Denmark, on May 5, 1813, when his father was fifty-six years old. The father's religious piety, discipline in finance, and deep melancholy dominated the home. In 1843 Kierkegaard alluded to the atmosphere of his childhood home:

> I could perhaps reproduce in a novel called "The Mysterious Family" the tragedy of my childhood, the terrifying secret elucidation of the religious which a fearful presentiment gave me, which my imagination hammered out, and my offense at the religious. At the outset it should be thoroughly patriarchal and idyllic, so that no one would have any inkling before the words suddenly appeared and gave a terrifying explanation of everything.[14]

The family was plagued by both physical and psychological instability. Only two of the children lived past age thirty-four. Two children died before Søren was nine. His father was convinced that he had been allowed to prosper in order to suffer like Job, and to have everything taken away from him because of his sins. He believed that he would outlive all of his children, a conviction that Søren apparently shared. Søren's brother Peter was forced to resign his position as bishop because of emotional and physical difficulties, and Peter's son even spent some time in an asylum.

It seems strange that Kierkegaard never made any description or mention of his mother in his writings. It has been widely accepted that his mother occupied little more than a servant's role within the home and was of relative unimportance in Kierkegaard's life. However, that her death in 1834 affected him painfully is attested by H. L. Martensen's *At mit Levnet* (1883). Martenson's mother told him that she had never seen a person so deeply grieved as Kierkegaard was by his mother's death.[15] Stendahl suggests that Kierkegaard did not mention his mother in his writings because the relationship remained for the most part in his private memory. "To record it would have been 'gossip.'"[16] The apparently happy disposition of his mother could not offset the religious guilt and depression which dominated the Kierkegaard men. Kierkegaard noted:

> As a child I was eternally and seriously brought up in Christianity. Humanly speaking, it was a crazy upbringing. Already in my earliest childhood I broke down under the grave impression which the melancholy old man who laid it upon me himself sank under. A child—what a crazy thing—travestied as an old man! Frightful![17]

In numerous places Kierkegaard described how this morbid emphasis on religious suffering affected his childhood. One of the more vivid images that remained with him in later years was a picture of Christ on the cross, the subject of mass derision. That picture was intentionally placed among his toys by his father.[18] The idea of Christ against the world became increasingly significant for Kierkegaard. Thompson sees the picture of Christ in isolation from the world as a motif that would influence how Kierkegaard would see his own existence.[19] Late in life Kierkegaard wrote:

> Already as a small child I was told—and as solemnly as possible—that "the crowds" spit upon Christ, who was in fact the truth, [*in margin*: that *they* spit on Christ, that *the* crowd

("those who passed by") spit upon Him and said: Fie on you].
This I have hid deep in my heart [*penciled in margin*: even
though there have been moments, yes, times, when I seemed
to have forgotten it, it has always come back to me as my first
thought]. In order to conceal the fact that I hid this thought
deep in my soul, I have even concealed it under the most
opposite exterior, for I was afraid that I would forget it too
soon, that it might would be tricked out of me and be like a
blank cartridge. This thought. . . is my life. . . . and if I forgot everything, I do not forget . . . what was said to me as a
child, and the impression it made on the child.[20]

Kierkegaard was trained in the use of his imagination and
intellect as a child. Father and son would often take fantasy
walks, pacing back and forth in the drawing room. They
would meet friends and strangers, note the changing scenes,
and keep one another informed of details the other might have
missed. Thompson contends that the Kierkegaards' use of
imagination was a "refusal" of the real world. The result, ob-
serves Thompson, was that:

Slowly, inevitably, a singular thought has taken root in the
young boy's mind. It is not necessary to live in the world. On
the contrary, the world—its resistance, its burdens, its conflicting demands—can be transformed. One need only dream.
Narcissus has found his solitary pool, and Kierkegaard his
future: he will become a dreamer.[21]

S. K.'s father was, in many respects, educated simultaneously with his children. A lay student of theology and philosophy, his wealth and leisure afforded opportunities for
prominent teachers in these disciplines to visit his home. In an
incomplete unpublished work, *Johannes Climacus* or *De Omnibus Debitandum*, Kierkegaard appears to have traced his
own intellectual development through such experiences:

When for any reason his father engaged in argument with
anyone, Johannes was all ears, all the more so because everything was conducted with an almost festive orderliness. His
father always allowed his opponent to state his whole case,
and then as a precaution asked him if he had nothing more to
say before he began his reply. Johannes had followed the
opponent's speech with strained attention, and in his way
shared an interest in the outcome. A pause intervened. The

father's rejoinder followed, and behold! in a trice the tables were turned. How that came about was a riddle to Johannes, but his soul delighted in the show. The opponent spoke again. Johannes could almost hear his heart beat, so impatiently did he await what was to happen.—It happened; in the twinkling of an eye everything was inverted, the explicable became inexplicable, the certain doubtful, the contrary evident. When the shark wishes to seize its prey it has to turn over upon its back, for its mouth is on its underneath; its back is dark, its belly is silver-white. It must sometimes glitter so brightly as to hurt the eyes, and yet it is a delight to look upon. Johannes witnessed a similar alternation when he heard his father engage in argument. He forgot again what was said, both what his father and what the opponent said, but that shudder of soul he did not forget.[22]

Kierkegaard never fully resolved the strangeness of his relationship to his father. He often spoke of the melancholy bequeathed him by his father. In an 1846 *Journal* entry he observed:

> An old man who himself was extremely melancholy (why, I will not write down) gets a son in his old age who inherits all this melancholy—but who also has a mental-spiritual elasticity enabling him to hide his melancholy. Furthermore, because he is essentially and eminently healthy of mind and spirit, his melancholy cannot dominate him, but neither is he able to throw it off; at best he manages to endure it.[23]

Kierkegaard saw his own childhood distorted by his father's guilt and melancholy. In an 1848 *Journal* entry he lamented:

> The joy of being a child I have never had. The frightful torments I experienced disturbed the peacefulness which must belong to being a child, to have in one's hands the capacity to be occupied etc., to give his father joy, for my inner unrest had the effect that I was always, always, outside myself. But on not rare occasions it seems as if my childhood had come back again, for unhappy as my father made me, it seems as if I now experience being a child in my relationship to God, as if all my early life was misspent so dreadfully in order that I should experience more truly the second time in my relationship to God.[24]

A month before his father's death, Kierkegaard claimed to see his father as the source of his own knowledge of the meaning of Divine love.[25] This reflected a reconciliation between the two after a severe break in their relationship that had lasted for several years.

That break in the relationship between father and son occurred in 1835. The cause of the break is not clear. Kierkegaard skillfully hid this dark family secret from public view. It no doubt related to his father's confession of his childhood cursing of God, and perhaps his moral lapse, to his youngest son. Kierkegaard later recalled that crisis, saying:

> Then it was that the great earthquake occurred, the frightful upheaval which suddenly drove me to a new infallible principle for interpreting all the phenomena. Then I surmised that my father's old-age was not a divine blessing, but rather a curse, that our family's exceptional capacities were only for mutually harrowing one another; then I felt the stillness of death deepen around me, when I saw in my father an unhappy man who would survive us all, a memorial cross on the grave of all his personal hopes. A guilt must rest upon the entire family, a punishment of God must be upon it: it was supposed to disappear, obliterated by the mighty hand of God, erased like a mistake, and only at times did I find a little relief in the thought that my father had been given the heavy duty of reassuring us all with consolation of religion, telling us that a better world stands open for us even if we lost this one, even if the punishment the Jews always called down on their enemies should strike us: That remembrance of us would be completely *obliterated*, that there would be no trace of us.[26]

Kierkegaard did not respond to his father's confession with repentance, piety, or prayer. Instead, S. K. directly rebelled against his father. Kierkegaard became the consummate aesthete. He gave lavish parties, frequented the finest restaurants and coffee houses, and was a regular at the theater, opera, concerts, and other artistic events. He ran up large bills at the bookseller, wine shop, tobacco store and even had an ill-fated experience at a brothel. Inwardly he felt a gnawing sense of the "silent despair" that characterized his family. He could not escape the shadow of his father's melancholy.

After their reconciliation, S. K. moved back home. Only a few months later Michael Kierkegaard died. Kierkegaard was deeply grieved over the loss of his father. He quickly discovered that his father had left an indelible mark on his life. In a *Journal* entry after his father's death Kierkegaard wrote:

> My father died on Wednesday (the 8th [of August, 1838]) at 2:00 A.M. I so deeply desired that he might have lived a few years more, and I regard his death as the last sacrifice of his love for me, because in dying he did not depart *from* me but he died *for* me, in order that something, if possible, might still come of me. Most precious of all that I have inherited from him is his memory, his transfigured image, transfigured not by poetic imagination (for it does not need that), but transfigured by many little single episodes I am now learning about, and this memory I will try to keep most secret from the world. Right now I feel there is only *one* person (E. Boesen) with whom I can really talk about him. He was a faithful friend.[27]

He could no longer argue against his father, so he became his father's son. He completed his delayed theological education in two years, finishing and successfully defending his thesis, *The Concept of Irony*. At the end of his studies Kierkegaard made a pilgrimage to the Jutland. Perhaps S. K. sought, through this trip, to understand more completely both his father and himself.

The youthful phase of Kierkegaard's life came to a close with the death of his father, yet he would never escape his father's pervasive influence. His sense of melancholy, his call to a life of religious service, his intellectual gifts and education were all part of his inheritance from his father. As he expressed it years later:

> An observer will perceive how everything was set in motion and how dialectically: I had a thorn in the flesh, intellectual gifts (especially imagination and dialectic) and a culture in superabundance, and enormous development as an observer, a Christian upbringing that was certainly unusual, a dialectical relationship to Christianity which was peculiarly my own, and in addition to this I had from childhood a training in obedience, obedience absolute, and I was armed with an almost foolhardy faith that I was able to do anything, only one thing excepted, to be a free bird, though but for one whole

day, or to slip out of the fetters of melancholy in which another power held me bound. Finally, in my own eyes I was a penitent.[28]

The Engagement to Regina

Next to his relationship to his father, no aspect of S.K.'s life stands as more important than his relationship to Regina Olsen. The influence of their relationship shaped and molded his self-understanding and his writing. In *Point of View* Kierkegaard observed:

> Before my real activity as an author began there was an occurrence, or rather a fact (*factum*—to use a word which etymologically implies that I had an active part to play, since presumably an occurrence would not have been sufficient, for I had to be the active agent in the affair . . . . It was a duplex *factus*. However much I had lived and experienced in another sense, I had, in a human sense, leapt over the stages of childhood and youth; and this lack, I suppose, must (in the opinion of Governance) be somehow made up for: instead of having been young. I became a poet; but with my predisposition for religion, or rather, I may say, with my decided religiousness, this *factum* was for me at the same time a religious awakening, so that I came to understand myself in the most decisive sense in the experience of religion, or in religiousness, to which, however, I had already put myself into a relation as a possibility. The *factum* made me a poet.[29]

The *factum* was Kierkegaard's engagement to Regina. They first met in May of 1837 when she was only fourteen. Kierkegaard was fascinated by her immediately. He observed, "Even before my father died my mind was made up about her. He died. I studied for the examination. During all that time I let her life become entwined with mine."[30] They were engaged in September, 1840. Kierkegaard lamented:

> The next day I saw that I had made a mistake. Penitent that I was, my *vita ante acta*, my melancholy—that was sufficient. I suffered indescribably during that time. She seemed to notice nothing.[31]

For nearly a year Kierkegaard struggled with his decision. He variously sought to reassure himself and disentangle himself. Should he marry her but hide the family secret, or live with her as a mistress, or share some sort of platonic relationship with her? The internal debate continued. He even considered suicide. He said, "There was a divine protest, so it seemed to me. Marriage. I would have to keep too much from her, base the whole marriage on a lie."[32]

The end came in 1841, when S. K. broke the engagement. He wrote Regina a note, returned her ring and recorded the final break saying:

> It was a frightfully painful time—to have to be so cruel and to love as I did. She fought like a lioness; if I had not believed there was divine opposition, she would have won.
>
> . . . .
>
> To spare her all the humiliation, I offered to give the affair the turn that it was she who was breaking up with me. She would not have it. She answered that if she could endure the other she could endure this too, and not unsocratically remarked that very likely no one would let her detect anything in her presence and what they said about her in her absence would make no difference.
>
> Then the break came. . . . She was heartbroken.[33]

Kierkegaard was unprepared for his own grief following the break. While he attempted to maintain an external air of undetached indifference to the whole episode, leaving her meant death to any hope of a normal life for him. Thompson contends that Kierkegaard had confused a "flesh and blood Regina with an ideal image."[34] Stendahl appears to see in Regina a challenge to Kierkegaard's acceptance of stereotypical sex roles. His break with her thus saw him become increasingly insensitive to feminist issues of the day.[35] Dru saw this episode in Kierkegaard's life as indicative of his "secret"—the inability to directly reveal himself, which became the focus of his creative genius.[36]

In the years that followed Kierkegaard increasingly withdrew from the world. Stendahl surmised that the break with Regina was a crucial turning point in Kierkegaard's life, noting that:

> Now he had also become free from every conceivable tie. The engagement was broken, he had fulfilled his father's wish

that he finish his studies and defend his dissertation. He was neither planning a teaching career nor contemplating becoming a minister of the Church.

He was free to act for himself, exploring himself as an object, the Regina affair had killed him as a subject, or so he thought. The experience had given him a fundamental insight and a new outlook on the world.[37]

This was the second great crisis of Kierkegaard's life. From the first crisis, his relationship to his father, Kierkegaard inherited the melancholy and the religious and intellectual stimuli that would shape his later life. From the second, the broken engagement, S. K. learned what he was not about. His life was not to be invested in fulfilling a universal ideal. Thus, the search for what he was to be had begun.

Kierkegaard regarded his task as one that he must accomplish alone. Years later he wrote:

> As far back as I can remember I was in agreement with myself about one thing, that for me there was no comfort or help to be looked for in others. Sated with the many other things bestowed upon me, filled as a man with longing after death, as a spirit desirous of the longest possible life, my thought was, as the expression of a melancholy love for men, to be helpful to them, to find comfort for them, above all clearness of thinking, and that especially about Christianity. The thought goes very far back in my recollection that in every generation there are two or three who are sacrificed for the others, are led by frightful sufferings to discover what redounds to the good of others. So it was that in my melancholy I understood myself as singled out for such a fate.[38]

Regina appears to have understood something of this. Near the end of her life she communicated to a friend that:

> Kierkegaard's motive for this parting was his conception of his religious task; he dared not bind himself to anyone on this earth, so that he might not be checked in his calling, he had to sacrifice his dearest possession in order to labor as demanded of him by God; he therefore sacrificed his love . . . in favor of his literary activities.[39]

Within two weeks of his break with Regina, Kierkegaard left for Berlin. During the next several months Kierkegaard produced an unbelievable body of literary works that culminated in the publication of six major works within a year's time. Kierkegaard's formal literary output during the next six years was astounding.[40] In addition, his voluminous journals and papers (twenty volumes in the Danish critical edition) give some indication of the creative force that drove Kierkegaard's authorship.

Kierkegaard's first major work, *Either/Or*, was an instant success. The part called "The Diary of the Seducer" was the talk of Copenhagen.[41] Kierkegaard's spirited debate between the consummate aesthete and Judge William over the ideal marriage was intended as an explanation to Regina of his inability to marry. Yet when he saw Regina in church at Easter and she gave him a friendly nod, Kierkegaard was thrown back into uncertainty.

Back in Berlin, Kierkegaard wrote *Repetition* and *Fear and Trembling*, which reflect his intense religious struggle. He prayed for Regina daily and continued to struggle with the possibility of a reconciliation. Even after her marriage to a former suitor, Friedrich Schlegel, S. K. proposed a platonic relationship in a letter she never received.[42] Regina saw Kierkegaard for the last time in 1855. Her husband had been appointed Governor of the West Indies. On the day of their departure, March 17, she intentionally encountered S. K. on the street and said, "God bless you—may all go well with you."[43]

It was Regina that first caused S. K. to develop "indirect communication." She also contributed to his self-understanding as a religious poet and as an "exception."[44] He remained devoted to her for the rest of his life. Years later he wrote:

> She was the beloved. My life will unconditionally accent her life, my literary work is to be regarded as a monument to her honor and praise. I take her along into history. And I who sadly had only one single desire—to enchant her—*there* it will not be denied to me. There I will be walking by her side; like a master of ceremonies I will lead her in triumph and say: Please make way for her, for "our own dear little Regina."[45]

The broken engagement to Regina had made Kierkegaard the subject of gossip and ridicule in Copenhagen. Kierkegaard cultivated the image of the idle aesthete. Meanwhile his authorship proceeded along two lines, the aesthetic and the religious. *Concluding Unscientific Postscript* was to be his last work. He had struggled with his future for some time. In a *Journal* entry dated February 7, 1846, he wrote:

> It is now my intention to qualify as a pastor. For several months I have been praying to God to keep on helping me, for it has been clear to me for some time now that I ought not be a writer any longer, something I can be only totally or not at all.[46]

In 1848 he wrote *The Point of View of My Work as an Author*, a report to history that would reveal his religious purpose and its relationship to his person. Locked in his desk for posthumous publication, S. K. considered his authorship finished. However, all this changed quickly. Kierkegaard's retirement from public view was halted abruptly by the third great crisis of his life.

The "Corsair" Affair

The Corsair was a widely circulated Danish weekly begun in 1840 by a Jew, Meir A. Goldschmidt. The Danish *Corsaren* literally means "pirate," "privateer," or to paraphrase, "gadfly."[47] The publishers of *The Corsair* were inspired by the ideas of the French revolution (1830) and the agitation for liberty that swept Europe in its wake. In Denmark the conservative papers supported the status quo and the liberal press sought a constitutional monarchy, while *The Corsair* advocated the complete abolition of the institutional monarchy.[48]

Its radical political views brought the paper into frequent conflict with the government. The real owners and editors hid behind various stooges who were hired as "editors" to face various fines and brief prison terms imposed by state censors. The paper skillfully used satire, literary reviews, gossip, and editorials to champion the lower classes. The prominent citizens of Denmark complained vigorously about the paper, but its pages were so popular that *The Corsair* maintained a circulation of nearly 5,000 more than that of any other Danish journal.

Kierkegaard bitterly complained that "Subscriptions to *The Corsair* increased; subscriptions to the other papers decreased; it was read by the higher and the lower classes and with enormous curiosity; it was a power, sheer tyranny."[49] No one appeared powerful enough to be immune to its scathing ridicule. No one, that is, except Søren Kierkegaard.

Goldschmidt admired Kierkegaard's intellectual and writing gifts. After the publication of *Either/Or* he hosted a banquet in Kierkegaard's honor. Kierkegaard did not attend and was offended by a favorable review given him by the scandalous tabloid. In no way did he want to be associated with the paper. Kierkegaard was no democrat. He opposed the "leveling process" of incipient socialism. He was against:

> the rule of the masses, the futility of endeavoring to discover truth by means of the ballot, and against the right divine of mobs to govern wrong. He was not opposed to change as such, but contended against the efforts to impose upon Denmark the abstract ideas of the French Revolution, without taking into account the character of this northern race, the history of the nation, and the institutions which had grown up in conformity with the genius of his people. In his day the Jews (men without political attachments) were prominent as instigators of liberal reform in Denmark, as they were also in other lands.[50]

He reflects this in an 1836 *Journal* allusion where he observed, "The present age is the age of despair, the age of the wandering Jew (many reforming Jews)."[51]

Other intellectuals were not so selective. Paul L. Møller occasionally contributed anonymously to the journal. Møller, who aspired to the chair of aesthetics at the university, severely criticized "Guilty/Not Guilty," a section of *Stages on Life's Way*, in another literary yearbook, *Gaea*, on December 22, 1845. He believed that Kierkegaard had unfairly exposed Regina. Kierkegaard was incensed and saw his opportunity to respond.

Kierkegaard retaliated the next week in *The Fatherland* in an article, "The Activity of an Itinerant Aesthete, and How After All He Had to Pay for the Banquet," signed by Frater Taciturnus, one of the chief characters in *Stages*. In the article Taciturnus referred to Møller's review of his authorship as a "Corsair assault" and indicated publicly that Møller was associated with Goldschmidt and *The Corsair*. Taciturnus sarcastically lamented:

> Finally, one wish: if only I might appear in *The Corsair* soon. It is very difficult for an author to stand singled out in Danish literature as the only one (assuming that we pseudonyms are one) who is not abused there. Yes, even Victor Eremita has had to experience the hitherto unheard of disgrace— of being attacked?—no, of being immortalized—by *The Corsair*. No doubt it would be highly desirable that this disgrace to literature did not exist at all, that there be no literary publication making money by prostitution, for what is a woman's loveliness if it is for sale for money, and what is a bit of talent when it is in the service of vile profit ... *ubi spiritus ibi ecclesia ubi* P. L. M. [Møller] *ibi Corsair*. Hilarius Bookbinder, my chief, has been flattered in *The Corsair*.[52]

Møller responded with a letter to the editor of *The Fatherland* and, disgraced, quietly left Denmark for Germany, where he later died in anonymity and poverty.

However, the battle with *The Corsair* had just begun. The next issue contained a satirical article by Goldschmidt entitled "How the Itinerate Philosopher Found the Itinerate True Editor of *The Corsair*." He "immortalized" Frater Taciturnus who, as everyone knew, was really Kierkegaard. There was more satire and whimsy than malice in the article. However, the next several issues of *The Corsair* featured cartoons that depicted Kierkegaard as a laughable and eccentric individual. One caricature of Kierkegaard noted the uneven length of his trousers, another depicted him training a young girl by riding on her shoulders, one showed Frater Taciturnus inspecting his army of men and women without legs and arms, and yet another featured Kierkegaard as the center of the universe.

On January 10 Kierkegaard fired his second and last public shot in the battle with *The Corsair*. "The Dialectical Outcome of a Literary Police Action," also signed by Frater Taciturnus, noted that this previously ignored journal now had the dubious distinction of having turned against one it had previously praised as a result of a command given by the subject of these attacks. Kierkegaard claimed that this showed the prostitution of this kind of journalism, noting, "We now see that you can order *The Corsair* to insult."[53]

This feud with *The Corsair* had enormous consequences for Kierkegaard. Previously he had been known in the educated circles of Copenhagen as an odd but gifted writer. Now he was familiar to all as a target for ridicule. He claimed that:

> Every kitchen boy feels justified in almost insulting me . . . young students titter and grin and are happy to see a prominent person trampled on; professors are jealous and secretly sympathize with the attacks, and spread them, too, with the appendage, of course, that it is a shame. The slightest thing I do . . . is twisted and distorted.[54]

Kierkegaard complained that "an insignificant pseudonymous little article" would create "more of a sensation . . . than all my writing put together."[55] "I am positive that my whole life will never be as important as my trousers."[56] He lamented this new and perverse interest in his person. Kierkegaard complained that he was "like a fish in a water to which a disagreeable ingredient has been added, making it impossible for fish to breathe in it. My atmosphere has been tainted for me. Because of my melancholy and my enormous work I needed a situation of solitude in the crowd in order to rest. So I despair. I can no longer find it. Curiosity surrounds me everywhere."[57]

By February of 1846 *The Corsair* had published a positive notice of Kierkegaard's *Concluding Unscientific Postscript*. It caused him to reflect that:

> They have not wanted to insult me, since they realize that according to my ideas that would have been an insult; so they have chosen a third course: an appreciative business style. But it just won't do: I want to be on unfriendly terms with them.[58]

Throughout this time Kierkegaard and Goldschmidt continued to greet one another and converse on the streets of Copenhagen. Slowly Kierkegaard's facade began to fade. Goldschmidt genuinely admired Kierkegaard. After one meeting on the street Goldschmidt records in his memoirs that:

> In the bitterness of that glance . . . there was something that verged on the comic. But this vanished and gave place to loftiness, the ideality, which were also present in his personality.

> There was something about that intense, wild glance that drew
> the curtain . . . . It accused and depressed me. *The Corsair* had
> won the battle, but I myself had acquired a false No. 1. On the
> way home I decided that I would give up *The Corsair*.[59]

The attacks on Kierkegaard became less frequent. By
summer Kierkegaard's name rarely appeared in the paper.
Publicly Kierkegaard claimed indifference. Yet his journals refer to the incident for the next three years and show a deep
hurt. He compared Copenhagen to a provincial market town,
complained of the vulgarity of his age, lamented the loss of reflection, and played the martyr—all in the privacy of his *Journal*. Numerous drafts of unpublished articles appear in his
papers. In the end, Kierkegaard chose to suffer alone. Thompson summarizes:

> Yet by far the chief importance of the *Corsair* episode was
> to suggest to Kierkegaard a new understanding of himself—
> that is, a revised scenario for the remaining years of his life. At
> first, he saw quite well that the feud had come about more
> through an accident of timing than from any deliberate deci-
> sion on his part. . . . As time went on, he forgot the accidental
> origin of the affair, and his role in it became more heroic.[60]

Kierkegaard's self-understanding of these events was that
they were providential. He claimed that "Governance himself
has kept me in the harness."[61] Further, he argued that he
would not have published his religious writings had he been in
a parish. "It was the tension of actuality which put new
strength into my instrument, forced me to publish even
more."[62] Stendahl said *The Corsair* "taught him what it means
to be scandalized and considered a fool by the masses. . . . His
personal image had no authority."[63] Kierkegaard in retrospect
observed:

> I had now reckoned out that dialectically the situation
> would be appropriate for recovering the use of indirect com-
> munication. While I was occupied solely with religious pro-
> ductions I could count upon the negative support of these
> daily douches of vulgarity, which would be cooling enough in
> its effect to ensure that the religious communication would
> not be too direct, or too directly create for me adherents.[64]

Kierkegaard's battle with the press was, in reality, a polemic against the "crowd," of which the press was simply an organ.[65] He anticipated the de-humanization of mass man. However, Kierkegaard longed for direct communication. He was still waiting for the right moment when he could speak in character.

Relationship to Christendom

The year 1848 was one of revolution and change throughout Europe. It also marked a "metamorphosis" in Kierkegaard's life. On Wednesday, April 19, of Holy Week he recorded in his journal that:

> My whole nature is changed. My concealment and inclosing reserve are broken—I am free to speak.
>
> Great God grant me grace!
>
> It is true what my father said of me: "You will never amount to anything as long as you have money." He spoke prophetically; he thought I would lead a wild life. But not exactly that. No, but with my acumen and with my melancholy, and then to have money—O, what a propitious climate for developing all kinds of self-torturing torments in my heart. . . . My resolution remains firm—to speak.
>
> [Additional note] Alas, she could not break the silence of my melancholy. That I loved her—nothing is more certain— and in this way my melancholy got enough to feed upon. O, it got a frightful extra measure. That I became a writer was due essentially to her, my melancholy, and my money. Now, by the help of God, I shall become myself. I now believe that Christ will help me to triumph over my melancholy, and then I shall become a pastor.
>
> . . . .
>
> Maundy Thursday and Good Friday have become truly holy days for me.[66]

This was evidently the "metamorphosis" S. K. had anticipated the previous summer as he reflected on the need to face and resolve his melancholy. Although in less than a week he seemed weakened in his determination to break his self-imposed isolation, this event marked a turning point in his life. Both Dru and Lowrie refer to this experience as a "conversion" which had a profound and lasting effect on Kierkegaard's subsequent career.[67] Yet the rapidity of Kierkegaard's backing away from this expressed desire to speak is seen in his "Easter Monday" journal entry, "No, no, my inclosing reserve still cannot be broken . . . . But to want to break inclosing reserve formally by continually thinking about breaking it leads to the very opposite."[68]

This religious experience marked the beginning of a new and different kind of authorship.[69] Kierkegaard's tone was sharper, his mode of communication became more "direct." These works were more specifically religious than anything he had previously written. Yet he continued to struggle with what it meant to speak "with authority."

Two things happened that would shape Kierkegaard's response to these problems. With regard to authority, Kierkegaard was intrigued with the case of Magister Abler, a priest who claimed to have a direct revelation from God. Long after Abler had renounced his "revelation," Kierkegaard continued to struggle with questions related to what it would mean to have a revelation from God today and what constituted religious authority. Kierkegaard's treatise *Authority and Revelation* went through several revisions and was never published during his lifetime. However, his conclusion was that only one willing to be a "martyr" could be a "witness for the truth." The established Church had lost its commitment through compromise with the world.

The second event that marked the last years of Kierkegaard's life was the death of Bishop Mynster. The primate of the Danish Church had been a pastor and friend to the Kierkegaard family for many years. When Kierkegaard was a child, his father had read him Mynster's sermons. He continued to listen to and read Mynster's sermons as an adult. Kierkegaard became increasingly aware of the wide gap between what he saw as true Christianity and the Christianity of Christendom.[70] He asked for an honest confession of this from the Bishop, a request which Mynster ignored.[71]

Kierkegaard remained quiet. After the publication of *For Self-Examination*, he wrote nothing for publication and little in his journals until early in 1854. He was awaiting a sign from God that he should speak. Two months after Mynster's death, Kierkegaard wrote:

March 1, 1854

So now he is dead.

If he could have been prevailed upon to conclude his life with the confession to Christianity that what he has represented actually was not Christianity but an appeasement, it would have been exceedingly desirable, for he carried a whole age.

That is why the possibility of this confession had to be kept open to the end, yes, to the very end, in case he should make it on his death bed. That is why he must never be attacked.[72]

Professor Martensen, one of Kierkegaard's former tutors, eulogized Mynster as "yet one more link in the holy chain of witnesses for the Truth."[73] Kierkegaard felt that Mynster had lied and misappropriated the term "witness for the truth." Mynster stood for Christendom—that caricature of genuine Christianity that Kierkegaard so strenuously opposed. Kierkegaard was coiled and ready to strike. Yet he wanted to avoid appearing to make a personal attack on Martensen, especially since Martensen was next in line to be Bishop of Denmark. He labored furiously at his desk but published nothing until after Martensen was installed as Bishop of Denmark.[74]

Kierkegaard published his response to Martensen's funeral eulogy of Mynster on December 18, 1854, in *The Fatherland*. Martensen replied that not even all the apostles were witnesses to the truth in the sense that Kierkegaard demanded. Kierkegaard launched a series of articles in *The Fatherland* and later in his own series of pamphlets entitled *The Instant*.[75] Kierkegaard was surprised at the popular response to his attacks. These works were the first of S. K.'s works to be translated into several foreign languages. The church responded weakly, and then attempted to ignore his complaint. The government looked the other way. Kierkegaard contended that "The Christianity of the New Testament simply does not exist."[76] In an article, "What Do I Want?" Kierkegaard underscored his protest saying:

> Quite simply: I want honesty. . . . I am not a Christian severity as opposed to Christian leniency.
>
> By no means, I am neither leniency nor severity: I am . . . a human honesty.
>
> The leniency which is the common Christianity in the land

I want to place alongside of the New Testament in order to see how these two are related to one another.

. . . .

And this in my opinion is the falsification of which official Christianity is guilty: it does not frankly and unreservedly make known the Christian requirement—perhaps because it is afraid people would shudder to see at what a distance from it we are living, without being able to claim that in the remotest way our life might be called an effort in the direction of fulfilling the requirement.[77]

Kierkegaard vigorously pressed his attack for almost a year. These attacks were widely read. S. K. had tapped a responsive cord. Popular opinion was anti-establishment in general and anti-Church in particular at this time. However, there were no reforms. Gradually, S. K. became disillusioned with the response of the educated upper class. The last issue of *The Instant* (unpublished in his lifetime) contains an appeal to the "plain man."[78]

Kierkegaard was hospitalized after fainting in the streets of Copenhagen on October 2, 1855. Kierkegaard refused to recant and would not receive communion from a priest. He was at peace and felt that his life's purpose had been realized. Kierkegaard died on November 11 of staphylococcus infection of the lungs.[79] His funeral a week later ended in near riot at the grave as a mob of students protested the way the Church had attempted to "steal" his body. Peter Kierkegaard refused to have his brother's grave marked. Later a simple marble slab inscribed with his name, leaning against his father's grave, was placed in the family burial plot to mark Søren Kierkegaard's final resting place.

2

Philosophical and Theological Foundations for Understanding the Function of Scripture in Kierkegaard's Thought

Kierkegaard's biographical crises are the foundation for understanding the function of Scripture in his thought. Chapter 2 deals with the foundational philosophical and theological issues related to Kierkegaard's understanding of the function of Scripture. Toward that end, the philosophical context for S. K.'s work will be set against the backdrop of his qualified acceptance of Kantian epistemology, his appeal to Lessing's famous "ditch" in relation to the problem of a historical point of departure for eternal happiness, and his rejection of speculative Hegelian rationalism. Kierkegaard assumed and worked from the authority of the biblical witness to Christ. There is no abstract or elaborate theory of biblical revelation in Kierkegaard's work. He was familiar with, and apparently unimpressed by, the options of Lutheran orthodoxy, on the one hand, and the emerging science of higher-critical biblical studies, on the other. S. K.'s understanding of the larger categories of revelation and authority is expounded in his book on Adler. Kierkegaard's understanding of the Christian purpose of his own authorship is developed in *Point of View*. It is here that he connects "indirect communication," speaking "without authority," and the transition to "direct communication" in his own authorship. The chapter concludes with a summary of the issues related to the function of Scripture in Kierkegaard's thought as indicated by this survey of his philosophical and theological context.

Philosophical Context for
Kierkegaard's Understanding of Scripture

Kierkegaard lived through a time of intellectual, religious, and political ferment in Europe. The Enlightenment, with its emphasis on the powers and positive value of human reason, had radically altered the intellectual climate. The history-of-religions school and various early quests for a "life of Jesus" marked the beginnings of modern biblical scholarship. The French revolution and the general turmoil in Europe added to the popular euphoric mood about the inevitability of human progress. Against this backdrop, Kierkegaard was both a child of his times and a protestor against them. His identity with the times is most obvious in his appropriation of a modified Kantian epistemology and his interpretation of Lessing's famous "ditch" between truths of history and truths of reason. His protest is most clearly seen in his rejection of "the system" of Hegelian speculation.

Kantian Epistemology

Immanuel Kant (1724-1804) is the father of modern critical philosophy. He sought to bridge the chasm between the two compelling philosophical options of his day, empiricism and rationalism. He agreed with the empiricist assertion that the mind has no knowledge a priori, but he sided with the rationalists in seeing an ordered structuring applied to reality within the mind. It is this raw structure that makes knowledge possible. Analytical judgments are a priori but provide the knower with no new information, they simply conform to the traditional laws of logical non-contradiction. The predicate is contained in the subject of such observations. Synthetic judgments are different. All a posteriori judgments are synthetic, but the converse is not necessarily true. Mathematical, geometrical, and causal concepts are synthetic a priori judgments. Kant argued in *Critique of Pure Reason* that mathematical and scientific knowledge find their basis and justification in the intuitions and categories of the understanding, since the latter are the necessary conditions of human thought.[1] Scientific knowledge, dependent upon the category of causation as the basis of inductive inference, guarantees that future experiences will follow a causal pattern similar to that of past experiences.[2] The mind has the capacity for receiving impressions (sensibility), forming representations, intuiting things through the senses, developing concepts with the understanding, and forming ideas by the use of reason. The understanding (*Verstand*) is the organizing principle of all knowledge, but it needs sense experience to provide any content to itself. Pure reason (*Vernunft*) is the realm of intuiting ideas based upon the understanding.

Kant was much more reserved regarding the possibility of metaphysical knowledge. Science (and mathematics and geometry) is an attempt to conceptualize about the world of sensory experience (the phenomena), hence the use of the categories of the understanding is appropriate. It is the categories of the mind which actually give the phenomenal world its reality. However, metaphysics is the study of the noumena— reality as it "really is." The application of the categories of the mind would be completely inappropriate since these phenomenal categories would distort the understanding of the noumena. Human knowledge is limited by the nature of the human intellect. Clearly, for Kant, metaphysics as it had traditionally been conceived is impossible.

Based upon the inapplicability of the categories of the mind to the noumenal world, Kant developed his devastating critique of the traditional arguments for the existence of God. The ontological and causal (cosmological and teleological) arguments are invalid because they attempt to arrive at conclusions about reality beyond the phenomenal world by means of the categories of the phenomenal knowledge and experience. They are abstractions empty of any factual content.

Kant spelled out his understanding of morality in *Critique of Practical Reason*. The type of reasoning to be employed in the realm of ethics is not speculative (pure reason with conceptual clarity as its goal) but practical (with moral action as its goal).[3] All persons everywhere are bound by the categorical imperative of duty. This principle is absolute, not requiring any entity or other principle as the ground of its existence. It is universally valid and universally recognized. The moral arguments are a justification of faith (practical reason) rather than a claim to knowledge (pure reason). The imperative to do one's duty implies personal freedom.[4] The incomplete realization of the ethical ideal in this life implies immortality.[5] Thus, God, as the guarantor of immortality, may be posited as existing based upon the implications of the categorical imperative.[6]

Kant established an epistemological and moral dichotomy; religion no longer made knowledge claims about ultimate reality, but was removed from the arena of conflicting interpretations and the criticisms of logic and science. Kant wanted to abandon such speculations in order to ground religion solely on morality, its true and proper basis. Thus, Kant "abolished knowledge in order to make room for belief."[7]

Kierkegaard basically accepted the broad dichotomy of Kant's program and praised the sobriety of "honest Kant."[8] Indeed, as Jerry Gill has pointed out, epistemology and ethics are the two major areas of Kantianism which are most important in Kierkegaard's own thought.[9] Although S. K. began by agreeing with Kant, he concluded by disagreeing at crucial points in each of these areas.[10] Kierkegaard distinguished between faith and reason. This was not a distinction between two forms of knowledge. Rather faith, as an experience and commitment, is set over against all forms of knowledge. As Gill points out, Kierkegaard is "not opting for subjectivity in matters of objective knowledge," rather his concern is for "subjectivity in . . . modes of existence."[11] The basic distinction between objectivity and subjectivity, knowledge and faith, the limitations of the former and the priority of the latter, and the association of religion with volition—all suggest an epistemological pattern which is essentially parallel to that of Kant.

However, Kierkegaard differed from Kant. Confronted with the impossibility of religious knowledge, Kant was content to "posit" the existence of God on the basis of the categorical imperative. In his master's thesis, *The Concept of Irony*, Kierkegaard rejected Kant's contention that thought must stop with "das *Ding an sich*".[12] Kant's error was, according to Kierkegaard, "a misunderstanding occasioned by bringing actuality as actuality into relationship with thought."[13] Rather than positing the existence of God based upon the catergorical imperative, Kierkegaard argued for a volitional "leap" of faith.[14]

Kierkegaard also differed from Kant on ethics.[15] Like Kant, he argued that morality must be defined in terms of the universal imperative of duty.[16] Further, the proper response to duty can be measured by motive more than by consequences.[17] However, for Kierkegaard, the leap of faith carries the individual beyond the universal, thus opening up the possibility of a "teleological suspension of the ethical."[18] Kant reduced religion to ethics as a horizontal relationship between persons. Kierkegaard transformed religion into a suspension of the universal and saw ethics as a vertical relationship between an individual and God.

Lessing's "Ditch" and Kierkegaard's Solution

Kierkegaard's opposition to objectivity in religion reflects not only a sympathy for Kantian epistemology, but also his appreciation for the pre-Kantian philosopher, G. E. Lessing (1729-1781).

No thinker, with the exception of Socrates, received such enthusiastic praise from Kierkegaard as did Lessing, to whom he dedicated the first section of his *Postscript*, "Something About Lessing."[19] According to S. K., the problem for theology was not the "what" of Christianity. Kierkegaard answered negatively the question raised by Lessing: "Is an historical point of departure possible for an eternal consciousness; how can such a point of departure have any other than a mere historical interest; is it possible to base an eternal happiness upon historical knowledge?"[20] Kierkegaard did not deny that there may be a proper question as to the essential doctrines of Christianity, but he insisted that the crucially important matters are not dealt with in answering this question. His concern was how one appropriates this objective content. The subjective problem is, "How can I become a Christian?" or more specifically, "How can I become a Christian in Christendom?"[21]

Lessing was an Aristotelian thinker; his thought preceded the historical-philosophical reason of speculative German idealism. He was also a deist. Lessing appears to have subscribed to a "quintessence Christianity . . . [of] universal brotherhood and a basic moral code."[22] He was also one of the first modern writers to stress that even if conclusions about historical events were more certain than they in fact are, any religious affirmation based upon them involves a transition to another plane of discourse, that of faith.[23] Therefore, no amount of objective evidence can be the basis for faith.

In *Philosophical Fragments* Kierkegaard gave the basic outline of his position, which is more fully developed in *Concluding Unscientific Postscript*. Here, drawing on Lessing, Kierkegaard indicated his agreement with Kant's dichotomy between objective knowledge and subjective faith. The attempt to establish the truth of Christianity on an objective historical basis has taken various forms such as appeals to scriptural reliability, ecclesiastical authority, Christian history, and the like. The results are always the same. Even if the objective truth of such arguments could be established, this would not establish a basis for faith. In fact, any attempt to do so simply demonstrates the loss of faith. Kierkegaard observed:

> Here is the crux of the matter, and I come back to the case of learned theology. For whose sake is it that the proof is sought? Faith does not need it; it must even regard the proof as its enemy. But when faith begins to feel embarrassed and ashamed, like a young woman for whom her love is no longer sufficient, but who secretly feels ashamed of her lover and must therefore have it established that there is something remarkable about him—when faith thus begins to lose its passion, when faith begins to cease to be faith, then a proof becomes necessary so as to command respect from the side of unbelief. And as for the rhetorical stupidities that have been perpetrated by clergymen in connection with this matter, through a confusion on the categories—alas, let us not speak of them.[24]

S. K. also briefly examined the relevance of objective, speculative reason for Christian faith. Philosophical speculation must never be confused with religious faith. He noted that Christian faith

> does not lend itself to objective observation, precisely because it proposes to intensify subjectivity to the utmost; and when the subject has thus put himself in the right attitude, he cannot attach his eternal happiness to speculative philosophy."[25]

Did Kierkegaard accurately appropriate Lessing? Scholars are divided on the relationship between S. K. and Lessing.[26] There are at least two reasons for this difficulty. First, Lessing was ambiguous with regard to theology. Second, there is a basic ambiguity between Lessing's and Kierkegaard's concepts of reason and history. Lessing, as an Aristotelian, believed that the mind has access to timeless propositional truths of reason, and that these are adequate to bring one to "religious" knowledge. Kierkegaard, a critical-idealist critic of speculative philosophy, saw a radical distinction between the "leap of faith" and other claims to knowledge, whether speculative or objective. He insisted that the human mind is limited to critical empirical knowledge.

Further, Lessing, as a deist, moved away from embracing incarnational Christianity. In contrast, the "Absolute Paradox," Kierkegaard's term for the Christian claim that God was incarnate in Jesus Christ, became the ultimate category for S. K.'s religious reflection.[27] Lessing stressed the role of the contemporary Christian tradition as the "place and possibility" of the individual Christian's mainstay.[28] Kierkegaard rejected any historical mainstay for faith; an existential "leap" was the only way the individual could appropriate Christian truth. Later in his career Kierkegaard became increasingly critical of Lessing and attacked his concept of truth in his *Journals* of 1849. Lessing advocated a romantic feeling for the truth, while Kierkegaard increasingly stressed the dialectic of existence faced in personal decision.

Kierkegaard's Rejection of Hegelian Speculation

Kierkegaard's writings contain, from the beginning, a sharp polemic against Hegelian speculation. G. W. F. Hegel (1770-1831) became, for Kierkegaard, the chief representative of the modern speculative philosophy that undermined Christianity. Hegel read his own thought back into that of Plato and classical idealism. He observed, "that which is really true is not things in their immediacy, but only things when they have been taken up into the Form of Thought, as conceptions."[29] Thought and the objects of thought have a harmony, and language expresses the affinity between them. Hegel rejected the Kantian dualism between phenomena and noumena. This "esoteric doctrine" that "understanding cannot go beyond experience" results in a "theoretical intelligence."[30]

The Science of Logic, indicative of Hegel's dialectical movement, claimed to be the system of pure thought. Hegel began with "Being," the most abstract of categories, which is "similar to itself alone," and having no differentiation within or relative to anything external to itself.[31] Being is juxtaposed by "Nothing," and the relationship between the two is understood only in "Becoming."[32]

The infinite is not realized or attained by a succession of finite steps. This is the mistake of rationalism, where the "essence of Being is studied in abstraction from the manifold particulars of finite existence."[33] The result, said Hegel, is that "the contents of the finite world were blindly accepted as empirical and contingent only. Thus rationalism lost itself in the empty forms of reason."[34] Hegel also repudiated empiricism, which "fell greedily on data . . . to get as many particulars together as possible" and nominalism, for which knowledge "became nothing but a formally consistent use of language and correct definition."[35]

As Hegel turned his attention to the doctrine of essence, he focused on the difference between a thing's nature and its appearances, between form and matter, and other polarities. He stated that:

> The Absolute is Essence. It distinguishes essential contradictions or polarities within itself while maintaining its concrete identity in this activity. This is its own dialectic. . . . Being posits the negation of itself as real: what seems to be also is. This is the ontological foundation of the subject-logic (*Begriff*) of truth and illusion: if illusion is known to be illusion, it is known in truth.[36]

Hegel exploits the artificial division of essence and appearance. Each is contained in the other and is only fully recognized in the "Doctrine of Concept."

The movement from being to concept is a major aspect of Hegel's understanding of the relationship between philosophy and religion. Religion is concerned with "image" (*Vorstellung*), while philosophy seeks "concept" (*Begriff*) or pure thought about thought itself. Hegel said, "The Concept grasps and focuses in itself the essential dialectic of Being."[37] The overall pattern of Hegel's logic of thought involves three aspects: (1) the logic of being, (2) the logic of essence, and (3) the logic of concept.[38] Being is the self-development of thought's inevitable object. "Essence" refers to the mind's reflection on being as it is reproduced in thought. "Concept" is the investigation of the dynamic structure of thought in which being and essence are united. Concept, then, is the structure of reality—the reality that thought seeks.

The totality of thought does not have to wait upon the unfolding of human history in order to be identified with the totality of reality.[39] The dialectic of thought resolves the "contraries" that appear as contradictions. Original abstractions are incomplete in themselves; when correlated with their opposites, a new and more complete reality emerges. However, the thesis, antithesis, and synthesis process only comes to a new beginning.

In *The Phenomenology of the Mind* Hegel analyzed consciousness coming to itself through history. The idealistic structure of Hegel's system is expressed in the assertion that only mind or spirit (*Geist*) is real. Aristotle said that the divine mind or mind fully actualized thinks itself, and its thinking is a thinking of thinking. Hegel sees divine mind as also being immanent in the world process. Subject (mind itself) and substance (mind for itself) are one for Hegel. He claimed that "the Truth is the whole."[40] The dialectic of mind is circular in motion. Mind is recovering itself at all levels through the process of the dialectic. In the beginning, mind is potentially everything but actually nothing. It is only through the processes identified as nature and history that mind realizes actuality.[41] The larger dialectic is that absolute mind exists first and only as idea, subjective mind. Mind finds its antithesis in nature by positing itself as object. It is reunited in the synthesis as the now fully realized absolute.

Several stages are evident in the emergence of individual or finite mind as an aspect of universal mind.[42] Subjective mind illustrates the potential that mind is capable of as mind. As finite mind thinks, it transcends spatio-temporal limitations. There are three historical stages in this process. In the anthropological stage, man discovers his nature. In phenomenology, by which Hegel meant the logic of the experience of consciousness, man becomes aware of personal transcendence. In psychology, man sees himself as subject determined by his own free activity.

Mind seeing itself as subject provides the transition to the next stage in the development of mind in which objective mind is manifest. The concern at this level is to describe what is true of man because he is free. Objective mind is presented in three stages. In the first stage, man as individual is characterized by rights. In the second, as individual, man lives under a relative, self-imposed morality (*Moralität*). In the third stage, the person exists as a member of society whose free will is oriented toward a higher morality (*Sittlichkeit*). In the *Phenomenology*, Hegel traces the journey of mind from "consciousness" to "self-consciousness" to the synthesis of the two. The movement is from epistemology through self-awareness to this last stage in which Hegel discusses reason, spirit, and religion before concluding with absolute knowledge.

Absolute knowledge moves beyond the images of religion to pure thought itself. Hegel said:

> It is spirit [i.e. mind] knowing itself in the shape of spirit, it is knowledge which comprehends through notions. Truth is here not merely in itself absolutely identical with certainty, it has also the shape, the character of certainty of self; or in its existence . . . it is in the form of knowledge of itself. Truth is the content which in religion is not as yet at one with its certainty.[43]

Hegel continues, "this knowledge is pure self-existence of self-consciousness."[44] The stage of world history is the logical place to observe the outworking of his philosophy of mind. Hegel saw history as " . . . the development of Spirit in Time just as Nature is the development of the Idea in Space."[45] Hegel claimed to see societal structure as the sphere of the concretion of Spirit.

Hegel's early religious writings had a Kantian starting point.[46] However, he was not satisfied with Kant's view of religion. His earliest fragments indicate a fascination with Greek religion. He appears to have attempted to mold a "religion of the people" (*Volksreligion*) from the Greek ideal. However, he questioned how qualified Christianity was for this. Hegel sought to move beyond a religion of incomprehensible doctrines and religious mysteries, stating that "reason must reject [such things]—in its demand for moral goodness it can permit no giving in."[47]

Hegel saw religion as the knowledge of God. Theology has the task of developing this knowledge. Hegel was severely critical of the theology of his time, which taught that one apprehends God in subjective feeling or certainty but that we may not know Him. Despite his claims to be a Lutheran, Hegel rejected the Lutheran principle of *sola fide* if the *sola* was taken to exclude knowledge. This seemed to him to be inconsistent in a religion which claimed to be revealed.[48]

Hegel did not deny the importance of faith as feeling; he stressed it. Faith seeks knowledge of God, and it cannot renounce that knowledge without self-stultification. However, faith provided only a pictorial representation of truths which are made conceptually real only in Hegel's system. The function of philosophy is to "demythologize" the representational form of Christian religion. Christianity is a religion of spirit. In his *Lectures on the Philosophy of Religion,* Hegel contended that:

> God is the one and only object of Philosophy; it has to do with Him, it recognizes all things in Him, it leads all things back to Him, so that as every particular is derived from Him and everything is solely justified and maintains itself in Him the particular lives in His radiance and has its soul from Him. Philosophy is therefore theology, and the pursuit of philosophy is in itself the service of God.[49]

In a passage fairly representative of his trinitarian conceptions, Hegel noted that Absolute Spirit posits itself in three forms:

> The three forms indicated are: eternal Being in and with itself, the form of Universality; the form of manifestation or appearance, that of Particularisation, Being for another; the form of the return from appearance into itself, absolute Singleness or individuality.
>
> The divine Idea unfolds itself in these three forms. Spirit is divine history, the process of self-differentiation of separation or redirection, and of the resumption of this; it is divine his-

tory, and this history is to be considered in each of these three forms.

Considered in relation to the subjective consciousness. . . . The first form is the element of thought. In pure thought God is as He is in-and-for-himself, is revealed, but He has not yet reached the state of manifestation or appearance, He is God in His eternal essence, God abiding with Himself and yet revealed. According to the second form He exists in the element of particularisation. . . . The third element is that of subjectivity as such. The third element is partly immediate, and takes the form of feeling, idea, sentiment; but it is also partly subjectivity which represents the Notion, thinking reason, the thought of free Spirit, which is free only when it returns into itself.[50]

With regard to space, Hegel sees three forms taking place—first, outside of the world in infinitude; second, in concrete form in history; and third, in the inner sphere of the Spiritual Community.[51] He also sees a similar triadic development with regard to time: beyond, past, and present.[52] It is this type of triadic development that is employed throughout the *Philosophy of Religion.*

There has been considerable debate concerning the extent of Kierkegaard's knowledge of Hegel.[53] Even a casual reading of the Kierkegaard corpus exposes an antipathy for "speculation," "Christian speculation," and "the System," S. K.'s code words for Hegel and Hegelianism. Despite his critical attitude toward Hegel, Kierkegaard confessed that he had "learned much from Hegel.[54] Kierkegaard saw Hegel as the chief representative of the trend in the modern world which undermined Christianity. Kierkegaard attacked and sought to refute several of Hegel's philosophical affirmations.

First, Kierkegaard repeatedly and with increasing vigor rejected the notion that philosophy is superior to faith. Hegel saw philosophy as giving conceptual clarity to the same truth that Christianity was able to provide only in the form of representation. Kierkegaard sought to show the limits of thought in dealing with Christian truth. He saw the Hegelian dialectic as destructive to the essential subjective character of Christian faith. He observed:

Christianity does not lend itself to objective observation, precisely because it proposes to intensify subjectivity to the utmost; and when the subject has thus put himself in the right attitude, he cannot attach his eternal happiness to speculative philosophy.[55]

Indeed, such an attempt at objective thinking is "wholly indifferent to subjectivity, and hence also to inwardness and appropriation."[56] Kierkegaard, noting Hegel's artificial removal of all contradictions through the dialectical development of thought, claimed that "personality will for all eternity protest against the idea that absolute contrasts can be mediated."[57] Thought encompasses only the immanental, the sphere of faith is concerned with the transcendent. Contradiction-free thought is the concern of the former, whereas the absurdity of the paradox is the key to the latter. The absurd points to a reality beyond the domain of reason and speculative philosophy.

Second, Kierkegaard rejected the Hegelian notion of the inevitability and supposed progress of the events of world history. Kierkegaard stressed the significance of human freedom in faith and repentance. In *Fear and Trembling* there is the reminder that, with regard to faith, "no generation begins at any other point than where the previous one did. Each generation must begin all over again."[58] In the denial of human freedom and responsibility implicit in the "necessity" of progress, Christian categories lose their meanings. Kierkegaard lamented that, "One thing continually escapes Hegel—what it is to live."[59]

Finally, according to Kierkegaard, Hegel's system had no ethics. The individual was reduced to an observer; intellectual contemplation had become "the ethical answer of what I ethically have to do."[60] Hegelian philosophy confounds existence. Ethics on the level of finitude is not ethics in the genuine sense. Kierkegaard maintained that there can be genuine ethics only when an individual is related to the eternal as a transcendent reality. Rather than engage in idle attempts to reinterpret Christianity for the modern age, Kierkegaard suggested that:

it doubtless would be better, for it would be a sign of life, if some people in our time were to admit bluntly to themselves that they could wish that Christianity never had come into the world or that they themselves had never become Christians.[61]

Human existence is, by its very nature, incomplete existence. Therefore it stands beyond the grasp of any speculative logic based upon timeless truths. Furthermore, the ethical is an open enterprise and not something already achieved with the arrival of a certain stage of history. Kierkegaard lamented the loss of the individual in Hegel's speculative system:

> It may be all very well from a scientific point of view to make thought the highest stage, and it may be quite plausible from the standpoint of world-history to say that the earlier stages have been left behind. But does our age bring forth a generation of individuals who are born without capacity for imagination and feeling? Are we born to begin with paragraph 14 in the System? Let us above all not confuse the historical development of the human spirit at large with particular individuals.[62]

The sum of Kierkegaard's encounter with and critique of Hegel's philosophy was negative because "it contained a wrong anthropology and a reprehensible theology" and because of the attempt by Martensen, and other Danish Hegelians, to "go beyond" Hegel.[63]

The division between philosophy and theology was not distinct in Kierkegaard's day. Just as he can be seen both as a reaction against the philosophical trends of the early nineteenth century and the father of twentieth-century existentialism, so Kierkegaard reacted against emerging trends in nineteenth-century theology and has significantly influenced twentieth-century neo-orthodoxy.

Theological Context for Kierkegaard's Understanding of Scripture

Kierkegaard opposed the spirit of rationalism which, he argued, had so infected the Danish Church that subjective appropriation of Christianity was largely lost. Kierkegaard reacted against the philosophical system of Hegel and the Danish Hegelians who attempted a synthesis between rationalism and theology based upon Hegelian speculation. He also steadfastly resisted the stale, objective formalism of the established Church of Denmark and of "Christendom" as a whole.[64]

The rationalism of traditional Lutheran scholastic orthodoxy had reduced the Scriptures to a textbook for objective doctrine. The same spirit of rationalism was also foundational to a new school of speculative theology and was instrumental in the development of the higher-critical study of the Bible. Kierkegaard was primarily concerned with theological trends in Denmark, but he vigorously opposed any approach to Scripture that would diminish the importance of personal and subjective appropriation of truth.

Danish Orthodoxy, Rationalism, and Hegelian Speculation

Kierkegaard was not particularly interested in Lutheran orthodoxy. Thulstrup notes that Kierkegaard "had in fact no knowledge of orthodoxy in its genuine form."[65] He had only a limited knowledge of Luther, claiming in early 1847, "I have never really read anything of Luther."[66] Further, classical orthodoxy was not one of the major theological options in the intellectual community of his day. Yet his own religious upbringing had been one of a conservative-type orthodoxy influenced by Moravian piety. Kierkegaard noted in a letter to P. W. Lund dated June 1, 1835, that he saw only two options in theology: the conservative and pietistic orthodoxy of his upbringing, which he referred to as the "enormous Colossus" and observed that "taken as a whole it actually is very consistent" but "difficult to get at," or rationalism, a "second rate" option.[67]

Danish theology was rooted in the scholastic Lutheran tradition.[68] Pietism and Rationalism grew in parallel movements beginning with the Renaissance.[69] Both attempted to answer the growing questioning of established authority in all areas, particularly of religious truth.

The early nineteenth century was a period of "somewhat conservative rationalism" as a repudiation of the utilitarian morality of the Enlightenment.[70] Political reverses in the war with Britain led to the state bankruptcy of 1813, and the subsequent loss of Norway added political instability to the other pressures, forcing a re-thinking of philosophical and theological options. Tolderlund-Hansen has observed:

These events abruptly put an end to the successful eco-
nomic expansion of the preceding period, plunging the country into dire poverty. In these circumstances, Kant's doctrine
of Duty became an important source of inspiration to many
Danish rationalists. Nevertheless, as a pointer to where man's
duty lay, the Categorical imperative was less often stressed
than the Bible, which was often cited as the source and norm
of the Christian faith. Still, there was no way back to the
Orthodox or Pietistic view of the Bible. The critical study of
the Bible had raised too many problems for that, and it proved
impossible to find a valid solution to this dilemma.[71]

The rationalist clergy wanted to free religion from the
trappings of superstitions. This more sober picture of true
Christianity focusing on "God, virtue, immortality, and
preaching was concerned almost exclusively with doing
[one's] duties."[72] As a result, an evangelical pietism grew more
popular among the lower classes. There was also a growth of
intolerance and persecution of sectarian groups on the part of
the state church.

H. N. Clausen, one of Kierkegaard's early tutors in biblical exegesis, was the chief Danish proponent of a rationalistic
religious view in Kierkegaard's day. Influenced by Schliermacher, he advanced a hermeneutic that focused on a somewhat
historical-critical understanding of the text of the Scripture.
He argued that "the study of the Scripture was the principal
discipline of theology, and its methods are the same as for all
other scientific philology and history."[73] The task of theology
was to guide the church in all areas of doctrine, liturgy, and
proclamation according to the canons of experience and critical reason.[74]

Clausen compiled a synoptic overview of the four gospels, the basis of later lectures on the gospels. He also produced a massive history of New Testament hermeneutics,
partly in reaction to the speculative theology of H. L. Martensen, which Clausen saw as a threat to the historical and
philosophical study of the New Testament. Clausen's biblical
theology also contrasted markedly with the Church tradition
movement of Grundtvig. Clausen's numerous commentaries
fairly consistently apply his hermeneutic. His moderate rationalism was a *via media* between evangelical Lutheran piety

and pure rationalism. Yet Clausen was seen as too liberal and was passed over for Bishop of Denmark following Mynster's death. Although Kierkegaard owned most of his major works, he remained respectful but unimpressed with Clausen.[75]

The major reactions to rationalism came from three distinct directions: Grundtvig and his church restoration movement, Mynster and his popular piety, and Martensen and his Hegelian speculative theology. As the German Romantic literary movement spread to Denmark, it influenced Henrik Steffens and Adam Ochlenschlager, who were significant in reviving Danish literature. In religion, this spirit of romanticism influenced N. F. S. Grundtvig and J. P. Mynster, both of whom were significant in the transformation of Danish spiritual life.

Nikolaj Frederik Severin Grundtvig was fascinated with Norse folklore. He wrote about the ancient folklore and history of his country and helped awaken a sense of Danish pride in his countrymen. He came to faith and entered the ministry after an intense personal struggle. Although he held a fundamental view of the Bible, Grundtvig felt he had not sufficiently dealt with problems of historical biblical criticism.[76] Seeking a secure grounding for faith, Grundtvig emphasized the Church as the "Living Congregation."[77] He turned to the sacraments and the Apostles' Creed, which he believed was the baptismal confession of the early church, and was a "word from the Lord's own mouth."[78] Kierkegaard was unimpressed with this movement. He dismissed them as sectarian for thinking that they were the only true Christians.[79] Kierkegaard also complained that "Grundtvig was limited to listening only to himself."[80] His doctrinal system was "propositional."[81] S. K.'s brother Peter was an adherent of the Grundtvig party, and much that Kierkegaard has to say about Grundtvig and the Grundtvig party is in relation to comments about his brother.

Mention has already been made of Bishop J. P. Mynster.[82] Originally trained as a rationalist, Mynster became dissatisfied with his religious position and through his own study of the Bible and a spiritual experience became convinced that "not only had Christ lived and taught as stated in the Gospels, but he was still a living force."[83] Mynster's preaching became warm and evangelical. His education and culture enabled him to have a wide influence over the life of Denmark. In addition, through his writings and role as a theological educator, Mynster influenced a generation of Danish clergy. A supernaturalist, Mynster was a conservative theological voice. He, like Kierkegaard, asserted the value of classical logic (as opposed to Hegelian speculation). He also argued against a philosophical justification of Christianity.

However, as Bishop, Mynster also functioned as an authoritarian and obdurate champion of the State Church. He resisted the revivalist movement of his time.[84] Although he had stressed individual conscience and the fervent acceptance of the mysteries of the faith, he proposed the compulsory baptism of Baptist children.[85] It was in the role as enforcer of the status quo that Kierkegaard reacted most violently against this former pastor and family friend. Mynster's significance for Kierkegaard's time includes:

> his activities as Church administrator, ecclesiastical politician, theological and edifying writer, and in particular, preacher. In none of these fields did Mynster show genuine originality. He was a bearer of tradition and an outstanding representative of a culture in which humanism and Christianity were united, a culture that was going into decline, just as, in its time, the medieval synthesis had broken up.[86]

Although Kierkegaard reacted against the moderate rationalism of Clausen and Mynster's Christendom, his major theological concern was with the rise of what he referred to as speculative theology. Pelikan has observed that "Hegelian intellectualism . . . had infected the Danish Church and Danish theology."[87] H. L. Martensen, one of Kierkegaard's university tutors who followed Mynster as Bishop of Denmark, was the chief representative of this trend.

Martensen sought to "go beyond Hegel."[88] He was in essential agreement with Hegel's philosophy of religion except as he thought it vulnerable to the charge of solipsism. Martensen argued that revelation was essential for a true knowledge of God, stopping short of Hegel's unconditional assertion of the seemingly unlimited scope of rationality. Martensen emphasized the "inviolable majesty of God, his sovereignty as Creator, and his opacity in relation to man's ability to acquire knowledge."[89] However, he also sought to maintain Hegelian speculation as the basis for the development of theology as a science.

Kierkegaard's initial appreciation for Martensen was shaken when Martensen returned from a study tour of Germany. Martensen appeared ambivalent about introducing Hegel and using his speculation as formal logic, even attacking his philosophy as theonomously rooted knowledge of God.

Second, Kierkegaard did not accept Martensen's attempt to distance himself from Hegel and considered him to be only a "reporter" and not an original thinker.[90] He failed to see any "balance" between revelation and philosophy in Martensen's thought. As early as 1837 Kierkegaard lamented the fog that such speculation had introduced into Christianity. He observed that:

> every Christian concept has become so volatilized, so completely dissolved in a mass of fog, that it is beyond all recognition. To the concepts of faith, incarnation, tradition, inspiration, which in the Christian sphere are to lead to a particular historical fact, the philosophers choose to give an entirely different ordinary meaning, whereby faith has become the immediate consciousness . . . and tradition has become the content of a certain experience of the world, while inspiration has become nothing more than God's breathing of the life-spirit into man, and incarnation no more than the presence of one or another idea in one or more individuals.[91]

Kierkegaard's whole discussion of the relationship between Christian truths and the truths of philosophy indicates that, in his view, the former were not merely logical extensions of the latter, nor are Christian truths mere assertions. The mistake of Hegelian speculation was its fundamental confusion of a philosophical "standpoint" with the "existing subject."[92] What are the existing subject's real interests? In the *Fragments* Kierkegaard observed:

> It is well known that Christianity is the only historical phenomenon which in spite of the historical, nay precisely by means of the historical, has intended itself to be for the single individual the point of departure for his eternal consciousness, has intended to interest him otherwise than merely historically, has intended to base his eternal happiness on his rela-

tionship to something historical. No system of philosophy, addressing itself only to thought, no mythology, addressing itself solely to the imagination, no historical knowledge, addressing itself to the memory, has ever had this idea: of which it may be said with all possible ambiguity in this connection, that it did not arise in the heart of any man. But this is something I have to a certain extent wished to forget, and, making use of the unlimited freedom of an hypothesis, have assumed that the whole was a curious conceit of my own; which I did not wish to abandon, however, until I had thought it through.[93]

Kierkegaard gloried in the contradictions of human existence and rejected any philosophical attempt at a false synthesis. He said, "As long as I live, I live in contradiction, for life is contradiction."[94] His polemic against Martensen reflected his increasing impatience with any system that attempted to bypass the central paradox of Christian revelation and the scandal of faith.[95] Kierkegaard noted that in previous generations philosophy allowed Christianity to be what it is, ". . . but Hegel was stupidly impudent enough to solve the problem of speculation and Christianity in such a way that he altered Christianity—and then everything went beautifully."[96]

The Rise of Higher Criticism

To completely appreciate Kierkegaard's relationship to the Bible, another major current of nineteenth-century scholarship must be noted, the rise of the historical-critical study of the Bible. The historical-critical method also had its roots in the Enlightenment philosophical presuppositions of Kant and Hegel.

Hegel's early attempts to establish a "religion of the people" were based upon both the Greek ideal of a people's religion and upon a Kantian view of metaphysics. Hegel questioned how well Christianity was qualified for this. His emphasis shifted as he attempted to move beyond a religion of incomprehensible doctrines and mysteries repudiating any doctrines that appeared to be above or against reason.

In an early essay on the "Life of Jesus," Hegel sought to establish a biblical basis for an ethical *Volksreligion*. In a later essay, "The Positivity of Christianity," (1795) Hegel moved away from a Kantian conception of Jesus and insisted that some of the flaws of Christianity, especially its authoritarianism, go back to Jesus himself. These early works influenced David Friedrich Strauss and others in the quest for a historical Jesus.

Grotius, Hobbes, and Spinoza are generally regarded as the pioneers of modern biblical criticism.[97] The Enlightenment and the English Deism which preceded it created an environment in which people were prepared to consider the scientific study of the Bible in a spirit independent of traditional or dogmatic positions. Lessing published the scandalous "Wolfenbuttel Fragments" by Hermann Samuel Reimarus in 1774-78. Although most of its conclusions are now discredited, the questions raised uncovered the central problems of a life of Jesus: the nature of the eschatological message, the strange surprise of the Resurrection if the passion predictions are historical, the possibility of a creative oral tradition, the Messianic secret, the connection of the sacraments with the life of Jesus, and the rivalry between the Synoptics and the Gospel of John.[98] Lessing's ditch between the accidental facts of history and essential truths also had a profound influence on New Testament interpretation.

Schliermacher assumed the validity of the historical-critical approach to the Bible and sought to move to the larger hermeneutical concern: the meaning of the biblical message for readers and hearers in the modern world.[99] Yet he was unable to escape his own rationalistic presuppositions. In his *Leben Jesu*, Schliermacher interpreted the resurrection of Jesus as his resuscitation after apparent death, the supernatural trappings of the Gospels are attributed to the presuppositions of the disciples. H. E. G. Paulus had, according to Schweitzer, a "distrust of anything that went outside the boundaries of logical thought."[100] His "Life of Jesus" was the most consistently rationalistic of this era. However, D. F. Strauss's carefully constructed replacement for the Gospel story, based on the typology of miracle and myth, displaced a rationalistic interpretation of the narrative with a mythological interpretation.[101]

In a *Journal* entry of 1848 S. K. sarcastically commented:

Things have been turned around in Christendom and thus that mythical Christ is supposed to have come from the time of childhood—the age of childhood composes myths. Charming! It is just the opposite. First comes the historical Christ. Then, after a long time, the mythical—an invention by the intellect, which then imputes it to that time of childhood, making it look as if the intellect now had the task of explaining this myth—this myth which it had itself composed.

. . . .

It is amazing to read an orthodox writer who is preoccupied with proving a particular item in Christ's life so that, being historical, we can accept it. —O, he who in faith has accepted the most absurd, humanly speaking, of all absurdities—that a simple human being is God—finds it impossible to be baffled by some detail.[102]

The inconclusive nature of the various quests for a life of Jesus led to the abandonment of this enterprise. Schweitzer, for example, sounds particularly Kierkegaardian in his observation that "there is nothing more negative than the results of the critical study of the Life of Jesus;" adding "Jesus means something to our world because a mighty spiritual force streams forth from Him."[103] What is significant is that Kierkegaard is omitted from all the major hermeneutical histories of the period.[104] Yet Kierkegaard had much to say that would have been relevant to the early quest for the historical Jesus. His exegetical skills have influenced the twentieth century "struggle for the recognition of the liberty and sovereignty of the Word of God against historicism."[105]

The Kierkegaardian Alternative

The Bible was the most important piece of literature in Kierkegaard's life. Victor Eremita, one of Kierkegaard's pseudonyms, observed, "The Bible is always on my table and is the book I read most."[106] Surely this is true of Eremita's creator. Over 1500 references to Scripture are indexed in his major works, with numerous other references in his *Journals and Papers*.[107] There is little doubt that Kierkegaard spent much time each day reading and reflecting on its contents. As Minear and Morimoto have observed, "We can be absolutely sure of one fact: his adult life was characterized by frequent, regular, thorough, and thoughtful listening to the Bible."[108] Yet Kierkegaard confessed his impatience with the Church's seeming inability to hear the Bible on its own terms. In an 1854 *Journal* entry he proposed:

> Let us collect all the New Testaments there are and bring them out to an open place or up on a mountain and then, while we all kneel, let someone talk to God in this manner: Take this book back again. We human beings, such as we are, are not fit to involve ourselves with such a thing, it only makes us unhappy.[109]

If Kierkegaard had given over his Bibles to God, his arms would have been full indeed. A cursory survey of his personal library indicates that Kierkegaard owned a Hebrew Old Testament, apparently from his student days, a Septuagint, six copies of the Greek New Testament (four were of the authoritative 19th century Knapp edition), three different editions of the Luther Bible, a separate Luther translation of the New Testament, a Luther translation of the Psalms, a sixteenth-century Latin Bible by the radical reformer Sebastian Castellio, and two copies of the Danish Lutheran authorized translation of the Bible. In addition, Kierkegaard had an impressive collection of exegetical aids and other Bible study tools of his day.[110]

Kierkegaard's major criticism of Lutheran orthodoxy was the faulty logic with which it approached the Bible as a textbook from which to draw doctrinal confessions rather than as a source of spiritual guidance.[111] This calls for an objective study of the Bible, raising historical and critical questions about the Bible. To the believer, these things are a "temptation for the spirit." The unbeliever, of course, does not wish the Bible to emerge as "inspired."[112] Therefore, asked Kierkegaard, "Who then really has interest in the whole inquiry?"[113]

The "objective" study of the Bible is a mistake from beginning to end, for faith does not need the promise of proof. Just as a historical accident cannot be the basis for an eternal happiness, neither can the Bible, objectively considered, be the basis of such a happiness. The higher critical method of studying the Bible was equally fallacious. Kierkegaard saw only two opposite options open with this approach: either a more scientific (and less dogmatic defense) of the biblical tradition, or the reverse, a more scientific rejection of the biblical faith on grounds beyond simple denial. In a 1850 entry in the *Journals* S. K. drew an analogy between the imperfections of the natural world and the imperfections of the Bible and declared that difficulties in the Bible were there precisely because "God wants the Holy Scripture to be the object of faith and an offense to any other point of view."[114]

Kierkegaard did not oppose critical scholarship per se. He frequently used insights on the background and context of biblical passages in his own Bible study. However, Kierkegaard recognized that historical study could only provide an "approximate" understanding of the Bible.[115] He warned that "the great mass of interpreters damage the understanding of the New Testament more than they benefit," comparing commentaries to "spectators and spotlights" that prevent the enjoyment of a play at the theater.[116] He suggested reading the New Testament "without a commentary" and asked rhetorically, "Would it ever occur to a lover to read a letter from his beloved with a commentary?"[117]

Kierkegaard never wrote an extended treatise on exegesis or hermeneutics, but his own hermeneutic is a principle of imitation through imaginative identification.[118] He argued for an active appropriation of Scripture by personal examination in the light of the biblical witness. The Kierkegaardian position is one of a "radical revaluation," which in the "personal and direct obedience of faith has the Bible appear as the bearer of the unconditioned and its messenger."[119] As one reads about the heroes of faith in the Bible one should not "doubt our likeness, however remote, to these men of God."

> The deep sorrow, the terrible battles within our attitudes, must not allow us to doubt completely our strength to bear what is our lot to bear. Inasmuch as such instances remind us of the dark and bright hours in our own experience, we shall not lose equilibrium, we shall not imagine that everything is accomplished in one stroke, and we shall not despair when we see that this cannot be done.[120]

Kierkegaard lamented that his generation had forgotten "that this letter [the Bible] is from God and entirely forgotten that it is to the single individual."[121]

Personal appropriation, then, is the standard by which Kierkegaard judged the value of Bible study methods. Kierkegaard saw simply learning the Bible by heart as an example of childishness. A mature person learns only "by appropriation."[122] Kierkegaard's concern was not that one should exegete Scripture in a certain way, rather that Scripture should be allowed to exegete life.

Authority and Revelation, and Kierkegaard's Own Authorship

The focus now shifts from the philosophical and theological context for understanding the function of Scripture in Kierkegaard's thought to his explicit statements regarding revelation, authority, and the purpose of his own authorship in two of his crucial works.

Kierkegaard worked from and assumed the truth of biblical material. There is no formal or elaborate theory of biblical revelation in his works. However, Kierkegaard explained his understanding of the nature of revelation and its relationship to religious authority in his book on Adler. He discussed his understanding of the Christian purpose of his own authorship in his posthumously published report to history. This work is essential for deciding how to interpret the Kierkegaard corpus and in determining the function of Scripture within that corpus.

On Authority and Revelation

The Book on Adler was written in 1846. Kierkegaard was reluctant to publish it because he felt no personal animosity toward Adler. Also, the Church had already resolved Adler's case when Kierkegaard finished his first draft of the book. Yet Kierkegaard continued to revise this treatise until his death. This work was not published until Walter Lowrie translated it out of the *Papirer* in 1955.

Adolph Peter Adler was a Danish priest who began to follow Hegelian philosophy during a year of study in Germany. He returned to Denmark, and after completion of his master's degree, was appointed pastor of two rural parishes, where he served faithfully and was loved by his flock. However, a year into his ministry, he had a "vision of light," a divine revelation, which turned him against Hegel. Jesus Christ spoke to him, bid him burn his earlier works on Hegel, and dictated the greater part of a large book Adler published as *Selected Sermons*. Later, under examination by the church, he claimed to have had a profoundly moving religious experience that was not inconsistent with Lutheran orthodoxy. Adler claimed the status of spiritual genius, and argued that with time for reflection and clarification, his writings would be edifying to Christianity. Initially ignored by the church, Adler was subsequently suspended by Bishop Mynster on the grounds that he was deranged. He was eventually defrocked.

Kierkegaard diagnosed Adler's confusion as indicative of his "imperfect education in Christian concepts."[123] He also saw in Adler the confusion of categories that reigned in the Christianity of his day. Christian categories had been readily assimilated into larger speculative philosophical systems, such as Hegelianism. In the process, Christendom had lost the true meaning of the grammar of faith. Kierkegaard noted:

> the holiest and most decisive definitions are used again and again without being united with the decisive thought. One hears indeed often enough Christian predicates used by Christian priests where the names of God and of Christ constantly appear and passages of Scripture . . . in discourses which nevertheless as a whole contain pagan views of life without either the priest or the hearers being aware of it.[124]

Kierkegaard's purpose was "essentially an ethical investigation of the concept of revelation" which concerned both "what it means to be called by a revelation" and "the concept of authority" which, according to S. K., "has been entirely forgotten in our confused age."[125] He used Adler's case "to throw light upon the age and to defend dogmatic concepts."[126] Kierkegaard, in relating the category of authority to that of revelation, indicated that the fundamental problem of his age was a

refusal to accept the authority of revelation. He observed,
"For the misfortune of our age . . . is disobedience, is unwillingness to obey."[127]

As Kierkegaard surveyed the plausibility of a claim to a
special revelation, he did not deny its possibility in the modern
era. However, Adler's retreat and qualified restating of his
claims to a revelation are incongruous. Kierkegaard noted that
the apostle Paul, if asked, would have simply said "yes" to the
question of "whether he really had had a revelation."[128] Any
justification of that claim would have raised doubts as to
whether or not it were true.

One indication of Adler's confusion was his publishing
of a book of sermons claiming to contain messages directly revealed from Jesus and some previous messages presumably of
his own composition. Kierkegaard noted that some of the
"pre-revelation" sermons also contain passages that claimed to
be written with the aid of the Holy Spirit. Although "Jesus
spoke to him," the "revealed" sermons show little substantial
difference from the earlier sermons.

Adler, in attempting to defend himself, claimed his "revelation" was consistent with the standards of Christian orthodoxy. He was still within the universal. Kierkegaard indicated
that a revelation is not needed where truths may be acquired
from the universal. Adler was unable to stand alone. Yet
"stand alone" is exactly what one with a revelation should be
prepared to do. Adler's defense and his "wish to be in the service of the Establishment is a self-contradiction, and to expect
of the Establishment that it shall keep him in its service is really to wish to make a fool of the Establishment"[129]

"Authority" is the key category with regard to "revelation." The confusion regarding the category of "revelation"
and uncertainty regarding religious "authority" demonstrate
the distance Christendom has moved from Christianity. The
idea of a "revelation" from God invokes Divine authority.
Kierkegaard said that the question is quite simple: "Will you
obey? or will you not obey? Will you bow in faith? . . . or will
you be offended?"[130] There is no such thing as neutrality toward a revelation from God.

Kierkegaard noted that many are uncomfortable with
revelation and seek to remove themselves from the biblical

revelation by "the parenthetical." The means used to keep one from confronting and being confronted by revelation include "exegesis," which Kierkegaard calls the "first parenthesis."[131] Exegesis seeks to determine "how this revelation was to be conceived whether it was an inward factor, perhaps a sort of *Dichtung* and *Warheit*, etc., etc."[132] Kierkegaard regarded this as an "excellent means of diversion."[133] Philosophy, and "the theology which caricatures philosophy," was the "second parenthesis." Kierkegaard said that these "people treat the Scriptures so scientifically that they might as well be anonymous writing."[134]

Thus, Adler's shift in categories, his later claim that his experience was essentially a spiritual awakening while failing to repudiate the initial claim of having had a "revelation," demonstrated his confusion. Furthermore, the claim that he could, with more time and reflection, clarify his position, proves that he did not have either a revelation or an awakening. Adler's claim ignored the category of "paradoxical religion."

He sought to explain religion back into the ethical. When this happens, observed Kierkegaard, it is "good-night Christianity."[135] Adler satirized himself. The true *extraordinarius*, the one with a revelation from God, is not concerned with whether he "prevails today or tomorrow or in a thousand years, for he *has conquered*, his relationship to God is his victory."[136] Kierkegaard concluded "that the whole thing about his revelation is a misunderstanding."[137]

Leaving the specifics of Adler's case, S. K. turned his attention to the larger issues it raised. The distinction between a genius and an apostle illustrates the difference between the wisdom of the world and the wisdom of God. The Paradox, Jesus Christ, is the ultimate confounding of the wisdom of the world.

The category of genius is different from the category apostle. The apostle has a revelation where "the Saviour communicat[es] a new doctrine."[138] Kierkegaard developed this difference noting that:

> A *genius* and an *apostle* are qualitatively distinct; they are categories which belong each of them to their own qualitative spheres: that of *immanence* and that of *transcendence*. (1) The

genius may well have something new to contribute, but this newness vanishes again in its gradual assimilation by the race, just as the distinction "genius" vanishes when one thinks of eternity. The apostle has paradoxically something new to contribute, the newness of which, precisely because it is paradoxical and not an anticipation of what may eventually be developed in the race, remains constant, just as an apostle remains an apostle to all eternity, and no immanence of eternity puts him essentially on the same plane with other men, since essentially he is paradoxically different. (2) The genius is what he is by reason of himself, i.e. by what he is in himself: an apostle is what he is by reason of divine authority. (3) The genius has only immanent teleology: the apostle's position is that of absolute paradoxical teleology.[139]

Christianity is both built upon a revelation and limited by the definite revelation it has received. It is a revelation marked by authority. Kierkegaard said:

Authority is the qualitatively decisive point. . . . The king's command has authority and therefore prohibits all critical and aesthetical impertinence with regard to form and content . . . . But what is it that has fundamentally confused Christianity, unless it is that people have at first in doubt become so nearly uncertain whether there is a God that in rebellion against all authority they have forgotten what authority is and the dialectic of it? . . . Doubt . . . has put God on the same plane as all those who have no authority, geniuses, poets, thinkers, whose utterances are appraised precisely by aesthetic and philosophical criteria; and in case a thing is well said, then the man is a genius, and in case a thing is unusually and especially well said, then it is God who has said it!!![140]

"The Paradox" is the model Kierkegaard appealed to as an illustration of what constitutes a true revelation from God. He noted that:

The fact that the eternal once came into existence in time is not something which has to be tested in time, not something which *men are to test*, but is the paradox by which *men are to be tested*; and the eternal proudly despises every pert and impudent argumentation from the many years.[141]

It is always important to distinguish between *the historical element in Christianity* (the paradox) and *the history of*

Christianity (the history of its followers). It is with the paradox that everyone must become contemporary.[142] This is a religious requirement and in the interest of Christianity.

Christ as the God-Man is the "specific quality of authority" which cannot be mediated. Kierkegaard said, "Christ therefore taught with authority. To ask whether Christ is profound is blasphemy and is an attempt . . . to annihilate him."[143] The Paradox, Jesus Christ, is the standard by which all other claims to revelation are to be judged. There is no point at which the paradox may be judged. In the same way, an apostle cannot prove his authority. The apologist and the skeptic, like Adler, fail to understand the radical nature of a true revelation from God. They succumb to the temptation to make "revelation" plausible.

Kierkegaard did not deal directly with the idea of general revelation. Yet he sharply distinguished between general revelation and a special revelation in which God reveals something specific to a particular individual. There would be no position of authority if revelation were general and universal.

Kierkegaard argued that revelation is not the same thing as a "spiritual awakening" or the rise of faith in an individual believer; it is a special and limited category that should not be confused with either the category of awakening or that of the genius. Kierkegaard indicated that a true revelation from God is a definite event and includes specific content conveyed to an individual. Uncertainty on these points is indicative that one has not truly received a revelation from God.

Joe R. Jones observed, "While God's authority may not be conditioned, it does seem that we cannot claim his authority without providing some criterion for justifying such a claim."[144] Kierkegaard would undoubtedly concede that the Christian concept of revelation is a form of question begging. There is no abstract account of Divine authority which would compel one to accept any particular claim to having such authority. It is the decisive point of the Christian faith that certain persons are acknowledged as bearers of divine authority. Kierkegaard saw Jesus and the apostles as defining instances of divine revelation and authority.

It appears that there was, in Kierkegaard's mind, a necessary circularity here. This circularity runs counter to traditional apologetic efforts to make Christianity plausible by reference to some outside point of reference. It should be clear that Kierkegaard's "defense of dogmatic concepts" involves clarifying concepts against any counterfeit which would obscure the true character and point of departure of Christian faith. It is the kind of defense which "thinks, lives, and speaks in the light of the new point of departure and within the limits of that point."[145] Dogmatic concepts do not render a higher understanding, rather they serve as sentinels demarcating the distinctive content of Christian faith.

Point of View

Kierkegaard wrote a brief "report to history" regarding his authorship in the posthumously published *Point of View*. This brief treatise provides a glimpse of the mature Kierkegaard's interpretation of his own authorship. There is, however, considerable debate among Kierkegaard scholars as to how seriously Kierkegaard's own view of his authorship should be taken.

Josiah Thompson, for example, has argued that "the claim . . . that the master plan for his books was in his mind from the beginning is contradicted by contemporary letters and journal entries."[146] Lowrie saw the pseudonyms as representing "sides" of Kierkegaard, but not the "whole" picture.[147] Brita Stendahl appears to take Kierkegaard's explanation of the stages of his authorship in *Point of View* at face value,[148] and Reidar Thomte sees in Kierkegaard's characters an existential identification with the stages of life.[149] Paul Sponheim has noted the "restless unity" of Kierkegaard's authorship.[150] James Collins, noting that Kierkegaard scholars have "outdone themselves" in interpreting the pseudonyms, seems more on target in arguing that initially Kierkegaard "had to resort the pseudonyms out of a natural inclination, and that only later on did reflection reveal to him his deeper significance and purpose of this practice."[151] Personal reasons, the ends of truth, and religious considerations converge as explanation for Kierkegaard's use of pseudonyms.[152]

Kierkegaard has contributed to this confusion. In his role as editor of Johannes Climacus' *Postscript* Kierkegaard claimed,

> So in the pseudonymous works there is not a single word
> which is mine. I have no opinion about these works except as a
> third person, no knowledge of their meaning except as a
> reader, not the remotest private relation to them.[153]

What Kierkegaard means by this and similar statements
is that these opinions do not directly reflect his own. He does,
however, acknowledge the unity of indirect and direct communication in his own authorship in *Point of View*.

The public debate in his own day over Kierkegaard's *persona* and his relationship to the pseudonyms was intense. He
stated that his purpose in writing *Point of View* was "to explain once for all, as directly and frankly as possible, what is
what: what I as an author declare myself to be."[154] His earlier
silence on this subject was due to the fact "that the authorship
was not yet in hand in so complete a form."[155] Furthermore,
he claimed, all his work could be understood as an expression
of his religious purpose, which dealt with the problem of "becoming a Christian" in Christendom.[156] He claimed that "the
religious is present from the beginning." He continued, "the
aesthetic is present again at the last moment."[157] However, he
claimed that if one only understood the later specifically religious works, then he, Kierkegaard, would not be unduly up-
set.[158]

The major importance of the pseudonymous writings is
that they become the vehicle for Kierkegaard's development of
the "stages" of the possible existence spheres of life.[159] Kierkegaard observed, "There are three stages: an aesthetic, an ethical, and a religious. But these are not distinguished abstractly .
. . but rather concretely, in existential determination."[160] These
existence spheres are not rigid categories for the classification
of human types. Nor is there any mechanistic necessity that
would move one along, like stages of human development.
Rather, Kierkegaard's "stages" describe existential options, the
basic choices that confront the concrete individual.

Collins has pointed out that the aesthetic, ethical, and religious stages constitute one of Kierkegaard's major contributions to philosophy.[161] These are not options excised from
Schliermacher or Hegel. Rather, the triadic understanding of
the possibilities of human existence appear to have grown out
of Kierkegaard's reflection upon his own experience.

The *aesthetic* is the first of the three existence spheres developed by Kierkegaard. According to S. K. the aesthete "overrates youth and this brief instant of eternity."[162] The early pseudonymous works develop a picture of the consummate aesthete—one who lives a superficial and indulgent lifestyle, pursuing beauty, art, pleasure, and immediated fulfillment. This existence sphere is developed most fully in *Either/Or* and *Stages on Life's Way*.[163] This lifestyle makes no ethical commitments and is therefore isolated from society. It is an "a-ethical" and an "a-religious" stage that can best be characterized by indifference that ends in despair.[164] In *Either/Or* Kierkegaard proposed the ethical as an answer to the aesthete's lack of commitment. The religious is only present as an aspect of the ethical.[165]

The Christian purpose of S. K.'s authorship at this stage was to dispel the illusions of the aesthete.[166] This involved a "maieutic" or indirect communication, and a hiding of his own religious purpose. He did this because, while it was impossible for him to compel belief, he felt "I can compel [one] to take notice."[167] Kierkegaard claimed that, in a Socratic sense, "the aesthetic work is a deception . . . for truth's sake."[168] What does it mean to deceive? Kierkegaard answered:

> It means that one does not begin *directly* with what one wants to communicate, but . . . by accepting the other man's illusion as good money. So (to stick to the theme with which this work especially deals) one does not begin thus: I am a Christian; you are not a Christian. Nor does one begin thus: It is Christianity I am proclaiming; and you are living in purely aesthetic categories. No, one begins thus: Let us talk about aesthetics. The deception consists in the fact that one talks thus merely to get to the religious theme.[169]

The *existence* sphere of the ethical is also represented in the pseudonymous works. The aesthetic category is criticized on the basis of the ethical. The ethical exists a priori (following Kant). Kierkegaard did not fully develop a system of ethics, but he directed his reader to an ethical way of living exemplified by the pseudonymous characters, Judge William in *Either/Or* and a Married Man in *Stages*. Only through absolute choice can one enter the sphere of the ethical. The sanctity of marriage, the order and structure of commitments in life, and the ethical value of immanental religion all stand in marked contrast to the nature of the aesthete. However, guilt is the category that the ethical cannot fully satisfy, except that one has the capacity to make the decision to be guilty for himself.[170]

Kierkegaard's engagement to Regina was central in his own struggle with the ethical ideal of a universal. Yet Kierkegaard gradually came to see himself as an "exception" to the universal, and in *Fear and Trembling* Kierkegaard dealt with the problem of whether or not it is possible to have a teleological suspension of the ethical. During the period of pseudonyms, Kierkegaard maintained an outward mode of existence which suggested he was living at the aesthetic level. He claimed that "seldom has any author employed so much cunning, intrigue, and shrewdness to win honour and reputation in the world with a view to deceiving it . . . in the interest of truth."[171]

The transition to his explicitly religious works was marked by the completion of the *Postscript*.[172] The *religious* stage is also subjective, but unlike the ethical, does not remain immanent but becomes the object of a "double reflection" based upon the Paradox.[173] In a *Journal* entry of 1850 Kierkegaard claimed:

> My thesis is not that the substance of what is proclaimed in Christendom as Christianity is not Christianity. No, my thesis is that the *proclamation* is not Christianity. I am fighting about a *how*, a reduplication. It is self-evident that without reduplication Christianity is not Christianity.[174]

This "reduplication" is the translation of truth intellectually apprehended into life.

S. K.'s distinction between the religion of immanence (Religiousness A) and the religion of transcendence (Religiousness B) is significant. The former consists of the ethical-religious justification of the universal. Fear of punishment and hope for reward are crucial aspects of this type of religion. The latter is based upon the solitary individual who stands by faith before God, with the hope of reward or fear of punishment no longer an essential part of his or her decision. Indeed, the crucial category for Kierkegaard was the "single individual"—the focus of both the ethical and the religious spheres.[175]

Kierkegaard's later religious writings and many of his discourses are "direct" communications, in contrast to the "indirect communication" of the pseudonymous aesthetic or philosophical writings. The contrast between the religious writings and the pseudonymous writings is itself a type of indirect communication. Kierkegaard was quick to warn his reader that he speaks "without authority" because he has no new revelation from God, nor was he ordained as a priest. "Christianity is an *existence-communication* brought into the world by the use of authority, it is not an *object of speculation* . . . ."[176]

After launching his attack on Christendom, Kierkegaard further qualified any claim to authority with the contention that an authoritative message was one lived as well as proclaimed.[177] He came to see "indirect communication" as something that could belong only to God as illustrated by the Paradox. He later claimed "the upbuilding [edifying discourses] is mine, not the aesthetic. . . ."[178]

This disclaimer not withstanding, it is evident that Kierkegaard used his pseudonyms to deal with various options in the quest for a meaningful life. They are caricatures. They reflect their respective stage as a means of indirect communication. As David Swenson has observed:

> This mingling of jest and earnest; their alternation between humor, irony and pathos; this illustration of abstract categories by the use of stories and anecdotes taken directly from the streets of Copenhagen, this constant shifting back and forth between logical abstractions and poetic imagery; this incorporation of a category in an imagined personality, who is permitted to speak for himself, so that we may see him as he is; this succession of different pseudonymous authors, each representing a distinct nuance of position; this teasing personality relationship which the style seeks to establish between the author and the reader, after the manner of a Socratic gadfly— all this is not mere idiosyncrasy of a versatile and capricious writer. It is rather a reflective maieutic, the sign of an author who has something more profound in mind than a mere appeal to the abstract understanding of the reader.[179]

In the end, Kierkegaard saw his role as that of a religious author seeking to build up true Christianity. He even claimed a sense of Divine, poetic inspiration for his writings.[180] The whole of his authorship reflected his own education before God, away from romanticism and speculative philosophy and back to Christianity.[181] In Kierkegaard, dialectic powers and philosophical thinking fused with creative imagination and literary ability. These skills combined with his desire for indirect communication and reserved and melancholy personality to produce a "philosophical production comparable only to that of Plato."[182]

Conclusion

Kierkegaard's qualified acceptance of Kantian epistemology, influenced by insights from Lessing and others, shaped his attempt to get beyond the ambiguities of the historical to the true essence of Christianity. His personal crises and the remoteness of Hegelian rationalism pushed Kierkegaard inward. However, Kierkegaard cannot simply be dismissed as an irrationalist. In the *Postscript* he observed:

> That thought has validity was assumed by Greek philosophy without question. By reflecting over the matter one would have to arrive at the same result; but why confuse the validity of thought with reality?[183]

Kierkegaard simply rejected the Hegelian equation of thought with reality.

Kierkegaard was also unimpressed with Lutheran orthodoxy and was an early critic of the emerging "scientific" study of the Bible. Drawing deeply from his own religious struggles, Kierkegaard focused his attention on the unique category of Christian revelation—the Paradox, the core of the Gospel.

3

The Function of Scripture
in Selected Philosophical Works

The preceding survey of the philosophical and theological contexts appropriated and reacted against by Kierkegaard provide parameters for understanding his views on authority, revelation, and Scripture. The specifics of Kierkegaard's biblical hermeneutic, based upon his philosophical presuppositions and their influence upon his understanding of the kerygmatic core of the Christian message and other key theological categories, are examined in this and the next chapter.

This chapter will focus on Kierkegaard's use of Scripture in his philosophical works, which are all pseudonymous. Kierkegaard saw all of his works as contributing to his ultimate religious purpose of reintroducing authentic Christianity into Christendom. In this sense, his works have a paraphilosophical purpose. These works could also be called "aesthetic." However, the term "philosophical" seems most applicable to this portion of the Kierkegaard corpus.

Kierkegaard's purpose was not to provide a systematic theory of biblical hermeneutics. His concern was "How does one become a Christian in Christendom?" In other words, how can the Word of God be heard as Word of God today? His answer was, in part, that modern persons must become contemporary with the Gospel or, to use his term, the Paradox. Therefore, the Bible, which is only a means to hearing the Word of God, not to be totally equated with that Word in itself, performs various functions in Kierkegaard's writings. The aesthete, who has no commitment to obeying the Word of God, would treat the Bible as little more than a novelty of culture—a literary device. The hermeneutic used by one interested in ethical commitment would focus on the external demands of Scripture. Appropriation through inwardness is the key to the hermeneutic of paradox.

This chapter deals with these works in chronological order, providing an examination of Kierkegaard's use of Scripture in relation to the development and use of pseudonyms. This underscores the dynamic transitions in Kierkegaard's appropriation of Scripture as he shifted from one existence sphere to another for the purpose of communication. Kierkegaard's allusions to and creative reinterpretation of the Bible are examined in these chapters in an effort to determine the flow of his hermeneutic of Scripture.

The Use of Scripture in Kierkegaard's Early Philosophical Works

Kierkegaard's first major work was *Either/Or*. Fictional prose shrouded in pseudonymity, it is Kierkegaard's circuitous attempt to explain his relationship with Regina. Much of the material in these volumes was written after the publicly embarrassing break in their engagement. *Stages on Life's Way*, written two years later, was written to further explain the themes treated in *Either/Or*. These works examine the "stages" of human existence. These "stages" are not mechanistic, like the normal progress in human development; rather they are options for existence or "existence spheres." Each contains elements of the other. Kierkegaard's pseudonyms were caricatures of an aspect of or point-in-time of each sphere. Another purpose of these, and the other aesthetic works, is to loosen the grip on their readers' false picture of reality.[1] This is particularly evident as the function of Scripture in these early works is examined.

However, before *Stages* was released, Kierkegaard had written several other works which were much closer to the religious stage. These works were more polemical in tone and focused on the hermeneutic of Paradox. The earliest of these was *Fear and Trembling*. Here Kierkegaard treated the well-known story of Abraham's willingness to offer Isaac as sacrifice, using it as a paradigm for "teleological suspension of the ethical," as the individual stands alone before God in "fear and trembling."

Either/Or

Kierkegaard's understanding of the doctrine of choice was set forth in *Either/Or*. The conflict is between the aesthetic mode of existence and the ethical. The protagonists are a young sophisticated aesthete, referred to as "A," and an older, mature "father figure" identified as Judge William or "B."

Originally published in one volume, the *Either* cannot be understood without the *Or* or vice versa. Since the latter was written first and is somewhat easier to understand, the book could have been called *Or/Either*. But that would have disrupted the progression. Kierkegaard clearly saw the ethical stage as an improvement over the detached and uncommitted nature of the aesthetic stage.

A wide world of culture, learning, and experience awaits the reader of Kierkegaard. This is nowhere more evident than in *Either/Or*. In a perusal of the essay "Diapsalmata," Dunstan has noted "the wealth of intellectual possessions" S. K. had, in the numerous passing references which fill the text: the story of Phalaris, a swineherder from Amager, insects which die in parturition, the royal dynasty of ancient Egypt, Dean Swift, Dr. Hartley, Cornelius Nepos, an English folk saying, the game of chess, the Arabian Nights tales, Noureddin, Hebrew grammar, the three-tailed Pasha, Don Juan, a poor man wearing a yellow coat, Nuremberg toys, Lyceus, and the absurd spectacle of a fly lighting on the nose of a business man.[2] However, of all the sources upon which Kierkegaard drew, none was more significant than the Bible.

The first volume, the *Either*, represented the aesthetic ideal through a variety of literary forms—dramatic and musical reviews, psychological analyses, and philosophical essays. This rambling collection of seemingly unrelated material provides a glimpse of S. K.'s own sense of the ambiguity of the aesthetic stage of existence. The literary style is heterogeneous; use is made of lyrical aphorisms, orations, psychological analyses, drama reviews, and philosophical formulations. Kierkegaard wrote as the consummate aesthete. If S. K. is to be believed, his purpose was "religious" at this early stage.[3] Here he introduced the notion of "immediacy" and "reflectivity" that became important in his development of Christian reflectivity.[4]

Judge William was the single author of the letters to the young aesthete that comprise volume II of *Either/Or*. William is not interested in love as an abstraction. True love can only be defined in a specific ethical context. The act of choice is the means whereby the ethical is intensified. Judge William was a rather dull replacement for the author of the first volume, the creative aesthetic. He personified, in life and in practice, the ethical virtues his treatise represented.

The Bible was one of Kierkegaard's most frequent sources, but the difficulty in deciphering these references in *Either/Or* and interpreting their hermeneutical function is compounded by the fact that he seldom used quotation marks.[5] Kierkegaard had complained that Adler ran biblical material together with his own "revelation," not distinguishing the one from the other.[6] The difference is that S. K. did not claim to have a "revelation" and wrote "without authority." Also, the Scripture passages and phrases S. K. appropriated are on the order of allusions and serve as literary devices rather than as the exposition of biblical teaching.

The most frequent use of Scripture in Kierkegaard's early writings was as a literary device. This is nowhere more evident than in volume one of *Either/Or*. Here there are no direct quotes of Scripture, no appeal to the authority of Scripture as the basis for a particular doctrine, and no exposition of a biblical passage to discover its meaning. Kierkegaard, writing as the consummate aesthete, restricted his use of Scripture to an aesthetic appropriation of the Bible. It is cited in the same way that a passage from any other classical source— literature, the theater, poetry—might be used. There is no particular significance in the fact that he dealt with Scripture. Indeed, the scriptural allusion could frequently be replaced by a more contemporary reference without any change in context and meaning of Kierkegaard's emphasis.

The most obvious illustration of this type of reference is
the passing allusions that, in a word or brief phrase, refer to
something that only someone as familiar with the Bible as
Kierkegaard would recognize as being references from that
source. For example, in the "Diapsalmata," the young aesthete
observed that:

> This is my misfortune: at my side there always walks an
> angel of death, and I do not besprinkle the door-lintels of the
> elect with blood, as a sign that he shall pass by, no, it is just
> their doors that he enters—for only the love that lives in mem-
> ory is happy.[7]

This reference to an angel of death and sprinkling the
door-posts is an allusion to Exodus 12:23. However, the passage, as cited, has nothing to do with the history of Israel's de-
liverance from Egypt. Rather it is the aesthete's idiomatic
expression for despair. Again, these kinds of references appear
to be only incidental.

Kierkegaard also used a number of biblical characters and
incidents. The immediacy of music is illustrated by alluding to
David playing for Saul.[8] David's census of Israel is compared
with the modern age, in which the individual is "counted."[9]
Reference is made to Saul and the witch of Endor,[10] Job,[11]
Adam and Eve,[12] David and Uriah,[13] Joseph and Pharaoh's
dream,[14] and numerous other allusions. Kierkegaard mistak-
enly had Rebecca, instead of Rachel, stealing Laban's gods.[15]
This indicates that these were not references cited after close
scrutiny. Rather, they were part of S. K.'s frame of reference.
As Dunstan has observed:

> Every writer borrows or develops phrases, which for him
> come to be typical ways of expressing himself. He uses them
> over and over again, for they pour out of his mind as he works
> as though they were waiting ready for his use. S. K. seems to
> have used the Bible in this way, having had its contents so
> firmly fixed in his memory that its words and phrases became
> part of his linguistic stock-in-trade.[16]

The diffuse allusions mentioned above continue into volume two of *Either/Or*. Here, S. K., through the persona of
Judge William, also used direct quotes from the Scripture to
establish a point of reference with regard to the issue under

discussion. Genesis 2:24, "A man shall leave his father and mother and cleave unto his wife" is the basis for analysis of the role of woman in marriage.[17] A misquote of 1 Timothy 4:4 ("Every gift is good . . . instead of "every good gift") is used as the basis for understanding the source of goodness in a gift.[18] The uniqueness of woman is indicated by a citation of the passage regarding the beauty of a woman's hair.[19] Numerous other passages are drawn upon in Judge William's discussion of the significance of marriage, love, and ethical commitment.

There are also numerous references where the meaning of the passage cited carries its own intrinsic implications with it in Kierkegaard's usage. These are in the text not as quotations, but as part of the sentences themselves. Scripture is used to give a wealth of meaning and could not be excised without doing violence to Kierkegaard's text. The aesthete asked, "For where can a young man be found who has not had moments in his life when he would have given half, or perhaps all of his possessions to be a Don Juan?"[20] Several biblical contexts are possible references for this quote. The most likely would be where Zacchaeus told Jesus that he would give half his goods to the poor. The point is that one would gladly give material resources for a spiritual gain, but the young aesthete sees a willingness to squander all for a sensual gain.

In an analysis of Hegel's treatment of "unhappy consciousness," the aesthete notes "we are not merely philosophers beholding the kingdom from afar," an obvious allusion to Moses' looking at the promised land without entering.[21] This implies that a speculative philosophical description of unhappy consciousness may be given, but it will always be an abstraction at a distance. Allusions to Scripture sometimes help convey a double meaning. Drawing upon the Old Testament story of Samson and Delilah, the aesthete, in "Diary of the Seducer," said, in response to questions regarding his faithfulness, "This is a secret, like Samson's hair, which no Delilah shall wrest from me."[22] Samson was seduced by Delilah, but the seducer refused to be seduced.

In the same vein, Kierkegaard frequently took a familiar passage and embellished it with a creative "addition," allowing the allusion as an illustration for his immediate literary purpose. An example of this is found in "The Rotation Method," where the creation and tower of Babel stories are unified under the theme of boredom.

> The history of this can be traced from the very beginning of the world. The gods were bored, and so they created man. Adam was bored because he was alone, and so Eve was created. Thus boredom entered the world, and increased in proportion to the increase of population. Adam was bored alone; then Adam and Eve were bored together; then Adam and Eve and Cain and Abel were bored *en famille*; then the population of the world increased, and the peoples were bored *en masse*. To divert themselves they conceived the idea of constructing a tower high enough to reach the heavens. This idea itself is as boring as the tower was high, and constitutes a terrible proof of how boredom gained the upper hand.[23]

The aesthete and Judge William represent their respective stages with regard to the Scripture. The aesthete utilized the Bible as part of his cultural background. It is the source of idioms and illustrations, but is not viewed as authoritative. In a telling passage from the "Diapsalmata" the aesthete speaks of the weakness of modern views of human pathos: "This is the reason my soul always turns back to the Old Testament and to Shakespeare. I feel that those who speak there are at least human beings."[24] Judge William, representing commitment to the ethical universal, explained his being "well versed in the Holy Scripture" saying that "one ought to be clear in one's own mind about the most important relationships of life."[25] Scripture is authoritative, and underscores the ethical universal. Dunstan has noted:

> Volume II has to do with marriage, and of necessity has to treat the relationship between the two sexes and the functions each performs in that relationship. In his discussion of these points, S. K. took the biblical teaching as correct and dealt with the attitude of his day in the light of the Bible. Adam and Eve appear again and again; S. K. followed their story through and dwelt upon the points of emphasis that are in it. Nowhere did he even suggest the question which the present age had popularized: did Adam and Eve really exist? From his writing one would conclude that he never really thought of that now common doubt. Yet actually that question has nothing to do

with the matter which he had at hand. He was concerned with the marriage relationship, and with the contribution respective partners made to it.[26]

However, William seeks to harmonize difficult passages and has no sense of either the paradoxical or the difficulty of following biblical commands.[27]

Beneath the ethical pseudonym of Judge William is, however, a clue to the confidence Kierkegaard had in the veracity of Scripture. In his numerous allusions to the Gospels, there is no evidence that he took seriously historical-critical doubts regarding the life, ministry, and words of Jesus.[28] Although Kierkegaard struggled with the "how" of appropriation of the Gospel, he appears to have had little doubt regarding its content. Dunstan has concluded that:

> Two things are clear; on the one hand, that S. K. took the words of Jesus as guideposts in that which he was writing; and on the other hand, that the words of Jesus he used bore upon the subjects with which he was dealing. It appears as though S. K. had found an authority to which he referred all questions which came to his mind, from whom he expected and found answers.[29]

The form and structure of the entire Kierkegaard corpus is shaped and influenced by Scripture. Biblical themes which had great significance in S. K.'s later works appeared in skeleton form in *Either/Or*. Primary in this work is the casual hermeneutic of Scripture as a literary device, which marks the aesthetic approach to Scripture, and the hermeneutic of the ethical, which marks the essays of Judge William. The limits of the ethical and the introduction of the religious stage are outlined in *Fear and Trembling*.

Fear and Trembling

Kierkegaard used the pseudonym Johannes de Silentio, suggesting silence and mystery, as author of *Fear and Trembling*. Built upon the eighteen-verse Genesis episode of Abraham's sacrifice of Isaac, with concentration on one verse (22:8), "Take your son, your only son Isaac, whom you love, and go to the land of Mount Moriah, and offer him there as a burnt offering upon one of the mountains of which I shall tell you." In addition to the extended treatment of the Genesis passage, there are numerous other references and allusion to Scripture in this brief treatise.[30] Edmund Perry has correctly observed:

> [Kierkegaard] maintained that the truth of human existence will be found only in the answers men give to the questions and demands of the God of the Bible rather than in the answers men find for the questions they frame. The Living God of biblical faith is the interrogator, human history is the witness stand, and we are the witnesses.[31]

S. K.'s interest was in understanding the possibility of faith and how it arises in the individual. He did not want a philosophical or systematic construction of a doctrine of faith. In an obvious slap at Hegelian speculation he observed:

> In our age, everyone is unwilling to stop with faith but goes further. It perhaps would be rash to ask where they are going, whereas it is a sign of urbanity and culture for me to assume that everyone has faith, since otherwise it certainly would be odd to speak of going further. It was different in those ancient days. Faith was then a task for a whole lifetime, because it was assumed that proficiency in believing is not acquired either in days or in weeks. When the tried and tested oldster approached his end, had fought the good fight and kept the faith, his heart was still young enough not to have forgotten the anxiety and trembling that disciplined the youth that the adult learned to control, but that no man outgrows.[32]

Kierkegaard was also concerned with the relationship between Abraham, saved under the Law, and salvation by grace.[33] The ultimate question posed by *Fear and Trembling* is whether one can acquire faith by simply imitating Abraham. Kierkegaard answered with a resounding "no."

As a child, Kierkegaard had repeatedly heard the story of Abraham and Isaac. He felt that it could possibly have taken place in Denmark. In an attempt to understand its significance, Kierkegaard noted that he was "not a thinker" and felt "no need to go beyond faith."[34] Further, in an obvious lampooning of the numerous exegetical commentaries that attempted to explain away the difficulty of this story, Kierkegaard observed that Johannes de Silentio "was not an exegetical scholar. He did not know Hebrew; if he had known Hebrew he perhaps would easily have understood the story of Abraham."[35]

The work opens with several possible scenarios of what might, but did not, take place with regard to Abraham and Isaac. These interpretations offer glimpses of how Abraham could have lost faith, disobeyed God, or lost his family if he had responded in any way other than the quiet obedience recorded in Scripture. Biblical faith always stands in tension, walking a tight rope between the arrogance of presumption and the sin of disobedience. Kierkegaard was impatient with any interpretations that removed this tension from faith.

Commentators of Kierkegaard's day were, by comparison, almost unanimous in seeing Abraham's willingness to offer Isaac as a great moral difficulty needing explanation. Further, as Pailin observed, "the canon of reason controls most of the interpretations of the story, making it incumbent upon the commentator to establish the reasonableness of God's command and Abraham's response" and, in what S. K. would have regarded as an ironic twist, the story is made "to illustrate the need for reason in matters of faith."[36] Various attempts were made to reconcile Abraham's action with the ethical. If it were simply a myth it could be ignored. It could be easily explained as a veiled rebuke of human sacrifice, or justified on the grounds of Abraham's belief that God would raise Isaac from the dead. Abraham's response would be reasonable if it were assumed he had full assurance that God had actually revealed himself. Kierkegaard complained of the easy answers offered and observed:

> If the rich young man whom Jesus met along the way had sold all his possessions and given the money to the poor, we would praise him as we praise every great deed, even if we could not understand him without working, but he still would not become an Abraham, even though he sacrificed the best. What is omitted from Abraham's story is the anxiety, because to money I have no ethical obligation but to the son the father has the highest and holiest. We forget it and yet want to talk about Abraham. So we talk and in the process of talking interchange the two terms, Isaac and the best, and everything goes fine.[37]

Kierkegaard used Abraham's willingness to offer Isaac as a basis for analysis of religious consciousness in contrast to ethical consciousness. *Fear and Trembling* went beyond *Either/Or* in developing Kierkegaard's struggle with the inadequacy of moral law as a basis for relationship to God. The ethical involves an awareness of universal moral obligation. In Abraham's case the ethical was, according to Kierkegaard, "Thou shalt not kill."[38] One must conclude that either Abraham was a murderer or he stood under the paradox of the teleological suspension of the ethical.

S. K. took the story of Abraham's offering of Isaac seriously. In it he saw a radical disjunction between the ethical universal and the command of God. He focused on becoming contemporaneous with the event. However, Johannes de Silentio was unable to explain Abraham, so he simply admired him, holding up his faith as a mystery to be observed and praised. When the sacrifice of Isaac was aborted, Abraham exercised the same joy at receiving him back that had been experienced in anticipation of his birth. Johannes observed that by "faith" one would

> receive everything exactly in the sense in which it is said that one who has faith like a mustard seed can move mountains. It takes purely human courage to renounce the whole temporal realm in order to gain eternity. . . . But it takes the paradoxical and humble courage to grasp the whole temporal realm now by virtue of the absurd, and this is the courage of faith.[39]

The "Problemata" develops Johannes's concern with the difference between the ethical and the religious categories. Johannes's first question was, "Is there such a thing as a teleological suspension of the ethical?" When one's duty to humanity and duty to God agree, there is no difficulty. However, when they do not agree there is a terrifying dilemma to which there is no direct answer, as illustrated by Abraham's silence.

Abraham is different from the tragic hero, Agamemnon, in that he gladly accepts his circumstances. Agamemnon remained within the ethical and, thus, can be understood. Kierkegaard observed:

> The difference between the tragic hero and Abraham is very obvious. The tragic hero is still within the ethical. He

allows an expression of the ethical to have its *telos* in a higher expression of the ethical, he scales down the ethical relation between father and son or daughter and father to a feeling that has its dialectic in its relation to the idea of moral conduct. Here there can be no question of a teleological suspension of the ethical.[40]

If the ethical realm were all that existed, then the philosophy of the Greeks would suffice. Larger-than-life heroes would reinforce the rules of human behavior as given in universal ethical laws. Abraham would make no sense. His act of "courage" would amount to murder and he would be condemned by all.

When the religious category of faith is introduced, however, every particular situation stands higher than the universal. Abraham is a true "knight of faith," for "by his act he transgressed the ethical altogether and had a higher *telos* outside it."[41] Although numerous biblical allusions fill this section of the work, it is the story of Abraham which contained "the teleological suspension of the ethical" and was thus cited as the basis for the emphasis on paradox.[42]

The second question raised in the "Problemata" is, "Is there an absolute duty toward God?" Kierkegaard noted that simply to equate love of neighbor with duty towards God is a tautology.[43] Luke 14:26, where Jesus said that one must "hate father and mother" and other family relations in order to be his disciple, is an example of absolute duty towards God.[44] Johannes indicated that this is a "hard saying" which persons have difficulty in hearing.[45] Further, the theological exegetes try to substitute the meaning "love less than" for "hate," thus escaping the harshness of this demand. But if the passage is to have any meaning it must be understood literally.

God is the one demanding absolute love. The key to understanding this is to "regard the task as paradox."[46] Only the knight of faith can seize its significance in the passion of faith. If this dictum were allowed to become an ethical command of the church, the tragic hero is reintroduced and the very denial of family is placed at the level of the ethical. Abraham is significant because he made the double movement from resignation to faith. He thereby regained the temporal and finite and

Isaac's life was spared. The absurd is accepted through faith. Johannes concluded:

> Therefore, either there is an absolute duty to God—and if there is such a thing, it is the paradox just described, that the single individual as the single individual is higher than the universal and as the single individual stands in an absolute relation to the absolute—or else faith has never existed because it has always existed, or else Abraham is lost, or else one must interpret the passage in Luke 14 as did that appealing exegete and explain the similar and corresponding passages in the same way.[47]

The third question raised in the "Problemata" is "Was it ethically defensible for Abraham to conceal his understanding from Sarah, from Eliezer, and from Isaac?"[48] Abraham is a "witness" to the reality of faith, there being no such thing as a "teacher." Yet he witnesses in silence. What Abraham had heard within himself could not be communicated—others would have only translated his action for themselves. In resignation he gave up all earthly hope for his son Isaac; in faith he silently obeyed the command of God with fear and trembling. Abraham's only words answer Isaac's question regarding the sacrifice, saying simply "God will provide. . . ."[49] He speaks truthfully, yet he speaks another language.

Abraham lay beyond Johannes's grasp. He could not understand him. He could only admire him from afar. Abraham remained true to his call to faith. S. K. concluded:

> Anyone who loves God needs no tears, no admiration; he forgets the suffering in the love. Indeed, so completely has he forgotten it that there would not be the slightest trace of his suffering left if God himself did not remember it, for he sees in secret and recognizes and counts the tears and forgets nothing.

> Thus, either there is a paradox, that the single individual as the single individual stands in an absolute relation to the absolute, or Abraham is lost.[50]

In the "Epilogue" to *Fear and Trembling* Kierkegaard reminds us that "the highest passion in a person is faith" and that "no generation begins at any other point than where the previous one did. Each generation begins all over again."[51]

Kierkegaard scholars are divided concerning S. K.'s intentions in *Fear and Trembling*. Walter Lowrie regarded it as a "guided" communication to Regina to explain the broken engagement. Kierkegaard, according to this view, identified with Abraham and saw Regina as his Isaac.[52] Kierkegaard did seek to resume the relationship with Regina after her marriage. Gregor Malantschuk believed that Kierkegaard identified with Isaac, thus he was trying to tell Regina that he was the one being sacrificed because of his father's sin. It was only later when Kierkegaard had a more detached view of his relationship to his father and Regina and could "confide more freely on paper" that "he attaches primary importance in his journal entries about Abraham and Isaac to what must have taken place between his father and him, and only secondary importance to what occurred between him and Regina."[53] Fishburn has suggested that the work is Kierkegaard's "propaedeutic to Christian faith" distinguished from *Sickness Unto Death* by the "omission of any reference to sin," simply paving the way to faith "by clearing away false expectations."[54]

The religious orthodoxy of Denmark in Kierkegaard's day had been saturated with an infusion of Hegelian rationalism, which sought to go beyond faith. This led, in S. K.'s view, only to resignation, not to Christian faith. The confession by de Silentio that he was "not a learned exegete" because of his lack of knowledge of Hebrew can be seen as suggesting that he could not understand Abraham because they lacked a common language.[55] Christendom had lost sight of the Paradox— Christ, who is the common denominator illuminating the faith of both Abraham and the Christian. Again, citing Fishburn, "*Fear and Trembling* is a preliminary 'expectoration' that anticipates the later, very direct, *Attack upon Christendom.*"[56] However, the hermeneutic of paradox was also given fuller explication in *Philosophical Fragments*, *The Concept of Anxiety*, and *Concluding Unscientific Postscript*.

The Use of Scripture in Kierkegaard's Later Philosophical Works

Casual indifference characterized the attitude of the aesthete toward Scripture. Judge William personified the hermeneutic of the ethical universal. Dissatisfaction with the ethical resulted in the emergence of religious consciousness. Thus, the hermeneutic of paradox was introduced in an ancillary way in *Fear and Trembling*. However, *Philosophical Fragments* and *The Concept of Anxiety* represent a clearer understanding and explication of the hermeneutic of paradox and the religion of transcendence.

Philosophical Fragments

Kierkegaard's *Philosophical Fragments* was published in 1844, just four days before the publication of *The Concept of Anxiety*. Johannes Climacus is the pseudonymous author of this work. The purpose of the work was to explain Kierkegaard's understanding of what is involved in becoming a Christian in contrast to the Socratic or idealistic perspective, which saw truth as originating within the individual. Few philosophers would entitle their work a "Fragment" and attempt in only one hundred and thirty-nine pages to call attention to the major thesis of their life's work.

In the *Fragments* the language of Idealism is employed as a means of both comparing and contrasting the truth of Christianity with the approach of speculative philosophy. The religious language of biblical and theological categories is present in modified form throughout the work. There are a number of references to Scripture contained in *Fragments*.[57] The vast majority of these are appropriated as allusions. However, the allusions are more directly related to the flow of the text than was the case with the earlier hermeneutic of the aesthete. There are also a number of places where the hermeneutic of paradox is developed more fully than in any work considered thus far in this study. This work is brief enough and its contents significant enough for understanding S. K.'s religious thought that the hermeneutical uses of the Scriptures just mentioned are examined in an exposition of this treatise.

Climacus was concerned with the question of truth, specifically "How far does the Truth admit of being Learned?"[58] The problem is set in the context of an examination of the Socratic and Idealistic approach to epistemology.[59] Either one already knows what one is to come to know or one does not. If one already knows, then there is no need to seek knowledge. If one does not know, then by what criteria does one recognize what one has discovered as the object of the quest for truth?

Plato resolved this paradox via the pre-existence of the soul, thus in coming to know one is not discovering truths of which there was previously total ignorance. In Plato's *Meno* Socrates taught a slave geometric truths that he was unaware he knew. The teacher is but a "mid-wife" for the truth, for "between man and man the maieutic relationship is the highest" whereas "begetting belongs to God alone."[60] If the truth merely lies dormant within the individual, time and the teacher are but vanishing moments. This knowledge would be ahistorical for "the temporal point of departure is nothing."[61]

"The Moment [of learning] must have a decisive significance" if the quest for truth is genuine.[62] S. K. said that "the seeker must be destitute of the truth up to the very moment of his learning it."[63] The would-be "learner" thus must be considered as in "Error" with regard to the truth.[64] In this case, a teacher could not simply "remind" a student of innate realities. Kierkegaard said, "If the learner is to acquire the Truth, the Teacher must bring it to him . . . he must also give him the condition necessary for understanding it."[65] The Teacher of eternal truth is God. Only God can transform an individual so that the eternal can be known and appropriated on a personal basis.

As Kierkegaard sets the stage for his understanding of Christian truth, he offers provisional definitions that incorporate biblical and theological concepts in his philosophical discussion. Thus, for example, he notes:

> The teacher is then the God himself, who in acting as an occasion prompts the learner to recall that he is in Error, and that by reason of his own guilt. But this state, the being in Error by reason of one's own guilt, what shall we call it? Let's call it *Sin*.[66]

What should this Teacher be called? He is the one who restores the lost condition and gives the "learner" the requisite condition and the Truth; he is called "Saviour or Redeemer."[67] Furthermore, the Teacher becomes an "Atonement" by "taking away the wrath impending upon that which of which the learner has made himself guilty."[68] Unlike the Socratic teacher who is but a "mid-wife to truth . . . this Teacher," observed Kierkegaard,

> The learner will never be able to forget. For the moment he forgets him he sinks back again into himself, just as one who while in original possession of the condition forgot that God exists . . . . The condition was a trust for which the recipient would always be required to render an account.[69]

The Teacher also serves as "Judge."[70] The Moment of decision has a peculiar character. It is brief and temporal, transient and past in the next moment, yet it is decisive and filled with the eternal. In an apparent allusion to Galatians 4:4, this moment is called the "Fullness of Time."[71]

In Error the "learner" was constantly departing from the Truth; once the truth is learned, the direction of the individual's life is changed. The "learner" forgets the world in the discovery of self. The self is forgotten in the discovery of the Teacher. Then the "learner" becomes "disciple."[72] The disciple who receives the condition of the truth is called, in an obvious allusion to 2 Corinthians 5:17, "a man of a different quality . . . a new creature."[73] This change is called "conversion" and, in an allusion to John 3:3, the "new birth."[74] There is a grief at having remained so long in the former state. "Repentance" is looking backward "to quicken the steps to that which lies before"—a veiled allusion to Philippians 3:13.[75] The disciple "owes no man anything," save the Teacher, adapted from Romans 13:8.[76] Such a transaction can only take place on an individual basis. The Moment is of decisive significance.

S. K. utilized a fairy tale involving a king who loved a peasant girl to illustrate the difficulty of a transaction between the Divine and the human.[77] The key is to communicate so that the object of affection is not overwhelmed and yet not to be so secret as to prohibit communication. The failure to communicate between these potential lovers is the greatest of all griefs. Is all this just fanciful speculation? What could move God to come and to seek after humanity? The Divine motive can only be explained as love.

The God has reserved to himself this unfathomable grief: to know that he may repel the learner, that he does not need him, that the learner has brought destruction upon himself by his own guilt, that he can leave the learner to his fate; to know also how well-nigh impossible it is to keep the learner's courage and confidence alive.[78]

How can this divine love be fulfilled? How will any union between the God and the "learner" be brought about? God cannot simply elevate the "learner" to the Divine level. Nor can He be satisfied with worship from a distance. Since the union cannot be brought about by an elevation, a descent is required. Echoing the theme of the kenosis passage of Philippians 2, S. K. concluded that the God must come in servant-form.[79] This form is no mere disguise, but must be "his true form and figure."[80] He must suffer all things and endure all things. Kierkegaard said:

> Every other form of revelation would be a deception in the eyes of love; for either the learner would first have to be changed, and the fact concealed from him that this was necessary (but love does not alter the beloved, it alters itself); or there would be permitted to prevail a frivolous ignorance of the fact that the entire relationship was a delusion. (This was the error of paganism.) Every other form of revelation would be a deception from the standpoint of divine love.[81]

Biblical allusions are most numerous in the few pages where S. K. described the servant-form of the God-in-time.[82] Several examples illustrate the type of allusions used. The Teacher would guard his steps "more carefully than if angels guided them, not to prevent his foot from stumbling against a stone, but lest he trample human beings" is a reference to Satan's challenge to Jesus to throw himself off the pinnacle of the temple, recorded in Matthew 4:6.[83] Furthermore, mankind would be "offended" at him (cf. Mark 8:31).[84] Yet God, who could "sustain heavens and earth by the fiat of his omnipotent word," a reference to Hebrews 1:3, would choose to ignore this response.[85] In servant-form he suffered all things including "hunger in the desert" (cf. Matthew 4:2), "thirst in time of agony" (cf. the crucifixion, John 19:28), and he was "forsaken in death" (cf. Mark 15:34).[86] Appropriating the words of Pilate recorded in John 19:5, Kierkegaard exclaimed, "Behold the man."[87]

Kierkegaard also used a variety of biblical allusions in describing the servant-form as essential for God's self-revelation. S.K. said that if "my eyes were filled with more tears than those of a repentant woman" (cf. Luke 7:37), and if he were at Jesus' feet "more humbly than a woman whose heart's sole choice was this one thing needful" (cf. Luke 10:42), he still could not change God's way of revealing himself.[88] It would be a false response to seek a more direct revelation from the Teacher. Jesus would rebuke him (like Peter, cf. Mark 8:33) and would weep over him (like Jerusalem, cf. Matthew 23:37).[89]

The explication of the servant-form of God's coming in time was biblically based. However, as S. K. returned to a more philosophically oriented discussion in chapter 3, "The Absolute Paradox: A Metaphysical Crotchet," biblical allusions are used sparingly.[90] The relationship between the paradox and reason is examined. Kierkegaard argued that one cannot reason toward existence. Rather, one must always reason from existence. S. K. was concerned with "real being," not "being in the ideal sense" which is essence.[91] The paradox of the Christian faith is absolute, in that it cannot be explained, mediated, or resolved by reason. With tongue-in-cheek Kierkegaard taunted the apologists:

> Whoever therefore attempts to demonstrate the existence of God (except in the sense of clarifying the concept . . .) proves in lieu thereof something else, something which at times perhaps does not need a proof, and in any case needs none better for the fool says in his heart that there is no God, but whoever says in his heart or to men: Wait just a little and I will prove it—what a rare man of wisdom is he![92]

In the "Appendix" following this chapter, no references or allusions to Scripture are found. Here Kierkegaard dealt with the issue of an offended conscience. Any true knowledge of the God will come only as the individual realizes that he is absolutely unlike God. However, "if the encounter is not in understanding" when reason and the Paradox come together then "Offense" is taken at the Paradox.[93] Basically, to be offended is to be passive to the Moment of encounter. Yet this offended consciousness is an indirect witness to the power of the Paradox. In its active form the offended conscience attempts to explain the Paradox away, "for why do we have our philosophers if not to make supernatural things trivial and commonplace?"[94]

There are twenty-six allusions to Scripture in chapter 4, "The Case of the Contemporary Disciple." Many of these are used to further describe God in time. For example, Kierkegaard said, in an allusion to the *kenosis* passage of Philippians 2, "The God's servant-form however is not a mere disguise, but is actual . . . ."[95] God sent a forerunner to "arouse the learner's attention."[96] God did not assume this servant-form to hide Himself from persons. But the condition for believing the signs of His divinity still rest with God and not the "learner." The contemporary disciples did not see God simply because they witnessed the incarnation. The rejection of Jesus by many in his day is evidence of this.

Since the God's relationship to the "learner" is the key to determining who will become a disciple, what advantage do first-century believers have over later generations of Christians? Here again the Paradox is central. The "learner" could understand the Paradox only as God gave the opportunity. Kierkegaard said:

> It comes to pass when the Reason and the Paradox encounter one another happily in the Moment, when the Reason sets itself aside and the Paradox bestows itself. The third entity in which this union is realized (for it is not realized in the reason, since it is set aside: nor in the Paradox, which bestows itself— hence it is realized *in* something) is that happy passion to which we will now assign a name. . . . We shall call this passion: *Faith*.[97]

If the encounter with the Paradox "has merely historical significance," then one does not become a disciple.[98] The contemporary who followed the Teacher might gain an accurate historical knowledge. But, in an allusion to the thief on the cross, one may know little of the historical life of the Teacher and have only a brief encounter before death, and still become a disciple.[99] It is the decisive Moment that is important.

Faith is not simply a form of knowledge. Faith is a happy resting in the Paradox. In order to have the power to provide conditions for this faith, the Teacher must be God. In order to place this in the learner's possession, he must be man. Kierkegaard said that "the disciple of faith is so related to his Teacher as to be eternally concerned with his historical existence."[100] The object of faith is not the teaching but the Teacher.

The disciple who is contemporary with the historical Jesus may appear to have the advantage of being able to see with the eyes, but the gift of faith is a miracle of God. The contemporary disciple does not have to deal with years of tradition that might encumber faith. The radical departure from the established order without any precedence for faith would appear to be a hindrance. Before dealing with "The Disciple at Second Hand," Chapter V, Kierkegaard included a philosophical "Interlude."

In the "Interlude," a veiled attack upon Hegel, Kierkegaard posed the question, "Is the past more necessary than the future? or, When the possible becomes actual, is it thereby made more necessary than it was?"[101] In other words, what is the importance of history for faith? In the only reference to Scripture in this section, Kierkegaard alludes to Hebrews 11:1, "Faith believes what it does not see. . . ."[102] In the context of the discussion, this reference is related more to a sense of the historical and coming into existence than to the Christian idea of faith as previously discussed.

Kierkegaard argued that "coming into existence" is not a step in logic.[103] Nor is it "necessary" because the necessary does not come into existence, it simply is. The historical is immutable in that "what has happened has happened."[104] However, it does not contain the necessary. Therefore, the necessary exists without reference to the historical. S. K. pointed out, "The change involved in coming into existence is actuality, the transition takes place with freedom."[105] The real question regarding the past is not concern with the specifics of what did or did not happen. The real question is, what does one believe about what has happened? The belief that God has come in time is an object of faith. Attempting to avoid the risk of faith is like refusing to get into the water before one is able to swim.[106] Belief and doubt are opposite passions.

> Belief is not a form of knowledge but a free act, an expression of will. It believes the fact of coming into existence, and has thus succeeded in overcoming within itself the uncertainty that corresponds to the nothingness of the antecedent nonbeing; it believes the "thus" of what has come into existence, and has consequently succeeded in annulling within itself the possible "how." Without denying the possibility of another "thus," this present "thus" is for belief most certain.[107]

The past itself never becomes necessary, for it is only "belief and coming into existence [that] correspond to one another."[108] Applied to religious faith, this means that there is in fact "no difference between an immediate contemporary and a successor."[109]

Chapter 5 develops this argument with regard to second-generation Christians. There are ten allusions to Scripture in this final chapter. Again drawing upon the *kenosis* passage of Philippians 2, Kierkegaard asked rhetorically whether or not the contemporary disciple would "gain anything by reason of the reliability of his account?"—that is, his nearness to incarnation. Kierkegaard replied, "Historically speaking yes, but otherwise not," for "he was after all only in the form of a servant" and "divinity is not an immediate characteristic. . . the Teacher must first develop in the learner the most profound self-reflection, the sense of sin, as a condition for the understanding."[110] Further, "The historical fact that God has been in human form is the essence of the matter," for the absurdity of faith "makes all petty difficulties vanish."[111]

Since Christian faith is not based upon mere probability, it is folly to consider any proximity to the historical aspect of the God in time as an advantage. According to Kierkegaard, "It is and remains the Paradox, and cannot be assimilated by any speculation. This fact exists for Faith alone."[112] The thought "that it is profitable for the disciple that the God should again leave the earth, is taken from the New Testament; it is found in the Gospel of John."[113] In an allusion to John 21:25, Kierkegaard noted that the disciple at second hand does not want so voluminous a contemporary testimony "filling so many books that the world cannot contain them."[114] The Par-

adox "did not arise in the heart of man."[115] Thus, in contrast
to the Socratic doctrine that truth lies within the individual,
Kierkegaard has proposed Faith as a new organ, the consciousness of Sin the new presupposition, the Moment as the
new decision, and God in Time as the new Teacher.[116]

The hermeneutic of paradox is most evident as Kierkegaard discussed God in Time. Scripture, not existential philosophy, was Kierkegaard's primary source for describing what
the incarnation entailed. His philosophical interest is in the
"how" of appropriation of the Christ-event. The themes outlined in this brief work are given "historical clothing" in Kierkegaard's last philosophical work, *Concluding Unscientific
Postscript.*

The Concept of Anxiety

There are clues to Kierkegaard's aesthetic understanding
of "anxiety" in *Either/Or* in the diagnosis dealing with sensu-
ousness in Mozart's *Don Giovanni.*[117] In that work, sensuous
anxiety is contrasted with its tragic and pathological counter-
parts. In contrast, *The Concept of Anxiety* was constituted as
a phenomenological or psychological treatment of human sin
and sinfulness. This work was penned under the pseudonym
of Vigilus Haufniensis, which means "the watchman of
Copenhagen." It introduced the religious stage and its inwardness by means of a systematic analysis of human sin.[118]

The Concept of *Anxiety* was an extended examination of
Genesis 3. S. K. took Adam seriously as an historical individual. However, he refused to accept the Augustinian and Lutheran notion of inherited sin.[119] He was not Pelagian, at least
not in the traditional sense. In arguing for the historical reality
of Adam, Kierkegaard concluded that everyman is Adam.
Thus, everyman's sin is both the first and, paradoxically, everyman shares in the guilt of the race. Only Christ represented
the truly universal man.

Kierkegaard said that sin was properly "the subject of the
sermon."[120] He rejected the attempt to introduce Hegelian
speculation into Christian theology concerning anxiety and
sin. Since "actuality" was a late entry in Hegel's logical
scheme, he was an inadequate source for dealing with sin as it
exists in reality.[121] In contrast, traditional dogmatics "begins

with the actual in order to raise it up into ideality."[122] Ethics is limited to the ideal of possibility, but can not raise actuality to a full and ideal possibility.[123] As S. K. moved toward the direct communication of his later religious authorship, the Bible became increasingly important. Kierkegaard's use of the Bible in *Anxiety* included the same type of allusions found in the earlier works, but also included a more detailed discussion of a variety of specific passages that relate theologically to understanding the causes, consequences, and cure for sin.[124]

In the first portion of the book, Kierkegaard dealt with the relationship between anxiety and hereditary sin. Anxiety is both the origin and the explanation of hereditary sin. He rejected any interpretation of Adam's sin that equated the first sin as the source of all hereditary sin. Kierkegaard specifically mentioned Catholic theology, which focused on Adam's loss of "the wonderful gift of God," and Federal theology, which saw Adam as a "plenipotentiary" for the whole race.[125] Such views really place Adam outside history and outside the atonement.[126] S. K. observed:

> The doctrine that Adam and Christ correspond to each other explains nothing . . . . It may be an analogy, but the analogy is conceptually imperfect. Christ alone is an individual who is more than an individual. For this reason he does not come at the beginning, but in the fullness of time.

The influence of years of human sin cannot be denied. However, the biblical account of the origin of sin is an accurate picture of every individual's first sin. As Kierkegaard said,

> Adam is the first man. . . . He is not essentially different from the race, for in that case there is no race at all; he is not the race, for in that case also there would be no race. He is himself and the race. Therefore that which explains Adam also explains the race and vice versa.[127]

The "first" sin is a "quality" constituting a new reality and it cannot simply be considered "numerically."[128] Adam's sin defined a new and previously unrealized human potential. The first sin is a "leap" from one quality of existence to another. Otherwise, Adam's sin could not be explained and every other individual's "first sin" would be of no consequence. Hereditary descent only expresses the continuation of human history, not the necessity of sin. The biblical account of the first sin is "care-lessly regarded as myth" according to S. K. because its reality has been lost in the theological explanations that have encum-bered it.[129] According to Kierkegaard, "The Genesis story pre-sents the only dialectically consistent view. . . . *Sin came into the world by a sin.*"[130] One is born into sin in the sense that that is every person's potential.

Kierkegaard analyzed anxiety as moving from a dream-ing state (the self is indeterminate), to objective anxiety (the self in relation to creation), and finally, to subjective anxiety (the self in relation to the other).[131] In innocence a person is "not qualified as spirit but is psychically qualified in an imme-diate unity."[132] At this stage the spirit is dreaming.[133]

The Genesis account also gives an accurate explanation of innocence as ignorance.[134] The human synthesis of physical and psychical is held in balance by transcendence or spirit. In-nocence is canceled by transcendence. Adam was innocent be-cause he was ignorant. The potential for sin was present with him from the beginning. One is born in sin in the sense that that is an individual's potential. However, each person must choose to sin. An allusion to the pathos of guilt over sin (cf. Psalm 51:5) is woven together with a reflection on the work of Christ (cf. Hebrews 7:29 and 9:28), as S. K. observed:

> It is true that a person can say in profound earnestness that he was born in misery and that his mother conceived him in sin, but he can truly sorrow over this only if he himself brought guilt into the world and brought all this upon himself, for it is a contradiction to sorrow *esthetically* over *sinfulness.* The only one who sorrowed innocently over sinfulness was Christ, but he did not sorrow over it as a fate he had to put up with. He sorrowed as the one who freely chose to carry all the sin of the world and to suffer in punishment. This is no esthetic qualification, for Christ was more than an individ-ual.[135]

The fall cannot be explained away by blaming it upon the prohibition regarding the tree of knowledge. Nor can it be blamed on the serpent. Kierkegaard cited James 1:13-14 as proof that temptation arises not from God or externals, but from within.[136] Neither can sin be simply equated with sensu-ousness, although S. K. noted that the sexual came into the world as a result of sin for "without sin there is no sexuality, and without sexuality, no history."[137]

Kierkegaard observed that "anxiety is a qualification of dreaming spirit," in that it involves the ambiguous sense of the difference between the self and the self's potential.[138] It arouses the individual from the dreamlike state of innocence and is the presupposition to hereditary sin. Persons today are derived creatures and thus share in Adam's initial nature of innocence and dreamlike anxiety. Sin coming into the world is a truth each person understands within the self. Kierkegaard observed:

> . . . anxiety means two things: the anxiety in which the individual posits sin by the qualitative leap, and the anxiety that entered in and enters in with sin, and that also, accordingly, enters quantitatively into the world every time an individual posits sin.[139]

. . . .

> Anxiety as it appeared in Adam will never again return, for by him sinfulness came into the world. Because of this, Adam's anxiety has two analogies, the objective anxiety in nature and the subjective anxiety in the individual, of which the latter contains a more and the first a less than the anxiety in Adam.[140]

As individuals are awakened to their nature, anxiety is expressed at first objectively. However, it is in subjective anxiety that personal estrangement is realized. There is a qualitative increase in the sinfulness of humanity as a result of heredity. Sinfulness is like a habit that has been reinforced through successive generations. Yet, one's actual sin is still the "first" for each individual.

Anxiety is not only the source of sin and expressed in the progression of sins, it is also a consequence of sin.[141] Mankind is not only a synthesis of spirit and body, but is also a synthesis of the temporal and eternal.[142] "In the individual life," wrote Kierkegaard, "anxiety is the Moment."[143] All sin takes place in time. However, "time" viewed as a succession of the past, the present, and the future does not make sense of the concept of the eternal. Time can only be understood from the perspective of the eternal. According to Kierkegaard, "The moment is that ambiguity in which time and eternity touch each other, and with this the concept of temporality is posited, whereby time constantly intersects eternity and eternity constantly pervades time."[144] Further, "the Moment is not properly an atom of time but an atom of eternity."[145] The eternal is present in "the moment" of temporal/eternal synthesis. As Dunning noted,

> Temporality is posited on the basis of the Moment, and history begins with it. In short, although the Moment occurs in the blink of an eye, it brings a qualitative change within the temporal sequence. . . . But if the Moment is the limitation of time by eternity, then temporality is seen as a relation to that time-stopping eternity, not simply to infinite succession.[146] The Moment determines the condition of temporality. Thus, the God who "makes all things new" (an allusion to 2 Corinthians 5:17) does so in "the fullness of time" (a reference to Galatians 4:4).[147]

The individual is thrust into this dialectical relationship between time and eternity and the finite and the infinite. Spiritlessness,[148] appeals to fate,[149] and guilt[150] (corresponding to paganism, Greek ideals, and Jewish legalism) are the dialectical poles that anxiety travels before the individual can arrive at a personal guilt over sin. Other solutions are unsatisfactory. Adam points to individual responsibility for sin.

Kierkegaard dealt with anxiety in-and-for-itself saying, "By a qualitative leap sin entered into the world, and it continually enters into the world in that way."[151] S. K. contrasted "anxiety about evil," in which there is still hope for redemption and "anxiety about good," which is the demonic. However, anxiety about evil may simply be a delusion when sin is not faced individually. S. K. said, "Anxiety wants to have the actuality of sin removed, not entirely, but to a certain degree. . . ."[152] Unchecked, this anxiety will result in total self-negation. In the confession of sin and repentance the self first realizes itself. However, the self may flee this realization via "anxiety about the good" or "the demonic."

Kierkegaard called "the demonic" an "unfree relation to the good."[153] Fear of disclosure characterizes the demonic. Numerous biblical passages are cited as evidence of this fear. In the New Testament, the appearance of Christ frequently coincided with the manifestation of the demonic.[154] The demonic asked of Christ, "What have I to do with you?"[155] The demonic may express the loss of freedom either "somatically-psychically"[156] or "pneumatically."[157] The former has to do with excesses of the body or "a bestial perdition."[158] The latter is expressed through an absence of inwardness. Unbelief and superstition, hypocrisy and offense, and pride and cowardice are the various polarities that may accompany the absence of inwardness. Kierkegaard concluded, "Whenever inwardness is lacking, the spirit is finitized."[159]

Anxiety is the avenue to faith. As every finite possibility is exposed, anxiety drives the individual to God. Kierkegaard observed that it is the "synthesis" of human nature that allows anxiety to arise in the individual.[160] This anxiety about self is nothing more than the admission that one is a creature of finitude challenged by the infinite, of freedom abused in sin, of transcendence, and of possibility. Kierkegaard observed:

> The only thing that is truly able to disarm the sophistry of sin is faith, courage to believe that the state itself is a new sin, courage to renounce anxiety without anxiety, which only faith can do; faith does not thereby annihilate anxiety, but, itself eternally young, it extricates itself from anxiety's moment of death. Only faith is able to do this, for only in faith is the synthesis eternal and at every moment possible.[161]

Kierkegaard concluded, "With the help of faith, anxiety brings up the individuality to rest in providence."[162] The one thus educated will "rest only in the atonement."[163] The psychological analysis of anxiety is concluded—further explication of these truths is the task of dogmatics.

Kierkegaard saw each individual's sin as both personal and incorporating the fallen state of the race. Anxiety is the means whereby the realities of sin are acknowledged and resolved through faith. As summarized by Dunning:

> Anxiety can be analyzed as follows: an initial abstract unity in which the self has not yet consciously distinguished itself from its external world; a negative dialectic of opposition between the self as inner and an external power that determines it; and a final reconciliation in which the determining power is inwardly revealed and appropriated and the self finds in faith the culmination and fulfillment of its dialectical education by anxiety.[164]

Kierkegaard's treatment of the self and anxiety are among the most dynamic of his philosophical conceptions. Reinhold Neibuhr, for example, appropriated the polarities of human existence in his doctrine of man.[165] Man stands at the juncture of nature and spirit, freedom and necessity, both limited and limitless. The God-relation, for Kierkegaard, provided the ontological quality to the self necessary for the self to be able to know properly and to actualize itself. Apart from God, the self remains in estrangement. The centrality of Scripture in an analysis of these and related religious concerns is even more evident in Kierkegaard's last philosophical works.

The Use of Scripture in the Final Philosophical Works

Kierkegaard's *Either/Or* was a commercial success. A portion of it, "The Diary of the Seducer," was the rage of the day. However, S. K. was dissatisfied with the popular misunderstanding of the larger message and purpose of *Either/Or*. Although he was well into his philosophical exposition of the religious themes of sin, guilt, anxiety, and the Paradox, Kierkegaard wrote *Stages on Life's Way* to explain clearly the aesthetic, ethical, and religious existence spheres. The use of Scripture in *Stages* is a corroboration of the hermeneutical patterns associated with the aesthetic and ethical existence spheres noted in the earlier works.

Understanding the existence spheres is also important for the work that S. K. intended to be the *finis* of his authorship, *Concluding Unscientific Postscript*. Circumstances, however, redirected his energies toward an even more prolific "second literature" of religious works. The *Postscript* more fully developed the themes of *Philosophical Fragments* and included the major emphases of all the earlier philosophical works, also developing the distinction between the religion of immanence and the religion of transcendence (religiousness A and B). The *Postscript* included aspects of the various hermeneutical patterns associated with the earlier works as well as an extensive use of the hermeneutic of paradox. Also, there are elements of the more polemical use of Scripture characteristic of Kierkegaard's later attack on Christendom.

Stages on Life's Way

Published on April 30, 1845, *Stages* reiterated the themes of *Either/Or* and provided a deeper and richer reinterpretation of the existence spheres.[166] In this work Kierkegaard also offered another attempt at a veiled explanation of his broken engagement to Regina Olsen. *Stages* contains fewer biblical references than the other works examined in this chapter.[167] However, the references and allusions to Scripture are consistent with the usage of the Bible found in more prominent and frequent display elsewhere in the Kierkegaard corpus.

The "Preface" by one "Hilarius Bookbinder" purported to explain how the manuscript of such a strange work came into his possession and to be published. Despite his claims to the contrary, there is ample evidence of a carefully crafted scheme in the writing of this work.[168] Various pseudonymous characters fill the pages.

The use of Scripture as a literary allusion with no particular authority is typical of the aesthetic portion of *Stages*. An allusion to the riddle of Samson, "out of the eater cometh forth meat," reminds one of the difficulty of keeping a secret and sets the stage for the telling of the tale of the Banquet.[169] There is an extraordinary scene from "In *Vino Veritas*," the first section of the book, written by S. K., under the pseudonym of William Afham. A glimpse of the aesthetic stage is provided through the story of an uninterrupted evening of food, wine, and fellowship. The after-dinner speeches of the various guests examine love, the erotic, and womanhood. There are few direct references to Scripture in any of the speeches. These speeches were extemporaneous and not reflective in nature.

There are several allusions to Scripture in preparation for the banquet. However, there is no appeal to the authority or religious significance of the Bible. Victor Eremita, for example, offered a toast with the observation that "the good Lord satisfies the stomach before the eye is satisfied, but the imagination acts inversely."[170] There is also an allusion to setting one's house in order,[171] and the banquet is described with "they ate and drank largely."[172] While in solitude, the author looks back at the banquet and weaves his tale. The characters depict Kierkegaard's struggles with aesthetic ideals associated with perfect love.

The first speaker, identified simply as "the young man" referred to "unhappy love" as the bitterest grief.[173] He desired to understand the true meaning of love before committing himself. He wanted to know the proper object of love before loving. The love of God is not included in the erotic.[174] One of the few allusions to Scripture, actually in an after-dinner speech, came as the young man lamented the folly of choosing a mate, noting that "Adam chose Eve because there was no other."[175] He rejected any basis for commitment to another. The notion of ideal love, when contrasted with the realities of marriage, is a contradiction and, thus, comic.[176]

Constantine Constantius spoke second. He urged the participants to forget their speeches as soon as they were spoken.[177] His speech focused on the illogic of woman. Viewed ethically, woman is jest, therefore Constantius concluded she could only be appreciated aesthetically.[178]

The third speech is that of Victor Eremita, the pseudonymous editor of *Either/Or*. He argued that woman is incomplete without man. She is the ideal that drives him, but she lacks particular identity. He urged his friends to avoid any relationship to her by declining to be wooed into marriage. It is "a strange invention" and a contradiction.[179]

The other unnamed speaker, The Ladies' Tailor, spoke fourth. He contended that the others failed to appreciate woman for what she is in reality: a slave to fashion. He observed that fashion is "a contraband trade in indecency licensed as decorum."[180] As such, fashion reflects the flirtatious changeableness of the feminine. Since all things are merely a matter of fashion, the tailor warned, "Forego love as you would the most dangerous neighborhood."[181]

Johannes the Seducer spoke last. He chided his colleagues for their fear and intrepidation and urged that they learn both to abstain from and enjoy the romantic, thus avoiding commitments.[182] Pure thought about love is a waste to time; the imperative is to enjoy. The gods created woman in order to harness and preoccupy man. Thus, for every woman there is a corresponding seducer.[183]

As the guests departed the banquet they encountered Judge William, the ethical speaker of volume two of *Either/Or* and his wife. The tender scene of their mutual and loving relationship stood in marked contrast to the cynicism that characterized the after-dinner speeches.

Victor Eremita, dashing into the Judge's home, discovers a letter from the Judge. It is published as "The Aesthetic Validity of Marriage." In contrast to the Banquet scene, Judge William communicates directly and in an open manner with the reader. The letter is introduced by one identified simply as "A married man." He argues that most objections to marriage are as ludicrous as Jewish misinterpretations of Esau's reunion with Jacob. Based on Genesis 33:4 (where it is recorded that Esau greeted Jacob with a kiss), this off-hand observation is indicative of the depth of S. K.'s knowledge of a variety of hermeneutic approaches to the Bible. This passage was commonly reinterpreted by changing vowel points to imply that Esau "begged" rather than "kissed" Jacob because Jewish interpreters refused to attribute any affection to Esau.[184]

Judge William argued that marriage is the most important journey a man may embark upon, comparing getting married with getting faith. Marriage is the highest expression of love and the ultimate expression of faith in God.[185] Although paganism had a god for the erotic, only in Christianity does one find a God for marriage. Marriage expresses the *telos* of man.

In contrast to the banquet speakers who focused on the transitory nature of woman's beauty, the Judge saw a woman's beauty as enhanced by maturity. Her seeming lower estate manifests her strength; motherhood fulfills her potential, and marriage makes all these possibilities a reality.[186]

There are several allusions to Scripture in Judge William's defense of marriage and answer to the objections raised by the young aesthetes. In a reference to John 5:24 taken out of context, William said that the man who refused to marry "cometh into judgment."[187] The bachelor is removed from the joys of life "in gnashing of teeth."[188] Though this unhappy man "cares for the sick, feeds the hungry, clothes the naked, visits the prisoner, comforts the dying," he shall not lose his reward or be regarded as "an unprofitable servant," yet he re-

mains unhappy.[189] A favorite expression of Kierkegaard's regarding the coming of Christ, "the fullness of time," is applied
to marriage.[190] Marriage is salvation from vanity.[191] Deity has
favored the married man for "whoso findeth a wife, findeth a
good thing."[192]

Unlike the second volume of *Either/Or*, Judge William
does not even allude to the major biblical passages concerning
marriage in this treatise. The assumed truth of these passages
is only remotely in the background of his discussion. The references and allusions to the Bible cited are only incidental and
are characteristic of the few references discussed above.[193]
William is a religious man. There is, however, only an immanental element to his faith. Faith, for the ethical, is resolved-
ness without reflection. Even the legitimate "exception" to the
validity of marriage only strengthens the case for its being universal.[194]

The largest section of *Stages*, entitled "Guilty/Not
Guilty," was penned by Frater Taciturnus. "Quidam's Diary," with many entries paralleling Kierkegaard's own *Journals*,
comprised the largest portion of this part of the book. It was
autobiographical in that it provided a picture of Kierkegaard's
psyche during the time of his relationship and break with Regina. The most direct autobiographical material appears in the
entries dated the fifth of the month at midnight. These are usu-
ally titled entries. However, they would appear to be autobiographical only in a parabolic sense. An example is the January
5th, midnight entry titled "The Quiet Despair," an obvious allusion to S. K.'s relationship with his father.[195] Also, many of
the entries begin "Today, a year ago" which would appear to
indicate S. K.'s prolonged internal battle.

There are numerous biblical references and allusions in
this portion of *Stages*. Taciturnus, reflecting on the need for
his beloved, quoted Luke 10:41, "Martha, Martha, thou art
careful about many things, but one thing is needful" and concludes that she, the lost love, is the beloved and the one thing
needed.[196] He compared his struggle with the competing options he faced to Rachel, who had twins within her womb.[197]
Unfulfilled plans correspond to labor pains that produce only
wind.[198] Jesus' delay in telling all to his disciples was cited as
an illustration of the teleological suspension of the ethical.[199]

These references show the unresolved ethical conscience struggling with the meaning of the religious.

"Solomon's Dream," another 5th of month entry, provided an interesting and creative emendation to the biblical material on the life of Solomon, similar to the creative retelling of Abraham's sacrifice of Issac in *Fear and Trembling*. The entry served as a reminder of S.K.'s frustration with speculative philosophy and concluded:

> And Solomon became wise, but he did not become a hero; and he became a thinker, but he did not become a man of prayer, and he became a preacher, but he did not become a believer; and he was able to help many, but he was unable to help himself. . . . He tossed through life, tossed about by life.[200]

There is also a creative monologue which speculated whether or not Adam reminded Eve of the garden of Eden after the fall.[201] But perhaps the most creative monologue is based upon Daniel 4, "Nebuchadnezzar's Dream" regarding the monarch's time as a beast.[202]

The sermon, "What It Means to Seek After God," was intended to accompany *Stages* and is printed in the back of this edition. In his "Preface" S. K. spoke of "appropriation—the reader's surrender" as the goal of the concluding sermon.[203] This indicates that the normative use of Scripture in the religious sphere is "appropriation." S. K. observed, "Worship therefore is mingled fear and bliss all at once" and that it involved a sense of wonder and wishful searching of the human heart after God.[204] The application of the principle in Hebrews 12:14, "without purity no man can see God," is, Kierkegaard said,

> The deeper the sorrow, so much the more does a man feel himself to be nothing, less than nothing, and this precisely for the reason that the sorrower is the seeker who begins to take note of God. . . . the individual was a sinner, but he became such only by God's presence. He, however, who seeks to understand himself in the consciousness of sin before God does not understand this as a general proposition that all men are sinners, for it is not upon this generality the emphasis falls. The deeper the sorrow, so much the more does a man feel himself as nothing . . . and . . . to take note of God.[205]

In an echo of the theme of *Anxiety*, consciousness of sin is seen as the beginning of the God relationship. Fear is aroused as one realizes personal sinfulness. The instant God is gained, He is lost. One is convicted of sin only in relation to God. This God-inspired awareness is essential if one is to be holy. The sinner who finds God and then loses Him is on the way to holiness and on the way to seeing God.

Concluding Unscientific Postscript

The *Postscript* was published on Feb. 27, 1846. It was intended as a sequel to *Fragments*. The earlier work employed the fundamental categories of Christianity without referring directly to the historical events of its origin. The *Postscript* provided the historical clothing for understanding S. K.'s conception of Christianity. The designation "Unscientific" distinguished this work from the "speculative" theoretical understanding of Christianity so anathematized by Kierkegaard. Although a *Postscript*, it was hardly a brief afterthought.

The *Postscript* summarized S. K.'s transition from the aesthetic to the ethical and then the religious existence sphere. Within the latter, a transition from religion A, the religion of immanence, to religion B, that of transcendence, is evident. Johannes Climacus, the "most personal" of S. K.'s pseudonyms, was the author.[206] It was intended to be Kierkegaard's last work. In an appendix titled "A Glance at a Contemporary Effort in Danish Literature," he alluded to all his earlier works.[207] He even expressed an interest in retiring to a country parish.[208] However, with the *Corsair* affair and Kierkegaard's subsequent attack on Christendom all this changed. His prolific writing continued and resulted in a "second literature" of exclusively religious works.

The Bible played a significant part in the development of the discussion in the *Postscript*.[209] The paradox, central to S. K.'s conception of Christian faith, is discussed. The polemical hermeneutic of the attack on Christendom, characteristic of the religious works examined in the next chapter of this study, is used in skeleton form in the *Postscript*. Finally, there are at least four major treatments of the "how" of biblical interpretation in this work.[210]

Kierkegaard rejected an "objectified" version of Christianity. Such a version is concerned only with historical and philosophical truth. It remains external. The question of "subjective truth" is concerned with "appropriation and assimilation."[211] The subjective thinker is the engaged thinker. The emphasis on subjectivity was simply another way of stating the need, stressed in *Anxiety*, for "inwardness." As was argued in the *Fragments*, Climacus repeatedly warns that historical certainty can only lead to an approximation at best.[212] As such it cannot provide an adequate basis for eternal happiness. Scripture, the church as an institution, and the history of Christianity are—when objectified—diversions from the central question of "how" one becomes a Christian. Indeed, historical-critical questions become a means of delaying commitment.

The objective approach to Christianity would turn naturally first to Scripture "as documents of decisive significance."[213] According to Kierkegaard, when the Bible is "a court of last resort for determining what is and is not Christian doctrine, it becomes necessary to make sure of the Scripture historically and critically."[214] This "making sure" would, it is assumed, precede the commitment of faith. Yet only through faith can the inspiration of the Bible be seen. Realized on any other basis, it remains nothing but an approximation. Kierkegaard did not doubt the historical veracity of the Bible. As has been observed, he took various biblical accounts at literal face value. However, he was skeptical about the nature and extent of faith offered by such certitude.

The real question is what is proved by "proving about the Bible everything that any learned theologian in his happiest moment has ever wished to prove about the Bible."[215] Even with the canon confirmed, traditional authorship attested, and complete trustworthiness demonstrated, "the most perfect realization would still remain an approximation."[216] Furthermore, "faith does not result simply from a scientific inquiry."[217]

On the other hand, what would happen if the critics "succeeded in proving what they desire about the Scriptures? . . . Have the opponent thereby abolished Christianity?" the answer is, "by no means" because:

> [Even if] these books are not written by these authors, are
> not authentic, are not in an integral condition, are not inspired
> (though this cannot be disproved, since it is an object of faith),
> it does not follow that these authors have not existed; and
> above all, it does not follow that Christ has not existed.[218]

According to Climacus, the crux of the matter is the nature of faith. "For whose sake is it that proof is sought? Faith
does not need it" and regards it as its enemy.[219] It is only when
faith loses its passion, when it ceases to be faith, that an appeal
to external proofs becomes necessary. In this context, S. K.
lambasted the clergy who, with false humility, spoke of their
struggles in faith. He contrasted that with the New Testament
emphasis on "the faith which removes mountains."[220] Objectivity breeds disinterest. Only in the passion of inwardness
"every iota will be of infinite value."[221] S. K. cited the concern
with "proof" as a negative fulfillment of the "anxious prophe-
cy of Luke 18:1 'Nevertheless, when the son of man cometh,
shall he find faith on the earth.'"[222] He concluded:

> Christianity is spirit, spirit is inwardness, inwardness is
> subjectivity, subjectivity is essentially passion, and in its maxi-
> mum an infinite, personal, passionate interest in one's eternal
> happiness.[223]

Similarly, he dismisses the institutional church and tradition (the history of Christianity) as an adequate objective
foundation for establishing the truth of Christianity. Indeed,
no such objectivity exists, for "Christianity does not lend itself
to objective observation, precisely because it proposes to intensify subjectivity to the utmost."[224]

There is nothing particularly unique about the isolated
references to Scripture in the early philosophical portion of
Postscript, which consisted basically of a restatement of the
themes of *Fragments*. In an extended introduction to the subjective problem, Kierkegaard acknowledged his debt to Lessing's dictum that "accidental truths of history can never
become the proof of the necessary truths of reason."[225] Several
allusions to Scripture occur in the discussion.

The following are among the more interesting examples.
With regard to the inwardness of truth realized through appropriation, the idle laborers in the marketplace were not

called to the vineyard by an objective call, but by a Divine call.[226] Jesus warns that the "inwardness of prayer" is not realized through external show, contortions, and the like (Matt. 6:6, 16-18).[227] The *Fragments* showed that there was no special advantage to the contemporary disciples. To argue for such is an "injustice and a distinction much more reprehensible than the one between Jews and Greeks, circumcised and uncircumcised, which Christianity has abolished"—an obvious reference to Gal. 3:28.[228] If one is limited to "every dogmatic determination [and] . . . philosophical theorem which has entered the heart of man" (a reference to 1 Cor. 2:9), then the paradox will never be realized.[229] Climacus drew on Luke 23:6-12 when he confessed to almost bowing the knee to Hegel after growing "weary from running back and forth between Herod and Pilate"—an allusion applied to philosophical options.[230]

Kierkegaard turned his attention from the "objective" problem to the "how" of becoming subjective. "If truth happens to be in only a single subject," he observed, "there is greater Christian joy in heaven over this one individual than over universal history."[231] The appeal to a universal ethical is compared to a Judas who "sells his God-relationship."[232] The problem with the modern age is that, like "the parable of the trees that wanted to make the cedar their king," everyone wants "a systematic Christian tree."[233] Speculation, the ethical, and systematic concerns must be put aside in order to become subjective.[234]

Speculative philosophy leads to "the modern mythical allegorizing tendency" and "declares out and out that the whole of Christianity is a myth."[235] Christendom has taken the biblical command "that one ought always to give thanks to God" and has reduced it to an occasional observance.[236] True thanksgiving should be expressed in all circumstances. Christian tradition, as popularly appealed to, is like "the flatness that salt takes on when it loses its savor."[237] The modern age has forgotten what it means to exist. Like the church at Laodicea, the modern generation "is neither cold nor hot [and] is nauseating."[238]

Kierkegaard saw all speculative system-building as a fantastic distortion of truth and an ingenious system of irrelevancy. Hegel (and Descartes) neglected the distinction between thought and reality, and thus each erected a system that excluded his own existence. In such a scheme, the individual becomes merely an expression of the abstract, universal, and timeless categories. Kierkegaard observed:

> It may all be very well from a speculative point of view to make thought the highest stage, and it may be quite plausible from the standpoint of the world-history to say that the earlier stages have been left behind. But does our age bring forth a generation of individuals who are born without imagination and feeling? Are we born to begin with paragraph 14 in the System? Let us above all not confuse the historical development of the human spirit at large with particular individuals.[239]

In contrast, the subjective thinker is passionately concerned with existence. The existentially decisive act for the ethically engaged subject is not an external action but an internal decision. Suppose, for example, the Levite in the story of the Good Samaritan had intended to help the man on the side of the road, but out of fear he went away. Leaving the victim, he was overcome by remorse and returned too late to the scene to be of any help. "Certainly he had acted [internally]" even though his action had no external consequence.[240]

The subjective thinker both thinks and exists.

> To understand oneself in existence is also the Christian principle, except this "self" has received far richer and deeper determination, still more difficult to understand. The believer is the subjective thinker.[241]

"The ethical and the religious example" should turn "the spectator's eye upon himself."[242] When one hears about Job's faith, it should "be so presented that it becomes a challenge, a question directed to me, as to whether I too desire to acquire a believing mind."[243] It should not be an occasion simply for aesthetic appreciation or ethical evaluation. The possibility of a faith like Job's should rouse those who hear of it.

Humor, related to the externalization implicit in the ethical, is the first step in the transition to religious. Suffering is the highest intensification of subjectivity. "Becoming a Christian is . . . the most fearful decision of a man's life" outside of

Christendom.[244] But in Christendom, everyone is a Christian "as a matter of course."[245] True Christianity is "not a doctrine but an existential communication expressing an existential contradiction."[246] S. K. observed that paganism erred in not having the will to venture everything; the Middle Ages ventured everything for the wrong reason; "the hodge-podge wisdom of our age mediates."[247] Christendom has replaced the offense of the Paradox and the intensity of inwardness with a temporal mediation.

As an individual examines the relationship between the temporal and the eternal, one faces "the absolute *telos* [where] there is a yawning chasm fixed between it and the relative ends."[248] Existential pathos arises from this tension. The believer comes to the place where everything is ventured. Certainty and venturing are mutually exclusive. Climacus, alluding to Matt. 13:45-46, observed, "When I give all that I have for a pearl, it is not a venture if I hold the pearl in my hand at the moment of making the exchange."[249]

The sense of absolute commitment underscores Kierkegaard's religious concern. He contrasted this as Religion B with the religion of immanence under the rubric of Religion A. Religion A is concerned with guilt, but not with sin. It is ethical and immanental. Guilt is a broken relationship within the individual. Climacus noted that "Religiousness A must first be present in the individual before there can be any question of becoming aware of the dialectic of B."[250]

The individual must realize through the transitory nature of existence, revealed through the dialectic of becoming, time, and the futility of death, that any claim to the ultimate is beyond the grasp of the self. These ambiguities give rise to religion B. S. K. argued in *Anxiety* that sin-consciousness can be disclosed only by God. The knowledge of sin is based on the absurd assertion that "the Diety, the Eternal came into being at a definite moment in time as an individual man."[251] This is the "Absolute Paradox" that separates Religion B from Religion A. The "strait entrance to the narrow way is the offense."[252]

In the conclusion to the *Postscript*, Kierkegaard contrasted the offense of the Gospel with the childish Christianity of his day. This section is both interesting and important. Here is an example of Kierkegaard's use of Scripture in establishing a point of reference for contrasting the Christianity of the New Testament with Christendom. Also, it is the most direct in a series of allusions that contrasted the true meaning of a biblical passage with the popular interpretations offered by the clergy.[253] The polemical tone developed here became even more strident in Kierkegaard's "second literature."

Climacus rebuked the childish Christianity of his day. The rich young ruler of Matt. 19:16-22 at least realized that he was unwilling to risk.[254] Christendom, in contrast, was unwilling to risk and explained that unwillingness away as a virtue.

> Rather than hold on to the name of Christian lukewarmly, it doubtless would be better, for it would be a sign of life, if some people in our time were to admit bluntly to themselves that they could wish that Christianity never had come into the world or that they themselves had never became Christians. But let the admission be made without scorn and mockery and wrath.[255]

Climacus argued that since "Christianity did not come into the world during childhood but in the fullness of time," its appropriation is for mature individuals.[256] In a veiled autobiographical statement, Kierkegaard observed, "To cram Christianity into a child is something that cannot be done . . . [for] the child has no decisive use for Christianity."[257] One must come in the "fullness of time" as mature individuals "whose strength is their weaknes."[258]

Christendom has misunderstood the "God who receives little children."[259] The clergy cite passages such as Matt. 19:12-15 where Jesus said, "Suffer the little children to come unto me and forbid them not, for of such is the kingdom of heaven."[260] Yet they ignore other passages in the same chapter of Matthew that speak of the difficulty of entering the kingdom of heaven such as "eunuchs who have castrated themselves" to enter, or declare that "it is easier for a camel to go through the eye of the needle than for a rich man to enter," or indicate the necessity "to forsake houses, or brethren, or sisters, or father, or mother, or lands for the sake of Christ's name."[261] In Jesus' teaching, entrance into the kingdom of heaven is made as difficult as possible.

In its biblical context, Jesus' statement regarding children was a response to the disciples' rebuking and sending them away.[262] Using a child as a paradigm for entering the kingdom of heaven was paradoxical. It served as a judgment on the Apostles. Christendom, according to Climacus,

> accentuates the sacrament of baptism with such exorbitant orthodoxy that one actually becomes heterodox on the doctrine of regeneration, forgetting the objection raised by Nicodemus and the reply to it, because with hyper-orthodoxy one decrees that a little child has actually become a Christian by being baptized.[263]

Childish Christianity produces childish orthodoxy with a romanticized picture of Christ that reduces the Paradox to nothing. The final section of *Postscript*, alluding to several biblical passages, returns to the theme of the Paradox.[264] S. K. reiterated that "The thing of being a Christian is not determined by the what of Christianity but by the now of the Christian."[265]

Conclusion

The pseudonyms of the aesthetic, ethical and religious existence spheres each have a slightly different approach to Scripture. However, hermeneutical patterns can be observed that roughly correspond to the stages.

The hermeneutic of the aesthete is characterized by an attitude of indifference to Scripture. Allusions to Scripture in the first volume of *Either/Or* and the aesthetic portion of *Stages* are of a very general nature. The Bible is not cited as proof of an argument. In fact, in most cases other non-biblical references could be used without a significant change in the meaning of Kierkegaard's text.

The hermeneutic of the ethical, as exemplified by Judge William in vol. 2 of *Either/Or*, the relevent passages of *Stages*, and discussion of the ethical in the other philosophical works, appeals to the Bible as a source for corroboration of universal law. The concern is with duty in religion to an external stan-

dard. Guilt is simply the result of violating the ethical standard. As the ethical state is expressed in "God-talk," the
religion of immanence (A) emerges.

The hermeneutic of Paradox characterized the transition
to transcendental religion (B) and was Kierkegaard's normative approach to Scripture when he sought to understand the
"how" of becoming a Christian. Faith is radically different
from truths of reason. This approach to the Bible involves active appropriation of its message. *Fear and Trembling, Philosophical Fragments, Anxiety,* and *Postscript* contained
examples of this approach. Also, in the *Postscript* there is evidence of the polemical hermeneutic that characterized Kierkegaard's later open confrontation with Christendom.

4

The Function of Scripture in Selected Works

From the "Second Literature"

The Bible played a variety of roles in Kierkegaard's early literary production, generally referred to as his "philosophical works." It served as a literary device for the pseudonyms of the aesthetic stage. It was a basis for appeal to universal law for the ethical stage. Immanental religion also appeared to glean wisdom by which to live from the pages of the Bible. *The Concluding Unscientific Postscript* marked a transition in Kierkegaard's literary production. It was the last of the "philosophical" works. Here, and in the earlier *Philosophical Fragments*, the emphasis on the Paradox characterized the introduction of the religion of transcendence. Although S. K. would at later times resort to pseudonyms in his religious writings, the connection between these and himself was much more direct than in the philosophical works.[1] However, most of the religious works were penned and published under Kierkegaard's own name. Thus, Kierkegaard's own view and use of the Bible appears most clearly in his later religious works.

These works have also been labeled Kierkegaard's "second literature."[2] This rather amorphous description simply indicates that, although there are elements of the earlier aesthetic or philosophical works contained in these later writings, the religious element dominates this material. Kierkegaard himself noted that the religious was present from the beginning, and, conversely, the aesthetic was present in the final re-

ligious works.[3] Since he referred to the whole of his
authorship as having a "religious" purpose, the "second literature" distinction seems a more appropriate way to differenti-
ate his later more "direct" communications from the earlier
"indirect communication." The *Edifying Discourses* are not
generally considered part of the second literature. They are,
however, "religious" in the immanental sense. Thus, while the
philosophical works move dialectically to the religious, the
Edifying Discourses are a sideways glance at the religious and
have been included under the category of "second literature"
in this study.

There is a slight alteration in the chronological format in
the treatment of the "selected works" in this chapter. The first
major section of the chapter deals with the use of Scripture in
selected discourses. In fact, the various "edifying" discourses
were published simultaneously with the earlier pseudonymous literature. Selections from these and the "Christian" discourses have been examined within their own chronological
flow in order to trace the development of Kierkegaard's
hermeneutic in this specific genera of literature. The *Works of
Love,* written in the same format as the discourses, is also examined in this section. The *Works of Love* is a mature statement of Kierkegaard's Christian ethic.

The polemical and prophetic works, *Training in Christianity* and *Attack upon "Christendom,"* are examined in the final section of the chapter. Here particular attention is focused
on Kierkegaard's direct appeal to the authority of the Bible
and the stark contrasts he paints of Christendom's divergence
from true biblical Christianity. A brief conclusion summarizes
the results of this survey of Kierkegaard's "second literature."

The Function of Scripture in Selected Discourses

While engaged in the production of his aesthetic works,
Kierkegaard's religious interest was expressed by the parallel
publication of several series of devotional essays. Kierkegaard
called them "discourses," not sermons, because its author has
no authority to preach; "edifying discourses," not discourses
for edification, because the speaker does not claim to be a
teacher.[4] A total of eighteen such discourses, published two,

three, or four at a time, was produced between 1843 and 1847. All were published under Kierkegaard's name and dedicated to the memory of his father, Michael Pedersen Kierkegaard. They were addressed to "my reader, . . . that individual who is benevolent enough to let himself be found."[5] Swenson, comparing them to the later religious writings, noted:

> Unlike the later religious writings, these edifying discourses do not make use of the transcendent categories of orthodox Christianity, but of the categories of immanence. The chain of continuity between the actual and ideal is not broken, and the relation of the individual to the divine is essentially passive. In thus exploring the possibilities of edification within the limits of an immanent religion, Kierkegaard again, as in the esthetic-ethical religious progress of the esthetic works, cleared up all the intervening territory before advancing to the transcendent categories of orthodox Christianity.[6]

There is, however, development within the eighteen discourses. One of the later discourses, "Man's Need of God Constitutes His Highest Perfection," stands on the threshold of transcendent religion.[7] *Three Discourses on Imagined Occasions* was produced in 1845 and has been published in an English translation, *Thoughts on Crucial Situations in Human Life*. These are transitional discourses that prepare the way for the later *Christian Discourses*.

Kierkegaard distinguished the *Works of Love* from both the edifying and Christian discourses, on the one hand, and the sermon, on the other. He observed that a Christian discourse "deals to a certain extent with doubt" whereas a sermon "operates absolutely and entirely through authority, that of Holy Writ and of Christ's apostles."[8] The *Works of Love* is intended to encourage reflection upon a single theme—the nature and manifestation of Christian love. That theme is the focus of Kierkegaard's Christian ethic.

Edifying Discourses

The Bible played a supporting role in Kierkegaard's early philosophical works. It moved center stage and became the dominant force in his discourses. The sheer number of biblical references and allusions increased dramatically in the eighteen discourses that constitute the four-volume *Edifying Discourses*.[9] There are more direct quotes from Scripture than has previously been observed. Frequently, a biblical incident is noted with chapter and verse reference given. Even passing allusions, the dominant characteristic of the aesthetic emphasis, were more often used in a manner consistent with their biblical context. These allusions frequently function as commentary on the biblical passage under examination in the discourse. The discourses themselves are often extended commentaries on the application of one specific biblical text. Selected discourses will now be examined in chronological order to demonstrate both the expanded function of Scripture and the emergence of the religion of transcendence in this literature.

The purpose of these "immanental" discourses is twofold. The limits of the immanental religion perspective are demonstrated. Also, there is an attempt to awaken the individual to the transcendent. The first discourse, for example, "The Expectation of Faith," was a new year's reflection based on Galatians 3:23-29. The biblical passage is concerned with the relationship between faith and the law—the latter being a "schoolmaster" that brings one to Christ. The meditation is concerned with the question of human wishes associated with the thought of a new year. The question of whether there is anything that one could devote one's self to completely is asked. "There is mention of worldly goods, of health, good times, wealth, power, fortune, a glorious fame," and, according to S. K., "the listener is warned against them."[10]

Faith, however, is a virtue of a different sort, for about it "a different kind of language is heard."[11] It is praised as the highest good, the most beautiful, and as the richest of all blessings. Yet few actually claim to possess it. While it is true that one cannot acquire faith for another, there is a fundamental misunderstanding of the true meaning of faith, if one can claim to describe it without possessing it.

On a purely natural level, "expectation" is based upon one's circumstances.[12] Those who are wealthy or successful generally expect continued prosperity. The only thing all expectations have in common is that they are concerned with the future. Kierkegaard said, "The fact of being able to occupy himself with the future is then an indication of man's nobility."[13] It is one thing to focus one's energies upon the present. That is a relatively simple task. However, "he who fights the future . . . fights himself."[14] One may be victorious in many battles of life, and ultimately stymied at some future challenge. The future portends only uncertainty. How can one meet and conquer an essentially ambivalent future? According to S. K., "Through the eternal can one conquer the future, because the eternal is the foundation of the future."[15] Faith is the evidence of the eternal in man. "The expectation of faith is victory!"[16]

This discourse views faith from an immanental perspective. Genuine faith contains its own reward. However, Kierkegaard did not, at this level, develop any detailed discussion of how faith arises in the heart of the believer. Rather, his description of faith is intended to be an interrogation of the human heart. Kierkegaard observed, "Doubt is a cunning passion, and it may well be very difficult to free one's self from its snares."[17] Silence is the best response when one is ensnared in doubt. It is only in solitude that the doubting self may be recovered.

True faith is not dependent upon corroboration by external events. In faith the soul remains true to itself.

> When the world begins its sharp testing, when the storms of life snap the vigorous expectation of youth, when existence, which seems so loving and so gentle, transforms itself into a merciless proprietor who demands everything back, everything which he gave so that he could take it back; then the believer looks with sadness and pain at himself and at life, but he still says: "There is an expectation which all the world can not take from me; it is the expectation of faith, and this is victory. . . . my expectation was not in the world, but in God."[18]

One can go no farther than the victory of faith. Ultimately faith rests in God, who cannot be changed and, in a reference to James 1:17, "with whom there is no variableness, neither shadow of turning. . . . He is truthful and keeps His promises."[19] Genuine faith is demonstrated in faithfulness. It is confident and can claim the words, "and so at last be saved."[20]

A later discourse, "Love Shall Cover a Multitude of Sins," based upon 1 Peter 4:7-12, queries the kind of love this text and title imply.

> We shall let our soul rest in the apostolic word, which is not a deceitful, poetic mode of expression, not a bold outburst, but a trustworthy thought, a perfectly valid testimony, which to be understood must be taken at its face value.[21]

There is, in this context, a clue to Kierkegaard's epistemology for transcendent and spiritual things. He said, "Insofar as the object of contemplation belongs to the external world, the nature of the observer is a matter of relative importance."[22] However, if the object of contemplation—in this case the kind of love that is able to cover a multitude of sins—belongs to the spiritual realm, "more important [is] the question of what the observer is in his inmost being," for it is here that appropriation must take place.[23]

There is a certain naivete to the kind of love that can cover a multitude of sins. S. K. observed:

> When love dwells in the heart, then a man comprehends slowly, and does not hear at all the hasty word and does not understand its repetition, because he ascribes to it a good intention and a good meaning; does not understand the long, angry or derisive speech, because he still expects one word which will give meaning to the speech. When fear dwells in the heart, then a man easily discovers the multiplicity of sins.[24]

In an interesting exposition of the biblical account of Jesus and the woman caught in adultery, Kierkegaard said that Jesus "wrote with His finger in order to blot out what He himself knew; for sin discovers a multitude of sins, but love covers a multitude of sins."[25] God's love is manifest in that, even with the sinner in sight, it covers. Jesus said, "Neither do I condemn thee, go and sin no more" because "the punishment of sin breeds new sin," but forgiveness breaks the cycle.[26]

The obvious challenge of this and the second discourse with the same title is for the individual, through self-examination, to see the extent of true love. However, there is more to these spiritual realities than merely being acquainted with biblical truths. In the discourse, "Strengthened in the Inner Man," based upon Ephesians 3:13-21, Kierkegaard comments on the teaching of Paul. "Was his doctrine quickly able to put an individual in possession of supernatural powers, was it sold like sorcery?"[27] The answer is an emphatic "No" for "it had to be acquired slowly, appropriated through experience" which began with the repudiation of all things worldly.[28]

This spiritual knowledge in the inner man is not a "more comprehensive knowledge," but is present only when appropriated as it "transforms itself in the moment of possession into action."[29] An individual's trying to "decide once for all" without appropriation results in "the inner man . . . [being] still-born."[30] Since God is Spirit, He "therefore can give only spiritual testimony . . . every external testimony . . . is only a deception."[31] Once this spiritual testimony is given then "both prosperity and adversity may serve . . . for the strengthening of the inner man."[32]

A discourse based upon the life of Job, "The Lord Gave, And The Lord Hath Taken Away, Blessed Be The Name Of The Lord," provides further illustration of the insightfulness of S. K.'s biblical exposition. The title of the discourse, a quote from Job, is significant not primarily because Job said it, but "in the fact that he acted in accordance with it."[33]

> At the moment when the Lord took everything, he [Job] did not say first, "The Lord took," but he said first, "The Lord gave." The word is short, but in its brevity it perfectly expresses what it wishes to indicate, that Job's soul is not crushed down in silent submission to sorrow, but that his heart first expanded in gratitude; that the loss of everything first made him thankful to the Lord.[34]

Job, because he had seen God, overcame the world. Even if one has not suffered like Job, "no man knows the time and the hour when the messengers [of suffering, destruction, and death] will come to him," therefore one should occupy one's mind with the example of his suffering.[35] Despite the deep pathos of this discourse, the religious outlook is still immanental. Both Job's wealth and honor were later restored. The paradox of Job (and even of Abraham) was not the absolute paradox.[36] However, if the individual falls short at the religion of immanence, how much greater the gulf between the self and the religion of transcendence.

The words of the Bible are always capable of more than one application. In the discourse "Every Good Gift," Kierkegaard observed that the Bible "can at different times be milk for babes and strong meat for adults, although the word remains the same."[37] S. K. claims in the discourse "Patient In Expectation" that "skepticism and the mistake of despairing do not lie in the understanding . . . the mistake is in the will which suddenly no longer wills."[38] In contrast to this loss of will, patience is a virtue that "submits its expectation to God and therefore the fulfillment always lies near at hand, however foolish this may seem in the earthly sense."[39]

The discourse on patience also illustrates the progression in the *Edifying Discourses* to the threshold of the religion of transcendence. For example, faith arises as one is emptied of self in the face of the transcendent.

> If a man truly understood how to make himself into what he truly is, into nothing; if he knew how to set the seal of patience on what he had understood, oh, then would his life, whether he were the greatest or the humblest, still today be spent in joyful surprise and blessed admiration, and would continue so all his days. For there is only One who is truly the everlasting object of wonder, and that is God; and only one who is able to halt the wonder, and that is man, when he himself wishes to be something.[40]

A further illustration of this progression is Kierkegaard's discussion of the folly of proofs for the existence of God. Attempting such arguments ignores the gap existing between the Divine and the human. In the discourse, "Remember Now Thy Creator," S. K. observed, tongue-in-cheek, that, "God in heaven must sit and wait for the fates to decide whether He exists, and finally He comes into being by means of some proofs."[41] Indeed, if one toiled long enough with the truth, "God might even become the creator!"[42]

In the discourse, "Expectation of an Eternal Happiness," Kierkegaard contrasted immanental ideas of faith, identified as "the wish," with a genuine expression of Christian faith. Modern people believe "that one should rely upon God in the same way that one relies on men, so that if one helps himself, then God does the rest."[43] Yet, according to Kierkegaard, if the expectation of an eternal happiness does not unite concern for the kingdom of God with the realities of earthly life, then "it is not an expectation of the eternal, but a superstition about the future."[44] Forsaking the grace of God renders any notion of eternal happiness meaningless. S. K. said that "concern nourishes uncertainty" and this in turn nourishes concern—there is no external security with regard to eternal happiness.[45] The only hope of eternal happiness is God's grace. Kierkegaard observed that

> every man acquires the eternal happiness of heaven only through God's mercy and grace, and this is equally near every man, so near, that it is a matter between God and himself. And let no third party who has himself received grace mar this by unwarranted meddling.[46]

In the prayer at the conclusion of this discourse, Kierkegaard rejoices in God's grace and the provision of faith, noting that "Peter stood more securely upon the waves of the sea, than does the one who stands on his own righteousness against Thee."[47]

Lillian Swenson contends that the *Edifying Discourses* attain "their supreme spiritual elevation in . . . Man's Need of God Constitutes His Highest Perfection."[48] Unlike the discourses previously reviewed, there is no specific biblical text expounded in this treatise. Rather, S. K. asks rhetorically what is essential to human existence. Once wealth, power, social relationships, and petty desires are removed and "take away . . . the little he has left. He does not suffer want; he is not compelled to go hungry to bed. But he does not know from whence his needs are supplied."[49] Such an individual would be in the position of complete dependence upon God.

> To let the grace of God suffice us! The grace of God is surely the greatest of all good gifts, on this point we do not propose to raise a controversy; this belief is at bottom the most earnest and blessed conviction of every human being. But we rarely evoke the thought; and if we wish to be honest with ourselves we must admit that in the last analysis, although without fully becoming aware of what we do, we quietly apply to this conception the old adage that "too much and too little spoils everything."[50]

The grace of God should mean more to the believer than mere consolation when the vicissitudes of life seem to turn against the individual. According to S. K., "To be in need of God is no shameful embarrassment, but precisely the perfection of human life."[51] The greatest tragedy of life would be for an individual to fail to discover personal need of God.[52] Echoing the Lutheran emphasis on the sovereignty of God, Kierkegaard maintained:

> It is God Himself who best knows how to utilize a man's own anxieties for the purpose of extirpating all his self-confidence; and when he is about to sink down into his own nothingness, it is again God Himself who can best keep him from continuing to maintain a diver's under-water connection with his earthly self.[53]

Divine consolation, or salvation, does not come simply because an individual is unhappy. As long as an individual believes "that he could . . . help himself if given the power," then he has not arrived at the place of absolute dependence upon God.[54] Kierkegaard repeatedly refers to the individual's "annihilation" as the means of becoming nothing.[55] This involves the self's inability to do anything apart from God, and thus underscores the need for absolute dependence upon God. S. K. conceded that a view of life focused on the self's need of God as the highest perfection "does indeed make life more difficult," but this is the only way "man learns to know God."[56]

Kierkegaard is not arguing that the individual get lost in mystical experience or that the knowledge of God is "otherworldly" to the exclusion of human existence. Indeed, he observed that:

> We do not wish to be understood as saying that a knowledge of God which consists of absorption in dreamy wonder and enthusiastic contemplation of Him is alone of the highest worth; for God cannot thus be taken in vain. Just as the self-knowledge which reveals one's own nothingness is the necessary condition for knowing God, so the knowledge of God is the condition for the sanctification of each human being in accordance with his specific end. Wherever God exists in truth there He is always creative. It is not His will that men should bask in the contemplation of His glory in spiritual sloth; but

He wishes, through coming to be known of man, to create in him a new man.[57]

How does God accomplish this task of recreating the individual? Through the word of God. In a discourse on "The Thorn in the Flesh," Kierkegaard noted that occasionally a biblical quote strays from its context, but "the function of the Holy Scriptures is to be the interpreter of the divine to men."[58] They "teach the believer everything from the beginning."[59] The Scriptures have produced "godly discourse about the divine" with "words and expressions repeatedly heard in the holy places."[60]

One of the transitional discourses, "What It Means to Seek God (on the occasion of a Confessional Service)," was published under the title *Thoughts on Crucial Situations in Human Life.* This discourse, along with two other discourses on imagined occasions, a wedding and a funeral, may also be considered "edifying." However, these discourses provide the transitional link to the *Christian Discourses.* David Swenson said that these treatises affirm, more directly than the earlier discourses, "supernaturalism in religion" and personal relationship to God.[61]

The opening prayer to the discourse, "What It Means to Seek After God," asks rhetorically, "How then should the sinner seek Thee, O God of righteousness!"[62] The place and occasion for asking this question is in the confessional. However, the question actually arises only in the stillness afforded by introspection and prayer which occasions true encounter with God. Kierkegaard observed that "no man can see God without purity, and that no man can know God without becoming a sinner."[63] This discourse is intended as a "mediation" of the principle that purity of heart is essential for knowing God.[64]

Kierkegaard, in tracing the various approaches to this essential "stillness" before God, was not speaking of mere poetic illusion. He noted:

> A poet has indeed said that a sigh without words ascending Godward, is the best prayer, and so one might also believe that the rarest of visits to the sacred place, when one comes from afar, is the best worship, because both help to create an illusion. A sigh without words is the best prayer when the thought of God only sheds a faint glow over existence. . . . But

if God is present in the soul, then the sigh will find the thought and the thought will find the word—but also the difficulty, which is not dreamed of when God is at a distance.[65]

The seeker after God who assumes he can do nothing to find the place of solitude is relegated to only wishing for its existence.[66]

Even wonder at its possibility, without seeking the place of contrition, is dismissed as an inadequate and incomplete response to God.[67] Kierkegaard said, "This state of wonder in the one who wishes corresponds to the unknown, and is thus wholly indeterminable, or rather infinitely determinable" and corresponds to a pagan response to the unknown.[68] As the "passion of wonder defines itself," the view of God that emerges includes the "inexplicable whole of creation."[69] S. K. claims that "idolatry purified becomes the poetic."[70]

Excessive emphasis on either "fate" or "human-freedom" may also characterize inadequate approaches to God.[71] Determinism or fate produces worship and wonder, but "its scope embraces the abhorrent as well as the ludicrous, the confused as well as the childish."[72] With the overt emphasis on freedom "the seeker is supposed to be able to do everything to find the thing sought, then is the enchantment over, the wonder is forgotten."[73]

Turning away from all externals and denying there is any object of wonder is also a deception. However, this response produces despair and can be the beginning of a transition in the individual. Kierkegaard observed, "the human being perishing in his despair discovers that he already has what he sought, and that the misfortune is that he stands and loses it."[74] Fear and trembling describe the true struggle to find God. The problem with objective proofs for the existence of God is that passion is mediated, for the apologist "places himself outside, he does not deal with God, but considers something about God."[75] This too is a diversion.

Kierkegaard argued, in contrast to the false start made by other efforts to approach God, that

> True wonder and fear first appear only when he, just he, whether greatest or humblest, is alone with the omnipresent God. The strength of power and wisdom and actions does not

determine the strength of the God-relationship. Did not the wise men of Egypt perform signs almost as great as Moses? Suppose they had performed greater, what would it have signified? Nothing, absolutely nothing with respect to the God-relationship. But Moses feared God, and Moses marveled about God, and this fear and this wonder, or the fear and happiness of the wonder, determine the strength of the God-relationship.[76]

In the emergence of a true God-relationship, the seeker realizes that the place of meeting God is within, or at least was within. However, awareness of sin and guilt means that the individual has changed from being the place where God is sought.[77] Now appearing to be at the end of seeking, the individual is at a true beginning. The greater the sense of personal nothingness, the greater the God-consciousness.

> If a man would have an essential understanding of his sin, he must understand it through being alone, just he alone, alone with the Holy One who knows all. This is the only true fear and trembling, only this is the true sorrow which the remembrance of God awakens in a man, this is the true repentance His love encourages.[78]

True humility before God will result in "not merely an enumeration of particular sins, but is an understanding before God, of the continuity of sin itself."[79] Sincerity is essential to repentance. Seeking God is not confined to the confessional. However, neither is it true that there are "different ways and different truths and new truths," rather "there are many ways which lead to the one truth, and each man walks his own way."[80]

There are a number of allusions to Scripture in this discourse. They are not as direct as either the earlier *Edifying Discourses* or the later *Christian Discourses*. The use of Scripture in this discourse is consistent with the hermeneutic of paradox. The basic question is how one may properly seek God. S. K. was not concerned with deducing a propositional formula for knowing God. He argued that, regarding the Bible, "a mature person learns only by appropriation, and he appropriates essentially only that which is essential to living."[81] Only God can communicate to each individual what is truly essential for her or him.

Christian Discourses

The *Christian Discourses* were published on April 26, 1848, just one week after Kierkegaard's religious metamorphosis. Of course they were written and sent to the publisher before that event, the greater portion having been completed in 1847.[82] These works are "direct communication" and are less subtle, containing no "mystification."[83]

The Bible plays a significant and direct role in the development of these treatises.[84] Each discourse is an extended exposition of a biblical text or theme given for that part of the book. Part I of this volume analyzes Matthew 6:24-34 in seven discourses under the theme "The Anxieties of the Heathen." Part II deals with the theme of suffering in seven discourses under the heading "Joyful Notes in the Strife of Suffering." Part III constitutes an attack upon Christendom in seven discourses taking up various biblical texts under the theme, "Thoughts which Wound from Behind—for Edification." Part IV, "Discourses at the Communion on Fridays: Christian Discourses," contains seven discourses on specific biblical passages. In addition, this edition of *Christian Discourses* includes "The Lilies of the Field And the Birds of the Air" and "Three Discourses at the Communion on Fridays." Only the first two parts of *Christian Discourses* are examined. They provide the best example of both an extended treatment of a single passage, and an extended treatment of a biblical theme.

These discourses are "Christian" in that they assume the transcendent categories only hinted at and pointed to indirectly in the earlier discourses. The *Edifying Discourses* analyzed Christian truth from the immanental perspective. They functioned as prompters to an awakening of a deeper faith. The *Christian Discourses* function as a prophetic voice calling the hearer to follow in the direction of religion of transcendence.

Kierkegaard said in his "Introduction" to Part I that "the edifying address [of the *Christian Discourses*] combats in many ways to bring it about that the eternal may be victorious in men."[85] The Sermon on the Mount is contrasted with the Old Testament giving of the Law.[86] The biblical passage which is the focus of this section is taken from Matthew. It proclaims, in part, that "No man can serve two masters." Furthermore, "the birds of the air" and "the lilies of the field" are contrasted to the anxieties present in the heathen, and according to S. K., within Christendom.[87]

The polarities of anxiety over external circumstances are analyzed in successive discourse in this section. "The Anxiety of Poverty" focuses on Matthew 6:31, "Be not therefore anxious, saying, What shall we eat? or, What shall we drink?—after all these things do the heathen seek."[88] The bird does not share this human anxiety for "the bird lives on the 'daily bread,' this heavenly food which cannot be too long kept."[89] The text of Matthew 6:11, "give us this day our daily bread," is tied to Exodus 16:4-30, detailing God's provision of manna for Israel.

The simplicity of dependence on God means that the poor Christian is not really poor for:

> Every day . . . the poor Christian has occasion to be aware of his Benefactor in prayer and thanksgiving. And his riches indeed increase with every time he prays and gives thanks, and with every time it becomes clearer that he exists for God and God for him; whereas earthly riches become poorer and poorer with every time the rich man forgets to pray and to give thanks.[90]

Kierkegaard dealt with the same passage of Scripture in the next discourse, "The Anxiety of Abundance." The Christian's response to wealth is examined. Just as the bird of the air does not worry because of any want, so it is unimpressed with its plenty.[91] Indeed the bird is satisfied with just enough to maintain life. The rich Christian, through the "cunning power . . . of thought" is able to realize that all that one really possesses is the "enough" for each day.[92] Indeed, the potential for loss of possessions or even of life itself are reminders that there is no security in external wealth. Kierkegaard argued that in true stewardship "the rich Christian understands precisely that in the highest sense riches are not his own property."[93] The Christian stands under the biblical command "To do good and to communicate forget not."[94] The rich Christian is "absent-minded" regarding personal wealth.[95]

The polarities with regard to dress and appearance are examined in the discourses contrasting "The Anxiety of Lowliness" with "The Anxiety of Highness." The text for both is taken from Matthew 6:25, "Be not anxious what ye shall put on—after all such things do the heathen seek."[96] The various colored sparrows do not divide themselves into classes according to their respective beauty for "the bird is what it is, is itself, content to be itself."[97]

Although the lowly Christian is surely aware of the distinctions made by the world, "by holding on to God with the tenacity of eternity he has become himself."[98] Christ is the Pattern, a frequent Kierkegaard theme, and the lowly Christian believes that "this Pattern exists expressly for him who in fact is a lowly man, struggling perhaps with poverty and narrow circumstances, or, more lowly still, being despised and rejected."[99] The lowly Christian "has God for his brother."[100] Whereas the lowly heathen has anxiety and is simply lowly.

The Christian enjoying a higher position in life, is, if truly a Christian, also oblivious to such distinctions.[101] S. K. cautions that while "Christianity is far too spiritual a thing to talk about outward lowliness," "the Scripture does nevertheless . . . talk of being literally a lowly man."[102] Christ, in resolving to be the Pattern, "was literally a lowly man."[103] In an interesting analogy, Kierkegaard observed:

> There is something in the spiritual life which corresponds to what spelling is in contrast to continuous reading. One spells, one advances slowly, distinguishing clearly and evidently between details, for fear of finally reducing the whole content of life to 'resolved moments' and life itself to much ado about nothing. So it is with the possession of external superiority in connection with becoming a Christian.[104]

The Christian faith cannot simply be equated with being lowly, but from "literal lowliness to the point of becoming a Christian there is however only one step."[105]

Similar polarities are sketched in the discourses dealing with "The Anxiety of Presumption" and "The Anxiety of Self-Torment," based upon Matthew 6:27—"No one can add one cubit unto his stature."[106] The final discourse exposes "The Anxiety of Irresolution, Fickleness and Disconsolateness" and is based upon Matthew 6:24, "No man can serve two masters."[107] In a theme developed more fully in the *Works of*

Love, S.K. reminds his hearer that the Christian serves God wholly because of love, "the firmest of all bonds."[108]

This portion of the *Christian Discourses* demonstrates Kierkegaard's skill as a biblical expositor. Part II demonstrates his skill in developing a biblical theme—in this case, the theme of "Joyful Notes in the Strife of Suffering."[109] These discourses do not expound a specific biblical text, although biblical allusions are numerous; rather the theme of joy in suffering is developed around the theme implied in the titles of each discourse.

These discourses intended to show that "the dismaying" may become that which edifies.[110] Suffering drives the individual to security in the reality of God. If not received in faith, however, "Christian consolation is more apt to drive to despair than are the heaviest earthly sufferings and the greatest temporal misfortunes."[111] In fact, since "what thou dost lose temporally thou dost gain eternally," S. K. said, "there is really no loss in the world."[112]

In these discourses, the temporal is repeatedly juxtaposed over against the eternal. For example, when S. K. said that the Christian suffers only once, he is contrasting the temporal (though it may last for seventy years) with the eternal.[113] Also, Christ is frequently alluded to as the Pattern. For example, in the discourse, "The Joy of it—that the poorer thou dost become, the richer thou canst make others," Kierkegaard noted that, "He was poor, yet surely made others rich! . . . His life is essential truth."[114] Suffering is a means to revealing the hidden God. In the discourse, "The Joy of it—that the weaker thou dost become, the stronger dost God become in thee," S. K. noted that God is not "directly present so as to be noticed in the world."[115] Indeed, His omnipotence is manifest in that He is able to create and love a creature "directly in opposition" to Himself.[116] Finally, these discourses emphasize that sin is the only thing that can ultimately destroy the work of God.[117]

The number of biblical references is greater in the *Edifying Discourses* and the *Christian Discourses* than in the earlier works. The kind of remote allusions characteristic of the aesthetic works is more infrequent. Biblical exposition is the normal pattern with the insights of Scripture illuminating Scripture. The fact that this straightforward appropriation of

Scripture is evident in the earliest discourses would indicate that this is indeed the normative Kierkegaardian approach to the Bible.

However, it appears that the closer Kierkegaard comes to the religion of paradox in the discourses, as illustrated by *Thoughts on Crucial Situations*, the number of explicit references to Scripture declines. This indicates that the paradox is the axiomatic center of Kierkegaard's theological interest and the prism through which the Scripture is interpreted. This theological focus on the paradox is taken for granted in the later religious works.

Once the paradox is assumed, the later "Christian" discourses return, with even greater emphasis, to straightforward exposition of biblical texts and themes. However, now the categories of transcendent religion are utilized with regularity. Increasingly, Kierkegaard's emphasis becomes more polemical, contrasting the demands of the biblical text with the realities of Christendom.

Works of Love

Published in 1847, *Works of Love* appears to be in the same style as the various discourses discussed above. However, these "discourses" are actually "Christian reflections."

> Reflections do not presuppose the qualifying concepts as given and understood; therefore they must not so much move, mollify, reassure, persuade as awaken and provoke men and sharpen thought. The time for reflection is indeed prior to action, and their purpose therefore is to rightly set all elements into motion.[118]

The treatise *Works of Love* is perhaps the most reflective and profound of Kierkegaard's works. Yet it has received surprisingly little attention from Kierkegaard scholars.[119] There are more references to Scripture indexed in this book than in any other volume examined in this entire study.[120] As with the various discourses just examined, the Bible is also center stage in *Works of Love*. Unlike the varied emphases of the diverse discourses, this book develops a single biblical theme—the nature of Christian love and the manifestation of the fruits of love in the life of the Christian.[121]

This work also embodies a direct and consistent effort to exegete significant biblical passages on Christian love.[122] Part One of the book provides a thematic foundation. The focus is on understanding the true nature of love as based on divine love, for in an allusion to 1 John 4:7-8, Kierkegaard said, "God is love."[123] Jesus' command to love one's neighbor constitutes one practical demonstration of divine love.[124] S.K. saw love as both a matter of conscience and a fulfillment of the law of God.[125]

Part Two of the book examines the love in action because love "builds up."[126] Several of the discourses in this section take as their text various aspects of love as described in 1 Corinthians 13.[127] Interestingly enough, the four discourses before the conclusion of the book are not based specifically upon a Scripture passage. However, each of these discourses generally contains the usual number of references to Scripture.[128] The concluding exhortation focuses on direct biblical exposition in a manner consistent with the work as a whole. It is an extended comment on the command to love one another, recorded in 1 John 4:7, the genuine sign that one is indeed born of and knows God.[129] The focus now shifts to an overview of the main themes of *Works of Love*.

Kierkegaard addressed this work, as he did the earlier discourses, to the "single individual."[130] He noted that:

> the divine authority of the Gospel speaks not to one man about another man, not to you, the reader, about me, or to me about you—no, when the gospel speaks it speaks to the single individual. It does not speak about us men, you and me, but it speaks to us men, you and me, and it speaks about the requirement that love shall be known by its fruits.[131]

Kierkegaard's own struggle with the nature of Christian love becomes the "schoolmaster" through which the gospel word is heard.

A discussion of love at any level must be informed by the Christian understanding of divine love. Kierkegaard argued that spiritual love is not a different kind of love or a higher form of love, as compared with erotic and philanthropic interest.[132] Rather, "Christianity knows only one kind of love; spiritual love; but this can lie at the base of and be present in every other expression of love."[133] Just as a tranquil lake is fed by a hidden spring, so human love originates from the hidden spring of divine love and is recognized by its fruits.[134] The reference to the "works" of love refers to the spiritual fruit or the qualities of life in which love is manifest.

Kierkegaard recognized that "all human language about the spiritual, yes, even the divine language of Holy Scriptures, is essentially transferred or metaphorical language."[135] Thus, it is not surprising that there is a marked contrast between the world's conception of love and the Christian conception, even though both perspectives appear to use the same vocabulary. It is, however, possible to distinguish between "worldly wisdom," which sees love as only a relationship between man and man, and Christianity, which "teaches that love is a relationship between: man—God—man, that is, that God is the middle term."[136]

Kierkegaard's conception is not simply one of love for love's sake. This would be an aesthetic and theoretical expression devoid of active reality. Christian love lacks the romantic charm of an idealized poetic expression. The exhortation to love one's neighbor, for example, could not be praised by the poet, for there are "invisible letters behind every word in Holy Scriptures . . . [that exhort] go and do likewise."[137] This practical exhortation is absent from all natural views of love. The focus of divine love is on expressing love, on learning to love, rather than being the object of another's love. It is only through divine love that one can be properly related to one's self as well as one's neighbor. Kierkegaard observed,

> For to love God is to love oneself in truth; to help another human being to love God is to love another man; to be helped by another human being to love God is to be loved.[138]

A proper understanding of the divine basis for loving is the beginning of the process of changing the heart. Any other form of love and basis for relationship entail a basic selfishness. But "wherever Christianity is . . . there is also self-renunciation."[139]

Christian love differs from sentimental and romantic notions of love in that it contains the imperative, "You shall love—this, then is the word of the royal law."[140] One does not simply fall into love, one obey's the divine command to love the neighbor. In answering the question that occasioned the parable of the good Samaritan, "Who, then, is one's neighbor?"[141] Kierkegaard indicated that "to love him who through favouritism is nearer to you than all others is self-love.[142] He observed, quoting Matthew 5:46-47, "Do not the heathens also do the same?"[143] Alluding to this same passage S. K. later observed that it is the "'pagan' way, 'to love those who can make repayment.'"[144] One's "neighbor" is thus simply any other human being—one who has the same potential for knowing and loving because of the image of God.

Reciprocity and mutuality in love are evidences that worldly love is essentially selfish. Kierkegaard was relentless as he sought to unmask any and all attempts to hide from the exceeding selfishness of all worldly loves. Even the Christian ascetic tendency to make much ado about its "indifference towards friendship, towards the family relationship, towards patriotism" is dismissed as "childishness."[145] True Christianity "does not seek to bring about external changes in the external; it wants to seize it, purify it, sanctify it, and thus make everything new, while nevertheless everything is old."[146] Thus while external relationships may appear to remain the same, the Christian is transformed from within. Love is a matter of conscience.[147] Love is the debt owed by every believer.[148] Love is, according to S. K., the "fulfilling of the law."[149]

Arbaugh and Arbaugh argue that Kierkegaard's conception of love based on duty is different from the Kantian "categorical imperative" for several reasons.[150] First, there is no universalization of the need of persons or human value. A Christian loves because it is God's will to do so. Second, S. K. is not interested in universal law per se but in the "absolutely personalized love for neighbor."[151] The neighbor is the particular individual nearest one at a given time. Finally, Kierkegaard's conception of love is based upon divine grace. Grace is the power behind the ability to love, and it is also manifest through the various acts of loving.

Thus, Kierkegaard wanted to evoke inwardness through reflection that would lead one to obedience to the divine command to love. The parable of Matthew 21:28-31, a "man had two sons," is cited as a warning that the commitment to love is not a commitment that should be too easily made.[152] The story tells of two sons, one who agreed to his father's command but never obeyed. The second son initially rejected his father's command but later obeyed.

> But what does the parable wish to point up? I wonder if it is not to show the danger of too great a hurry in saying "Yes," even if it is meant at the moment. The yes-brother is not presented as one who was a deceiver when he said "Yes," but as one who became a deceiver because he did not hold to his promise, more accurately, as one who by his very eagerness in promising became a deceiver—that is to say, the promise became his snare.[153]

However, once the imperative is heard, love is transformed into an act of both freedom and spontaneity. Now the love for neighbor (and all relationships include this level of love) is an act of joyful response to God and thus is not affected by the fluctuation of circumstances. Even the marital bond is transformed.

> The wife shall first and foremost be your neighbour; the fact that she is your wife is then a narrower definition of your special relationship to each other. But what is eternally basic must also be the basis of every expression of what is special.[154]

Kierkegaard's concern with how one becomes a Christian and how one lives the Christian life involves two distinct but related concepts. One becomes a Christian through introspection. The realization of sin—estrangement from God—opens the door for grace and faith. Once all false allurements have been repudiated and one is willing to rest by faith on the sufficiency of the Paradox as the communication of God to man, the Christian life has begun. However, the Christian life is lived in relationship to others. Even here S. K. does not succumb to the temptation of an idealistic humanitarianism. Rather, with God as the middle term of the love relationship, neighbor-love is transformed into a dynamic expression of obedience and service to God.

What then is the result of this kind of love? What are the "works" of love? The last half of the book deals with these questions. Kierkegaard was not particularly concerned with social reform. He was horrified by the "mass man" and repeatedly protested the "leveling" effects of democracy, for example.[155] Nor did he relegate the works of love to specific acts of kindness, benevolence, and the like. In fact, the works of love are not so much deeds as qualities of life—akin to the "fruit of the spirit."[156] Most of these discourses explain specific Scriptures related to love.

The first discourse of this section, for example, "Love Builds Up" is based on 1 Corinthians 8:1.[156] The expression "to edify" or to "build up" is one of those terms with an everyday usage and a particular spiritual usage in the Scripture. In the latter sense, "building up is exclusively characteristic of love."[157] Citing Scripture as evidence of his point, Kierkegaard observed that

> Wherever there is building up, love is present, and wherever love is, there is building up. Therefore Paul says that a loveless man, even though he were to speak in the tongues of men and of angels, would still be like a noisy gong and a clanging cymbal. And what is less edifying than a clanging cymbal! Worldliness, no matter how splendid and acclaimed, is loveless, and therefore does not build up.[158]

Love is also the ground, or the foundation upon which this spiritual "building up" occurs. Although no one can create or produce love in another, it becomes the presupposition for all relationships. S. K. said that

> the lover presupposes that love is in the other person's heart, and by this very presupposition he builds up love in him— from the ground up, insofar as in love he presupposes it present as the ground.[159]

This is not blind naivete, but confidence that God—the middle term in all love relationships—is at work in the love of the other. S. K. noted that "the prodigal son's father was perhaps the only one who did not know that he had a prodigal son."[160]

The second discourse in this section, "Love Believes All Things—and Yet Is Never Deceived," draws contrasts between worldly wisdom and the wisdom of love.[161] Stupidity involves deception. The wisdom of the world belies a spirit of mistrust which says "believe nothing in order never to be deceived."[162] Yet in relationship to God, persons do not deceive

Him, rather "a man can deceive only himself."[163] There is a superiority to love which allows it to stand above the fear of deception. In a play on Luke 12:4, Kierkegaard said, "One need not infinitely fear them who are able to kill the body . . . nor is the kind of deception the world talks about a danger."[164] The kind of love that does not focus on reciprocity may have "the appearance of being the weaker."[165] In reality, love that believes all things "overcomes the world."[166]

"Love Hopes All Things and Yet Is Never Put to Shame," based upon 1 Corinthians 13:7, is the third discourse in this section.[167] In contrast to worldly expectations, the eternal is the focus of the Christian's hope.

> Christianity does not lead you up to some loftier place from which you nevertheless can only survey a somewhat wider territory—this is still only an earthly hope and a worldly vision. No Christianity's hope is the eternal, and therefore in its sketch of existence there are light and shadow, beauty and truth, and above all the depth of perspective. Christianity's hope is the eternal, and Christ is the way; his abasement is the way, but also when ascended into heaven, he was the way.[168]

Fear is a negative "hope," an expectation regarding the possibility of evil. Hope for good is distinctively Christian. This hope sees good as the "possibility . . . present at every moment."[169] Christian hope "will not be put to shame."[170] Even if the prodigal had died estranged from his father, the father's love would have been honored. The expectation, not the result, is the basis for eternal honor and glory.[171]

"Love Seeks Not Its Own," based upon 1 Corinthians 13:3, is the fourth discourse in this section.[172] Love is not selfish. God created humanity in His image, to be like Him. Christ came as the prototype to "draw all men unto himself."[173] However, the goal was that in becoming like Him, each might become their own. In this sense, love is sacrifice. Kierkegaard said that

> in love there is no mine and yours. But mine and yours are only relational qualifications of "one's-own"; consequently, if there is no "mine" or "yours," there is no "one's-own," either; but if there is no "one's-own," it is indeed impossible to seek "one's-own."

. . . .

There are a you and an I and yet no mine and yours! For without you and I there is no love, and with mine and yours there is no love.[174]

These distinctions are not truly dissolved in either friendship or erotic love. Though the lover may be "outside of his own," there is still a basic selfishness which undermines the sacrifices of love at this level.[175] "Only spiritual love has the courage to will to have no mine at all, the courage to abolish completely the distinction between mine and yours, and therefore it wins God—by losing its soul."[176] Thus, the one who expresses unconditional love—creatively enabling the other to be his or her "own" in the proper sense—is God's co-laborer.[177] If this creative process is successful then the help given will not be evident. The one helped would not be "his own" if the help could be detected.[178]

"Love Hides the Multiplicity of Sins" echoes the theme of two of the earlier Edifying Discourses of similar title.[179] The sixth discourse, "Love Abides," is the last of these discourses to take its title and theme directly from a verse of the Bible—1 Corinthians 13:13.[180] Divine love persists. Kierkegaard said that "if one ceases to love, he has never been loving at all."[181] Since true love is "in compact with the eternal," one does not fall in or out of love based upon the response of the beloved.[182] The lover says "I abide" and thus, there is no break in the relationship. The eternal gain is its own reward in true love.[183]

The discourse "Mercifulness, a Work of Love, Even if It Can Give Nothing and Is Capable of Doing Nothing" stresses the importance of proper motivation in doing good works.[184] In a twist on the familiar story of the good Samaritan, Kierkegaard invites the supposition that there were two men who journeyed from Jerusalem to Jericho and both fell among thieves.[185] If one forgot his own suffering in order to speak a comforting word, dragged himself to a stream to get a drink for the other, or even breathed a silent prayer to God in the other's behalf—he was merciful. It is not what one does but how one does it that demonstrates proper motivation. Kierkegaard, for example, warned that even when aid is being given to the poor too often "mercifulness is not practiced."[186]

The discourse, "The Victory of Reconciliation in Love Which Wins the Vanquished," focuses on forgiveness.[187] Reconciliation is a matter of the spirit. Even if the prodigal's brother had been willing to do all for his brother, the most difficult thing to accept would be that "the prodigal should be the more important one."[188] Yet it is at this level that love wins over the vanquished. The final victory is realized when the beloved no longer feels it necessary to ask forgiveness.[189]

"The Work of Love in Remembering One Dead" is peculiar in that it does not treat a biblical theme or text in any direct way.[190] There is no concern with, nor even any possibility of, reciprocity in revering the dead.[191] In this sense, the work of remembering the dead is "the most disinterested, the freest, the most faithful love."[192] Revering deceased family and friends can therefore actually aid in developing love for one's neighbor.

The final discourse is "The Work of Love in Praising Love."[193] S.K. encourages the commending of love to others, not by poetic expression, but through "self-renunciation" and "sacrificial disinterestedness."[194] True love is "to love one's neighbour. . . finding the unlovable object to be lovable."[195]

Works of Love concludes with an exhortation based on 1 John 4:7, "Beloved, let us love one another."[196] Kierkegaard reminds his hearer that "a profession of faith is not enough."[197] Indeed, the same old commandment, to love one another, becomes new for each generation. The only change is "that the lover becomes more and more intimate with the commandment."[198] Hence, the relative mildness of the Apostle John's encouragement to love. True Christianity is a repudiation of all interest in reciprocity. Kierkegaard is not arguing that one "earns grace" by loving for "what you learn first of all in relating yourself to God is precisely that you have no merit at all."[199] Rather, love is the truest manifestation that one has been loved. A properly disposed Christian will maintain an "unforgettable fear and trembling even though he rests in God's love."[200]

Edifying Discourses contains religious exhortations based upon the religion of immanence. The *Christian Discourses* presuppose the paradox and develop themes from the perspective of the religion of transcendence. *Works of Love* is unique in its focus on a single theme—love. Relevant biblical passages are treated in a systematic and comprehensive manner to encourage "appropriation"—practical obedience to the Bible's message of love. Kierkegaard was convinced that Christendom had not heard the message of biblical Christianity. His use of Scripture is increasingly direct and poignantly prophetic in his later polemical works.

The Function of Scripture in Selected Polemical Works

Training in Christianity and *Attack upon Christendom* are examined in the final section of the chapter. As Kierkegaard became more open and prophetic in his religious stance, his appeal to the authority of the Bible became more direct. Correspondingly, he took an increasingly more critical view of the established church and the clergy.

Training in Christianity

Kierkegaard experienced a religious metamorphosis Wednesday of Holy Week, April 19, 1848.[201] Written later in 1848, *Training in Christianity* was published September 27, 1850. No veiled references to "the Christian tradition" or "Christian culture" obscure Kierkegaard's purpose. Training was his most direct repudiation of Religion A, cultural Christianity, and Christendom.[202] His was a "gospel" purpose. His concern was that persons might become "contemporary" with the Lord Jesus Christ.[203] Kierkegaard hoped that no further attack upon the church would be needed and even reported to a friend that his writing was finished.[204]

The Bible is central to this work, in new and pronounced ways, as Kierkegaard expounds his understanding of biblical Christianity.[205]

The frequent quotes make these the easiest to locate of any work examined thus far. S. K. had long ago abandoned the casual allusions of the aesthete. Now the sharp contrasts between the faith of the New Testament and Christendom stand in bold relief. The biblical message is authoritative, refusing to submit to any need for corroboration by human reason. The

Gospel message should either scandalize or evoke belief. There is no comfortable middle way.

Training is divided into three sections. Part I, subtitled "For Revival and Increase of Inwardness," focuses on Jesus' invitation, recorded in Matthew 11:28, "Come hither, all ye that labour and are heavy laden, and I will give you rest."[206] Part II deals with the believer's response to Christ's invitation in Matthew 11:6, "Blessed is he whosoever is not offended in me," and is subtitled, "A Biblical Exposition and Christian Definition of Concepts."[207] Part III, "He Will Draw All unto Himself," deals with the implications of entering into Christ's suffering for Christian discipleship and is an extended exposition of John 12:32, "And I, if I be lifted up from the earth, will draw all unto myself."[208]

In the opening "Invocation," Kierkegaard said that, though it has been more than eighteen hundred years since Jesus was on earth, his coming is more than an event of mundane history, for a believer today must be "as contemporary with His presence on earth as were those [first] contemporaries."[209] Although Jesus' purpose in coming was to "seek the lost," he was both "the sign of offense and the object of faith."[210] S. K. concluded his prayer, "Would that we might see Thee ... and then that for all this we might not be offended in Thee."[211]

The divine invitation to "come hither unto me" evoked the exclamation and praise of Kierkegaard, "Oh! Wonderful, wonderful! That the one who has help to give is the one who says, Come hither! What love is this!"[212] Jesus offers this help as if he were the one needing help. The one who in self-surrender offers himself is also the one who invites all to come. S. K. said, "He is true to His word, He is what He says, and in this sense also He is the Word."[213] Yet, each one must come as an individual.[214]

There is, however, a divine halt within this invitation "at the parting of the ways where the path of sin deviates from the hedge road of innocence."[215] The invitation is a call to return from the path of perdition. Eloquently Kierkegaard called to the sinner:

> If thou thyself art conscious of being a sinner, he will not inquire of thee about it, the bruised reed He will not further

break, but he will raise thee up if thou wilt attach thyself to Him. He will not single thee out by contrast, holding thee apart from Him, so that thy sin will seem still more dreadful; He will grant thee a hiding-place within Him, and once hidden in Him he will hide thy sins. For He is the friend of sinners.[216]

This invitation is not, however, open-ended. Kierkegaard warned that one who has ceased to seek and sorrow is not invited for the call grows "fainter and fainter."[217]

There is a "halt" more significant than the problem of guilt over sin. This halt comes from the Inviter himself, who speaks from his humiliation. Kierkegaard said just as it would be an "untruth" to ascribe words to Him that he did not in fact say, it would also be false to "represent him as essentially different from what he was when he spake certain words."[218] In this context, in order for modern persons to properly understand a biblical text, they must become contemporary with Jesus. The invitation to "come" is identified with Jesus in his servant-form. One must become contemporary with the paradox. But how is this possible?

Kierkegaard contends that one can neither learn nor prove from history that Jesus is the Christ. Indeed, "one can 'know' nothing at all about 'Christ'; He is the paradox, the object of faith, existing for faith."[219] Proofs from history are limited to probability—at best. At worst, attempts to prove who Christ is will result in an essential distortion of His ministry, message, and purpose. Proof is opposed to faith.

> The proofs which Scripture presents for Christ's divinity—His miracles, His Resurrection from the dead, His Ascension into heaven—are therefore only for faith, that is, they are not 'proofs', they have no intention of proving that all this agrees perfectly with reason; on the contrary they would prove that it conflicts with reason and therefore is an object of faith.[220]

Kierkegaard entertains modern skepticism regarding the historical veracity of these events. It is a "blasphemy" to avoid the offense of the paradox by making the gospel palatable.[221] Sacred history is qualitatively different from history in general.[222] The significance of Christ's life is that "God lived here on earth."[223] The offense of Christ's humiliation is not merely an accident, because he was misunderstood. His humiliation was essential.[224]

It is the "misfortune of Christendom" that this distinction has been lost.[225] People are content to know about Christ; however, the only proper way to relate to Him is to believe. Kierkegaard complained of Christendom's

> Sunday twaddle about Christianity's glorious and priceless truths, its sweet consolation; but it is only too evident that Christ lived 1,800 years ago. The Sign of Offence and the object of Faith has become the most romantic of all fabulous figures, a divine Uncle George. One does not know what it is to be offended, still less what it is to worship.[226]

The ultimate and often repeated charge is that "Christendom has done away with Christianity."[227]

The cautious response of various modern persons to the life and person of Jesus Christ is indicative of the blasphemous spirit of offense. There are numerous New Testament parallels to these various responses to Jesus. In the first period of his life, the multitude is carried away with him, and they would make him king. The "wise and prudent man" concedes that he appears to be unique, but he is hardly "extraordinary."[228] A "clergyman" comments that "for an impostor and seducer" there is something "uncommonly honest about Him."[229] The philosopher appreciates his "aphorisms," although they lack systematic clarity, and admires the fact that he is able to lead people to believe in him, even though he is guilty of "philosophical bestiality."[230] The "statesman" notes the colossal waste of opportunity—he has numerous strengths, "but He seems to annul them."[231] The "solid citizen" notes his idealism but appeals for moderation and notes that "Pastor Green," (who is better at the club on Monday than in the pulpit on Sunday) predicts a "terrible ending" for him.[232] The crowds appear to follow because of a few dubious miracles. The "mocker" exclaims, "I shall proclaim that I . . . am God."[233] These various responses are not exaggerations, for there is "only one, one single man, who seriously sought Him out, and he came to Him . . . by night."[234]

In the second period of his life, the offense became more apparent. S. K. observed, "The mighty drew the net closer—

and then the people, perceiving that they were completely deceived, turned their hate and the bitterness of their disillusionment against Him."[235] To identify "literally. . . with the most miserable" is "for men . . . 'too much.'"[236] When Christianity gets away from radical identification with Christ, or "absolute contemporaneousness," it is "toned down to the merely human" and becomes, in a play on 1 Corinthians 2:9, "what has 'entered into the heart of man.'"[237] Yet, according to Kierkegaard, "in relation to the absolute there is only one tense—the present."[238] If one is not contemporary with Christ then for that one He has no existence. S. K. cites Matthew 13:16, "Blessed are the eyes which see the things that ye see," saying that this must refer to becoming contemporary with Christ.[239] His glory was not directly visible, "for he humbled Himself and took upon Him the form of a servant"[240] and "there was nothing about Him for the eye, no glamour that we should look upon Him."[241]

Kierkegaard's complaint is that in Christendom, "To be a Christian has become a thing of naught, mere tomfoolery, something which everyone is as a matter of course, something one slips into."[242] The absolute paradox is that the God-man should suffer for sinners. Echoing a theme from the *Concept of Anxiety*, Kierkegaard says that sin-consciousness is essential if one is to become a Christian in Christendom.

> Everyone for himself, in quiet inwardness before God, shall humble himself before what it means in the strictest sense to be a Christian, admit candidly before God how it stands with him, so that he might yet accept the grace which is offered to everyone.[243]

The "torments of a contrite heart" make it possible to "enter by the narrow way," for it is "through the consciousness of sin" that one moves "into Christianity."[244]

In order to be properly trained in Christianity, there must be a recognition that the real Christ is offensive. In the "Prelude" to the second division of the book, Kierkegaard paints a picture of the earthly life of Christ, utilizing the various scriptural descriptions of his ministry. The challenge is to "Behold, the man" for, "Blessed is he who is not offended in Him but believes."[245] There is no salvation apart from him. S. K. affirmed,

"He is the Saviour, there is no salvation for any but in Him."[246]
Furthermore, Jesus is "the Truth and the Life" of whom all have
absolute need.[247]

The offense of Christ may be understood from several
different perspectives. It can, for example, be seen as simply
the collision between a mere human individual and the established order. The collision with the Pharisees, recorded in
Matthew 15:1-12, where Jesus said, "this people . . . honoureth
me with their lips, but their heart is far from me" occurs again
in Christendom when inwardness is juxtaposed to "empty ex-
ternalism."[248] In a state of complacency all fear and trembling
has ceased.

Hegel has deified the established order. This results in the
"secularization of everything."[249] The individual is lost in the
inevitability of progress. However, the essential offense of the
God-man is the paradox, and it is before this truth that all "understanding" comes to a standstill.[250] S. K. cites Jesus' instruc-
tion to take a coin from a fish's mouth to pay taxes and avoid
giving offense as an illustration that the true nature of the offense is more than mere collision with the established order.[251]

Socrates was persecuted accidentally. Jesus actually invited reproach and encouraged the offense. The idea "essential
offense" is associated with Jesus' exaltation.[252] His identity
during His earthly ministry was more obscure. This is illustrated by the fact that John the Baptist, the forerunner, questioned His identity.[253] Jesus did not answer John directly. He
simply reported His works—but not as proofs, for "a man
does not come to Him by the help of proofs" because, as S. K.
noted, "there is no direct transition to this thing of becoming
a Christian."[254] Christendom has painted a "fantastic" picture
of Christ.[255] The offense has been "abolished."[256]

The real key to the offense of the incarnation is not that
Jesus in His exaltation should be called the God-man; the true
nature of the offense is that in His lowliness, He who is the
God-man is poor and suffering. When His neighbors asked,
"Is not this the carpenter's son?" S. K. points out that they
were "offended that God should be the son of a carpenter."[257]
Peter's denial of Jesus illustrates the essential offense of
Christ's passion.[258] Kierkegaard exclaimed, "Oh, depth of suf-

fering . . . that He must be the sign of offense in order to be the object of faith!"[259]

> Only when the self-contradiction of suffering is present is the possibility of offence also present, and that in turn, as was observed, is inseparable from being a Christian, as Christ himself represents it.[260]

Since the disciple is not above the Master, then "to be a Christian in truth should mean in the world . . . to be abased."[261] Christendom, however, proclaims the church triumphant—"His disciples made a triumphal conquest of the whole world."[262] A "Hurrah!" would be more appropriate than an "Amen" to such preaching.[263] The parable of the sower and those offended when tribulation comes is one biblical text cited as demonstration of the true nature of the offense.[264] The Lord Jesus predicted that those who persecuted His followers would be seen as doing God a service.[265] The offense— that the God-man suffered—must be shared by those who would be disciples. The centrality of suffering is further illustrated in the account, recorded in Matthew 16:21-33, of Jesus' rebuke to Peter, "Get thee behind me, Satan," because Peter could not accept Christ's impending passion.[266]

Kierkegaard utilized these and several other biblical passages as "proof-texts" to show the paradox, the offense, and the ways in which the disciple should identify with Christ through suffering. Yet these texts do not constitute "apologetic" arguments as such. S. K. was not seeking to coerce faith by the persuasive weight of these biblical texts. The call to faith is not simply a response to their divine authority. Rather, he sought to paint an accurate picture of Christ, with whom each individual must become contemporary. He says that "the God-man is the object of faith."[267]

The later portion of this part of *Training* is focused on the implications of Kierkegaard's understanding of the God-man as an offense. The God-man is a sign, a negation of immediacy.[268] But the incarnation is a sign of contradiction. Jesus' humanity points away from itself, implausibly, to God.[269] Miracle and parable, like Jesus, are indirect communications— they are signs pointing beyond themselves to God. Thus, the revelation of God in Jesus is incognito.[270] The very real responses to the God-man are either faith or offense. There is no middle ground of accommodation. Indirect communication is essential because of the hiddenness of God, the person of the God-man, and the requirement for faith.[271]

The final third of *Training* interprets the life of discipleship for those who enter into the fellowship of Christ's suffering. This section is softer in tone than the previous two-thirds of the book, more akin to the emphasis of the various discourses. However, the contrast between Christianity and Christendom remains. Further, the concern with being a martyr, or witness, anticipates a major theme of the *Attack upon Christendom*. True following is to walk as He walked. One becomes a Christian in New Testament discipleship, which identifies with Christ's suffering and is far removed from the comfortable "Christians" of Christendom.

The words of Jesus, uttered when he was still in servant-form, recorded in John 12:32, "And I, if I be lifted up from the earth, will draw all unto Myself," are the basis for the seven discourses of this section. This is a reference to Jesus' "drawing all" from his present glorified state according to S. K.'s interpretation of the text.[272] The text actually applies the image of "being lifted up" to Jesus' death on the cross. John 12:33 says, "He said this to show by what death he was to die." Also, in John 3:14 a comparison is made between the "serpent in the wilderness" lifted up by Moses, a cure for sickness caused by sin, and Jesus' own being lifted up.[273] Kierkegaard's point is that it is after the cross, from his position on high, that Jesus draws all men unto himself. He observed:

> He is there—He from whom in a sense thou dost separate when thou departest from the altar, but who nevertheless will not forget thee if thou dost not forget him; yea will not forget thee even when, alas, thou dost sometimes forget Him, who on high continues to draw thee unto Himself, until the last blessed end when thou shalt be by Him, and with Him on high.[274]

Christ is the truth who helps each individual to see aright so that the self is realized even as it is drawn to Christ.[275] S. K. contended that Christ's whole life involved suffering, even from his beginning as "an illegitimate child."[276] It is a "misunderstanding" that applies "'the story of the Passion'" to only the last week of Jesus' life.[277] True followers are not content to simply walk where Jesus walked, or feel aesthetically the pathos of the cross. The disciples were content "to know nothing save Christ and Him crucified."[278] It is the image of Him as the suffering one that "may yet move thee to love Him" and desire "to suffer in His likeness."[279] Many are called, but few chosen—the invitation is for all, though not all will "permit themselves to be drawn."[280]

The individual's life should be examined in the light of the suffering of the God-man. Gradually the highest examination of life is faced. The ultimate question is "whether one will be in truth a Christian or not."[281] As Kierkegaard observed, "Christianly understood, the truth consists not in knowing the truth but in being the truth."[282]

Christendom "does not resemble the Church militant any more than a quadrangle resembles a circle," according to S. K.[283] The church is "militant" and victorious only as it is properly related to the Lord Jesus Christ, the truth. It is from his vantage point "on high" that victory is proclaimed. The individual Christian's spiritual victory is realized in "hidden inwardness," not in crass triumphantism.[284] The "single individual" stands above the "fellowship" of the church, for "the congregation" is primarily understood as a category of the eternal.[285]

Matthew 7:13f describes the path to heaven as "strait" and "narrow," but these are lost concepts when all are Christians in Christendom.[286] The triumphant church of established Christendom, through its false position of pretending to have already arrived, stands in opposition to the genuine church militant. Indeed, Christendom is the destruction of the church militant.[287]

The "sacred text" having been examined from several perspectives, Kierkegaard concludes *Training* with a benediction that all might be drawn to Christ, "In so far as a man is able—for Thou alone art able to draw unto Thyself, though Thou canst employ all means and all men to draw all unto Thyself."[288]

The discourse, "The Woman That Was a Sinner," was intended to accompany *Training* and is included at the end of this edition. Based on the Luke 7:36-50 account of the woman who wept at Jesus' feet, this is perhaps one of Kierkegaard's loftiest eulogies of womanhood. S. K. says that two things are taught by this woman's example. First, "we can learn . . . [to be] indifferent to everything else in absolute sorrow for our sins . . . to find forgiveness."[289] Second, "in relation to finding forgiveness she herself could do nothing at all."[290] Finally, the Christian today can view the completed life and ministry of Jesus, therefore, "we have a comfort which she had not."[291] Kierkegaard concluded:

> His death alters everything infinitely. Not that His death abolished the fact that at the same time He is the Pattern; no, but His death becomes the infinite guarantee with which the striver starts out, the assurance that infinite satisfaction has been made, that to the doubtful and disheartened there is tendered the strongest pledge—impossible to find anything more reliable—that Christ died to save him, that Christ's death is the atonement and satisfaction.[292]

Attack upon "Christendom"

Kierkegaard's prolific publication of works ended abruptly with the release of *For Self-Examination* in 1851. He wrote little in his journals until early 1854. He was awaiting the proper time to speak, a sign from God. That sign came with the death of a family friend and pastor, Bishop Mynster, the prelate of Denmark.[293] When S. K.'s former tutor, Professor Martensen, eulogized the Bishop as a "witness for the truth," Kierkegaard was enraged. Mynster had refused to respond to S. K.'s previous critiques of "Christendom." Indeed, he had become, for Kierkegaard, the personification of all that was wrong with the institutional state church. Kierkegaard expressed this and other concerns in a series of brief articles for *The Fatherland* and a later pamphlet series entitled "The Instant." These short and violent eruptions were among the first Kierkegaard works translated into other languages and earned him a popularity that was somewhat surprising. One familiar with the larger Kierkegaard corpus will recognize these bold outbursts as being in character with S. K.'s concern for the recovery of true Christianity.

The Bible is prominent in these essays, but biblical exposition does not occupy center stage.[294] Instead there is a repeated juxtaposing of "the Christianity of the New Testament" over against "Christendom" with Kierkegaard's oft repeated verdict, "Christianity does not exist."[295] Kierkegaard has lavish praise for the "truth" of the New Testament. He says, for example, that in it "The true is represented ideally" and that it has "high notions of what it is to be a man."[296] He frequently refers to "God's word" and in one case he even equates the words of Paul with "what God is talking about."[297] Also, he repeatedly condemns the failure of Christendom to appropriate the truth of the Bible. Instead of appropriation, he sees a "Biblical interpretation of mediocrity" that continually interprets Christ's words "until it gets out of them its own spiritless [trivial] meaning—and then, after having removed all difficulties, it is tranquilized, and appeals confidently to Christ's words!"[298]

It was the loss of the paradox, the loss of inwardness, and thus the loss of New Testament Christianity that burdened Kierkegaard. He indicated that if Christianity is to be equated with Christendom, then "the New Testament is . . . no longer a guide for Christians" and is only "a historical curiosity, pretty much like a guidebook to a particular country when everything in that country has been totally changed."[299] Yet, "we know from the New Testament how Christ judges official Christianity."[300] *Attack upon "Christendom"* is simply an edited collection of the essays and articles that addressed these concerns.

The articles in *The Fatherland* carried on the running battle Kierkegaard had with Martensen's characterization of Mynster as a "witness for the truth."[301] A genuine "witness" is one who faces sacrifice, poverty, suffering and is "at last crucified, or beheaded, or burnt, or roasted on a gridiron . . . thus a witness to the truth is buried."[302]

> Bishop Mynster's preaching soft-pedals, slurs over, suppresses, omits something decisively Christian, something which appears to us men inopportune, which would make our life strenuous, hinder us from enjoying life, that part of Christianity which has to do with dying from the world, by voluntary renunciation, by hating oneself, by suffering for doctrine,

etc.—to see this one does not have to be particularly sharp-sighted, if one puts the New Testament alongside of Mynster's sermons.[303]

Kierkegaard had tried to live by the messages he had heard Mynster preach. He even claimed, "I was his sermon on Monday."[304] The opulent life style, the public praise, the position of honor in society—all belied Mynster's failure as a genuine witness to the truth. The point was not simply that every witness must suffer death, rather that any genuine witness for the truth will live in accordance with self-denial implicit in willingness to become a martyr.[305]

In a later article, "What do I want?" Kierkegaard called for sincere honesty. He said, "The leniency which is the common Christianity in the land I want to place alongside of the New Testament in order to see how these two are related to one another."[306] He accused the official church of failing "frankly and unreservedly" to make known "the Christian requirement" out of fear that the population would see the gap between its orthodoxy and orthopraxy.[307] The concept of "grace" had been stretched too far if Christendom was acknowledged as Christianity.[308] Kierkegaard sought to dispel the illusion of Christianity. He did not presume that he was a Christian, he simply wanted the admission that Christendom did not meet the radical demands of the New Testament.

A later essay, "This Has to Be Said; So Be It Now Said," urged the "plain Christian" to disassociate from the "official worship of God" of the state Church because it was a "forgery."[309] Warnings regarding the collusion between Church and State in Christendom and a continued effort to dispel the illusion of Christianity are among the major themes of the later pamphlet series, "The Instant." This title refers to the moment of decision, when one takes the leap of faith. It is at that moment that time is intersected by eternity. Elsewhere Kierkegaard called it the "fullness of time."[310]

Here he was relentless in his attacks upon the clergy. He called for the disestablishment of the state-sponsored Church, although the government should continue to pay the salaries of the pastors to whom it was contractually committed.[311] S. K. satirized an imaginary theological student, Frederick, who had developed some doubts regarding the truth of Christianity. His fiancee, Juliana, is threatened at the prospect of losing the parsonage and an income. She says, "Sweet Frederick, . . . Why go and torment thyself with such thoughts? There are surely 1000 priests like thee; in short, thou art a priest like the others."[312] The priest is seduced. Later he preaches about "seek first the kingdom of God"—a good sermon that "produced the proper effect," according to the bishop.[313] Yet no one is concerned with what this passage should mean in daily living. The priests are "cannibals" living off sacred things in a profane way.[314] In a note of irony and humor, S. K. lampoons the church's worldliness saying:

> In the magnificent cathedral the Honorable and Right Reverend Geheime-General-Ober-Hof-Pradikant, the elect favorite of the fashionable world, appears before an elect company and preaches with emotion upon the text he himself elected: "God hath elected the base things of the world, and the things that are despised"—and nobody laughs.[315]

Kierkegaard's sarcasm is evident as he talks of Jesus who "won only eleven" in three and a half years of preaching,[316] and complains of one apostle who got carried away and "maybe in one hour, wins three thousand disciples of Christ."[317] Only the God-man can hold the proper balance between "extension" and the demand of discipleship.[318] The multiplied millions of Christian adherents stand in marked contrast to the small band of disciples around Jesus. The "success" of the modern Church makes the Pattern appear that much more unsuccessful. The point to all of this is that there is a fundamental cleavage between New Testament Christianity and Christendom.

"What Christ's Judgment Is About Official Christianity" tells of a poet who brought out a New Testament before a group of churchmen who had taken an oath upon it and were supposedly committed to its truth. What is Christ's judgment of the church? S. K. turns to the "woes" of Matthew 23 and by interjecting modern application, relates the text to the "leaders" of Christendom.[319]

Kierkegaard did not expect to reform the Church.[320] He simply wanted honesty and repentance. His was a "Gospel" purpose. He did not claim to have arrived as a Christian.[321] He simply sought to hold up the biblical ideal. In the end he addressed his message to the ordinary citizen:

> Thou plain man! The Christianity of the New Testament is infinitely high; but observe that it is not high in such a sense that it has to with the difference between man and man with respect to intellectual capacity, etc. Not, it is for all. Everyone, absolutely everyone, if he absolutely wills it, if he will absolutely hate himself, will absolutely put up with everything, suffer everything (and this every man can if he will)—then is this infinite height attainable to him.[322]

One of his contemporaries reported that there was great soul-searching, even on the part of the clergy, following Kierkegaard's death.[323] In a real sense, however, the attack fell on deaf ears. The emergence of modern mass society, secularism, and the decline of the church are all indications that Kierkegaard was indeed a prophetic—if somewhat strident—witness to the truth.

Conclusion

The hermeneutic of exhortation is most evident in the various discourses written throughout Kierkegaard's lifetime. The earlier *Edifying Discourses* are immanental and indirect in the communication of Christian truth. The *Christian Discourses* introduce the transcendent categories of "Religion B." They communicate Christian truth in a more direct fashion. However, there are a diversity of concerns evident in the biblical themes treated in these two levels of the discourse. *Works of Love* is unique in that a single theme—love and its manifestations—and the appropriate biblical material are developed in systematic fashion.

The polemical works return to the themes associated with the earlier exposition of the paradox: the offense of God-man, contemporaneousness, the leap of faith. In this sense, *Fragments* and *Postscript* are also polemical works. However, the tone is clearly more direct in both *Training* and *Attack*. *Attack* represents a departure from the extensive development of biblical themes so central to the rest of Kierkegaard's second literature. While the claims for biblical authority are "higher" here, he actually had less to say from the Bible. Instead, he launched a broadside attack that was intended to startle Christendom into making specific comparisons between the demands of the New Testament and itself. It is true that the whole of the second literature aimed at this kind of comparison. However, the subtleties and nuances of the earlier discourses and even *Training* give way to biting sarcasm in the *Attack*.

5

Kierkegaard and Scripture: An Evaluation

Kierkegaard's existential philosophy and religious concerns interacted in a creative and dynamic way in his use of the Scriptures. Even a cursory examination of Kierkegaard's biography indicates that religious concerns were part of his life from his earliest days. His intellectual interest in and ultimate repudiation of speculative philosophy grew out of his larger religious interests. It is therefore impossible to distinguish fully Kierkegaard's Christian concerns from his philosophical concerns. By his own admission, his understanding of the purpose of his various writings was that these contained the religious element from the very beginning.

This is not to say that there are not philosophical presuppositions, interests, and parallels in Kierkegaard's thought. He was a child of his times. He worked out of a modified Kantian epistemology. He presupposed human freedom, the discontinuity of an eternal God with time, and the corresponding limitations of human language for divine disclosure. He had a fascination with classical philosophy, pursuing the Socratic method to its logical dead end as he interrogated the nature of existence. Even his notion of paradox has parallels to Hegel's category of contradiction. However, on each of these points he developed a religious case for his position, frequently appealing to the Scriptures for justification. Thus, Kierkegaard's philosophical posture and religious concerns are intricately interwoven. Patrick Bigelow has observed:

Like Socrates, Kierkegaard the thinker thinks one thought and thinks this thought through to its completion until, in thinking this one thought, the thought has thought itself out and is no more to be thought. Kierkegaard the religious sage invites us to take "offense" at this thought, the thought that annihilates itself by announcing the "Absolute Paradox." He exhorts us to rejoice in the "shipwreck" of reason, the "crucifixion" of the understanding, that this thought betrays. Kierkegaard the prophet enjoins us to harken to the absolute loss of meaning disengaging the measured thinking of the philosopher. Kierkegaard the poet summons the silence harboring us in the wake of the withdrawal of the divine. Kierkegaard thinks one thought throughout these stations. This thought is the furtive, fugitive thought of the radical discontinuity of thinking with reality.[1]

Kierkegaard sought to "stick with the original difficulty of life."[2]

The complexity of Kierkegaard's interests is nowhere more evident than in dealing with the function of Scripture in his thought. He used the Bible as philosopher, sage, prophet, and poet. The various approaches to the Scriptures of both the early pseudonymous aesthetic and philosophical works and the later "second literature" display a diversity of models for "appropriation"—depending on the specific purpose and concerns of a given work.

Kierkegaard saw his work as a corrective to prevailing philosophical, theological, and popular religious trends of his day. He would no doubt repudiate an effort to systematize an approach to the Bible as a diversion from hearing its message. He certainly would not have ascribed any sort of normative status to his various uses of Scripture. He repeatedly noted that he spoke "without authority."

These reservations notwithstanding, an analysis of the function of Scripture in Kierkegaard's thought is in order. As is obvious from even a cursory reading of the Kierkegaard corpus, he had an intimate familiarity with and appreciation for the Bible as a literary work. The numerous passing allusions, aphoristic quotes, utilization of biblical characters and events, and other passing references of his earliest works illustrate this. He also had a deeper concern with regard to the Bible. Kierkegaard vigorously sought to reintroduce the radical demands of New Testament Christianity into Christendom. The vocabulary of faith was, for Kierkegaard, discovered, defined, and clarified through the revelation of God contained in the Scriptures. Regardless of the final verdict that one may reach concerning the accuracy of his biblical exposition and the validity of his theological position, there can be little doubt that his religious pilgrimage involved a deep and profound struggle to appropriate the message of the Bible.

A number of general characteristics of Kierkegaard's use of Scripture have been observed throughout this study. The aesthetic pseudonyms had a preference for Old Testament characters and illustrations. In the later works there was an obvious preference for the Synoptic Gospels, for Kierkegaard built his understanding of the life of Jesus upon traditional conflations of these accounts. He made frequent use of the Gospel of John. The Book of James, because of its practical concerns with faith and practice, was also a favorite source in Kierkegaard's "second literature."

Revelation was, for Kierkegaard, a unique category peculiar to Divine communication. As has been demonstrated, he was persistent in his criticism both of the orthodoxy of Danish Lutheranism and of cultural Christendom. Both represented an attempt to "accommodate" Divine truth according to the canons of human reason. Although he was aware of the emerging science of higher-critical studies in his day, Kierkegaard was, on the whole, indifferent to this line of inquiry. He also rejected the theological proof-texting and system building of those who attempted to offer an apologetic for the Christian message.

Frequently, in his own use of a biblical character, event or passage, Kierkegaard would bracket questions about the historicity of an event, specific exegetical issues, and conflicting traditional interpretations of a text in his effort to appropriate the Scriptures for daily living. Appropriation was the key to Kierkegaard's biblical interests. The numerous references to the Bible and its creative application in the Kierkegaard corpus are ample evidence that "Kierkegaard persisted in seeking the truth in Scripture through imaginative and total immersion in its content."[3]

The interaction of Kierkegaard's philosophical and religious concerns are evident in the different approaches to the Scriptures reflected in the various writings. An examination of these approaches and a critique of the strengths and weaknesses in Kierkegaard's use of the Scripture will conclude this study.

Kierkegaard's Approaches to Scripture and Appropriation

The pseudonyms of Kierkegaard's early works used the Bible in a variety of ways. The pseudonyms represent various aspects of the aesthetic, ethical, and religious existence spheres. Each of these "caricatures" has a slightly different approach to the Scripture. In general, the hermeneutical pattern of each corresponds roughly to the existence sphere it represents.

The Hermeneutic of Paradox

The hermeneutic of the aesthete is characterized by an attitude of indifference to the Scripture. Allusions to Scripture in the first volume of *Either/Or* and the aesthetic portion of *Stages* are of a very general nature. The Bible is used as a literary device. Theological concerns are not directly evident. Therefore, the Scriptures are not cited authoritatively or as proofs in the development of an argument. A reader's knowledge of the Bible may make some of the allusions more meaningful in terms of irony, humor, or their general illustrative value. Indeed, Kierkegaard appears to have assumed a general biblical literacy for his audience or he would not have used so many remote references to the Bible. However, in most cases, other non-biblical references could be used without a significant change in the meaning of his text.

The hermeneutic of the ethical, as exemplified by Judge William in volume two of *Either/Or*, the relevant passages of *Stages*, and discussion of the ethical in the other philosophical works, appeals to the Bible as a source for corroboration of universal law. This approach was also consistent with the immanental religion of what Kierkegaard later condemned as Christendom. Despite S. K.'s concern with duty in relation to an external standard, even here the Bible is not the foundation for the ethical point of view, it simply offers support. Dissatisfaction with an appeal to the ethical universal characterized the use of the Scriptures in *Fear and Trembling*. This work and *The Concept of Anxiety* stand on the transitional ground to the hermeneutic of paradox.

The hermeneutic of paradox characterized Kierkegaard's polemical approach to Christendom. This approach was evident in the transitional philosophical works, *Philosophical Fragments* and *Concluding Unscientific Postscript*, as well as the later, more directly polemical *Training in Christianity* and *Attack upon "Christendom."* In the earlier works, references to the Scripture with regard to the paradox are infrequent. There are enough allusions to indicate the importance of biblical sources for Kierkegaard's conception of the incarnation. There is, however, not the direct appeal to the New Testament characteristic of both *Training in Christianity* and the *Attack upon "Christendom."*

Kierkegaard's emphasis upon and understanding of the paradox of the God-man is not substantially different in *Training* and *Attack* from the conception in the earlier works. The major difference is that the lines of demarcation between Christendom and New Testament Christianity are more sharply drawn. However, the paradox was consistently the key to Kierkegaard's deepest religious understanding of the Scripture. The major difference between the earlier and later utilization of Scripture with regard to the paradox is two-fold. In the early works Kierkegaard himself was engaged in "indirect communication." In the later more polemical works, Kierkegaard communicated directly. However, the paradox itself, and hence, the message of the Bible, remained an "indirect communication."

The Scripture is also the major source from which Kierkegaard drew the two possible responses to the paradox. Faith or offense, and not doubt, comprise the only alternative responses to the Gospel. Kierkegaard viewed faith as not just another kind of knowledge—a justified, albeit spiritual, belief. It involved total commitment to the God-relationship. It was an active appropriation of the Bible's message. Kierkegaard's open confrontation with Christendom was a result, in part, of his commitment to the radical nature of the Christian message.

S. K.'s various discourses are characterized by a hermeneutic of exhortation. The earlier *Edifying Discourses* are immanental in nature. Only in an indirect way do they communicate transcendent Christian truth. They are, however, more direct than the aesthetic literature that S. K. was producing simultaneously with their writing. In these early discourses Kierkegaard stretched the limits of immanental religion. The transcendent categories of mature Christianity are only hinted at, with varying degrees of clarity and emphasis.

The discourses contained in the volume *Thoughts on Crucial Situations in Human Life* introduce the transcendent categories of "Religion B." Here the hermeneutic of paradox is intertwined with exhortation. These discourses are not generally as polemical as the other works characterized by a dominant emphasis on the paradox. They do, however, communicate Christian truth in a more direct fashion than the various *Edifying Discourses*. A diversity of concerns is evident in the *Christian Discourses*. These discourses treat various biblical themes. The polemical tone of the later works in this volume is more evident. The *Works of Love* focus on a single theme—love and its fruit. Here, the biblical material is developed in systematic fashion. This is still, however, a hortatory work.

Specific Questions

What aspect(s) of Scripture is (are) taken to be authoritative?[4] Kierkegaard, especially in his later works, claimed that the Scriptures are fully authoritative. However, he appeared to favor different parts of the Bible for different purposes. He used the Old Testament more than the New Testament in the numerous allusions of the aesthetic pseudonyms; and he did not cite the Bible for its authority in this context. The Old Testament characters of Abraham and Job were used as important pointers beyond themselves to the absolute paradox. Kierkegaard's analysis of sin in *The Concept of Anxiety* takes both the Old Testament account of the fall and its New Testament interpretation seriously.

The Christian demands of the New Testament are also significant for Kierkegaard. Repeatedly he contrasted these to the easy faith of Christendom. Although he had a personal preference for the Synoptics and the Book of James, there is no indication that these were any more authoritative than any other portion of the Scripture. He cited the Gospels as providing a complete picture of the offense of the paradox and the demands of the teaching of Jesus. James was important to Kierkegaard because of its emphasis on the relationship of faith to works. Both 1 Corinthians 13 and relevant passages from 1 John provided the biblical data for S. K.'s discussion of love.

The paradox is the key category for Kierkegaard. It is the prism through which he viewed the whole of the Scripture. His interpretation of the Bible was, in keeping with the Reformed tradition, intentionally Christocentric. In his journals, Kierkegaard said that "the Holy Scriptures are the highway signs: Christ is the way."[5]

What is it about this aspect of Scripture that makes it authoritative? Paradox is the Divine confrontation with and transformation of the human. Kierkegaard was not concerned with the "what" of Christianity, but with "how" one becomes a Christian in Christendom. Thus, it is the existentially compelling force of the Gospel message, addressed to the individual who would allow himself or herself to hear, that comprises its authority.

Kierkegaard generally assumed the historical accuracy of the Bible. However, in his understanding, Christianity is not a doctrine, it is the communication of personal truth. The Bible is intrinsically authoritative as it confronts the human heart. The nature of the God-man as a communication of the Divine and the response of the human heart in either faith or offense are indications of the Bible's authority. Human freedom guarantees the opportunity of either response, but these are the only options available. There is no middle ground of accommodation. Thus, the message of the Bible and its existential fit are the only "proofs" of its authority. There are no external proofs that can otherwise substantiate its authority or message.

What sort of logical force is ascribed to the Scripture to which appeal is made? The logic is not the development of a formal system of truth, for truth is personal and its appropriation is through inwardness. There is, however, a logic to subjectivity. The various aesthetic works are veiled apologetic works in the sense that they seek to strip away the veneer of unauthentic approaches to life. With regard to the Bible, the pseudonyms illustrate the various "false starts" made with regard to appropriation of its message. Christianity, as existential truth, relies on the spiritual force of its message, rather than upon the force of formal logic. Thus, the Bible's only "logical" force is that it, via the God-man, addresses the very nature of being—the longing of the human heart. It is a subjective and indirect communication that may even be objectively ignored—albeit to one's spiritual deprivation.

How is the Scripture that is cited brought to bear on theological proposals so as to authorize them? Kierkegaard used frequent allusions to the Bible to illustrate a variety of points. Theologically, he took the biblical account of the fall, the incarnation, the passion and resurrection of Christ all at face value. These were events that happened. But the paradox is more than mere history. It is a divine communication.

Kierkegaard carefully cited biblical evidence for his understanding of Religion B, the religion of transcendence. The Bible is used by Kierkegaard to demonstrate the essential otherness of God, the offense of the paradox, becoming contemporaneous with Christ, and the true nature of faith. He also develops the demands of the Christian life, the Christian ethic of love and related issues along biblical lines. When defining key concepts, Kierkegaard was generally a careful exegete of the text.

When he used the Bible along the way to the religion of transcendence, however, such as the account of Abraham's sacrifice of Isaac in *Fear and Trembling*, he was not nearly so careful nor was he even concerned with the larger contextual problems surrounding the historical meaning of a passage. He warned that exegesis and the science of biblical interpretation had become diversions from hearing and appropriating the message of the Bible.

Kierkegaard and the Function of Scripture: A Critique

The systematic pulling together and review of Kierkegaard's various uses of the Scripture require critical evaluation.
First, we will examine various problems associated with Kierkegaard's use of the Scripture. Issues related to competing
truth claims, Christian tradition and biblical interpretation, as
well as the individual and the Church are the focus of this section. Second, the positive value of Kierkegaard's approach are
explored. His apologetic approach via the "existential fit" of
the Gospel, his alternative to rationalistic understandings of
the Christian faith, both right and left, the Christological focus
of his theology, and his concern with "appropriation" of the
message of the Bible are the major contributions discussed. Finally, we will conclude with observations regarding the importance and validity of Kierkegaard's use of Scripture in
today's religious climate.

Problems in Kierkegaard's Approach

Kierkegaard rejected any appeal to the proofs, either
from history or reason, to substantiate the claims of Christianity. Such proofs could, at best, only render Christianity plausible. Of course, they also open the door for scientific
skepticism. Indeed, appeals to the historical accuracy of the
biblical record, the subsequent history and influence of Christianity, and philosophical proofs for the existence of God are,
in Kierkegaard's analysis, a betrayal of faith.

God's coming as a suffering servant is absurd. It is fundamentally an offense to human reason. The realization of one's
own sin and finitude is the catharsis that opens the door to
transcendence. The leap of faith and a life of repentance toward God cannot be mediated in any other way. The radical
demands of the Christian life are, in Kierkegaard's view, com-
promised by any attempt to settle for less.

Kierkegaard lived in Christendom. Knowledge of the
facts of the story of Jesus and familiarity with his sayings, the
reliability of the biblical narrative, and a superficial understanding of Christian confessions comprised Kierkegaard's in-

tellectual and religious universe. Modern culture has moved in the very secular direction he predicted. Pluralism, both religious and cultural, is now common. How does one settle on the Christian faith as opposed to other contradictory world views?

The modern situation has changed the philosophical and theological environment in which the Christian message must compete with the truth claims of other world religions and secular humanism. The accuracy of the biblical record, for example, may be called into question by scientific doubt, which S. K. anticipated, or other religious views not dreamt of in Kierkegaard's provincial market town. The options would appear no longer to be simply an either/or of faith or offense. The Christian message may not even get a hearing. The religious options are both of "what kind of faith" and also "faith in what kind of God."

Robert Adams chided Kierkegaard for being a simple fideist and has suggested that religious interest and ethical commitment are served in having "well grounded beliefs."[6] Gill's reinterpretation of Kierkegaard's emphasis as "a protest against the objective/subjective dichotomy than as an exponent of one side of it. . . " and that "faith is a *way of life* which includes both reason and commitment" is not widely accepted.[7] One might argue that if S. K. had lived in the twentieth century western world, his approach to the Gospel would have involved a more direct apologetic. However, this is only speculation. It is difficult to see how Kierkegaard could have offered much direct help in dealing with the matter of competing religious world views and their conflicting truth claims.

Another major area of concern with regard to Kierkegaard's use of Scripture is his almost total loss of the doctrine of the church. The word of God is heard in isolation—by the "solitary individual." Kierkegaard's Christology is surely orthodox. His critique of Christendom rings true on many points. However, his ecclesiology is suspect, as even his ardent supporters would concede.[8] Indeed, his view of the church denies any viable formal expression of the body of Christ. He was critical of Lutherans, Roman Catholics, and the free church tradition. Immediately before his death he refused communion, unless given by a layman.

Most in the free church tradition would agree with S. K.'s contention that appropriation of the Gospel takes place on an individual basis. However, the witness of the Spirit in the midst of the community of faith is also a vital biblical concept. Despite Kierkegaard's repeated claims that he lacked authority to preach, it would appear from the attack upon Christendom, that no one, in his view, gave evidence of that authority.

Kierkegaard did have a positive Christian ethic and was not as individualistic as is frequently assumed. The *Works of Love* demonstrate this. There is, in S. K.'s conception of "neighbor love," an unconditional love for the other that has practical expression in its "works." Even here, however, the formula is "man-God-man." There is little sense of the interdependence, accountability, mutuality of spiritual gifts, and the like within the Church as body of Christ. The New Testament has a decidedly corporate nature in most of its practical exhortations regarding the Christian life. One commentator has listed at least thirty-five imperatives in the New Testament that involve relating "one to another."[9]

Kierkegaard's doctrine of "contemporaneity" sidesteps the centuries of Christian interpretation of the biblical text. It is both naive and arrogant simply to assume one can leap back into the New Testament without at least being aware of how one's own dogmatic tradition has influenced one's reading of the New Testament message. Also, Kierkegaard does not fully develop his distinction between the historical element in Christianity and the history of Christianity. Various interpretative studies of the text may indeed be a diversion from appropriation of its truth, as Kierkegaard claimed. But they need not be. A better understanding of the Bible is not complete until appropriation has taken place.

Finally, there is little doubt that the New Testament demands regarding the Christian life are considerably more strenuous than cultural Christianity would ever maintain. A decision regarding the consistent "biblical" nature of Kierkegaard's theology is beyond the scope of this study. However, a few concerns should be noted. Kierkegaard did not have a strong focus on the completed work of Christ on the cross. Also, there is little emphasis on the doctrine of the resurrection, though there is no reason to doubt his belief in its reality. Here again, a more positive biblical word could be heard.

Many of these observations are mitigated by the fact that Kierkegaard was engaged in what he saw as an emergency measure. He was critiquing Christendom. He did not deny the importance of corporate elements in the life of the Christian. He simply denied their reality in Christendom. However, a positive view of the church and a deeper understanding of the creative role of theological tradition are correctives from which the Kierkegaardian emphasis could profit.

The Positive Value of Kierkegaard's Approach

These criticisms and reservations notwithstanding, there are a number of positive contributions to be noted in Kierkegaard's use of Scripture. First, and foremost, there can be little doubt as to the *centrality of the Scripture in Kierkegaard's thought*. He sought, for better or worse, to hear and appropriate the biblical word. It should be evident that Kierkegaard did not simply secularize the vocabulary of the Gospel via his psychological and existential interests. As a Christian believer, he sought to be a faithful expositor of the biblical message.

Second, Kierkegaard was surely correct regarding the *limits of apologetic proofs*. These can only lead to an approximation, and reduce the Christian message to the status of probability. This remained a strong and persistent theme throughout his works. A convinced mind is not a convicted heart. The absurdity and offense of the paradox is in the affirmation that "God was in Christ." Kierkegaard had no doubts about the "facts" of the Gospel. He had serious reservations about their significance as *only* facts.

It is frequently argued that there is an ample biblical basis and precedent for some sort of Christian apologetic. The Apostle Peter, for example, encouraged the believer to have an answer for those who query regarding his or her hope (1 Peter 3:15).[10] In the Book of Acts, Paul answers the questions of the Athenian philosophers (Acts 17:22f), and defends himself before the mob in Jerusalem (Acts 23:1ff), before Felix (Acts 24:1ff), and before Agrippa (Acts 25:1ff). The Gospels and the Book of Hebrews are also cited by J. K. S. Reid as giving evidence of apologetic activity. He concluded:

There is in fact no difficulty in identifying apologetic elements in the New Testament. They appear both early and prominently. Apologetic activity is built into the foundations of the apostolic witness.[11]

Kierkegaard did give reasons for his hope. The crucial issue for S. K. was both the type of apologetic offered and what one hoped to accomplish with it. He warned that the real propensity of traditional apologetics lay not in making a case for Christianity, but in opening the door to skepticism. Yet, his analysis of the Gospel's remedy for the human condition is an apologetic of sorts.

Nor can S. K. be fairly accused of being an "irrationalist" or believing in absurdity for absurdity's sake. He was simply describing what he saw in both the human condition and the Divine response to this condition in the Gospel. He contended that an individual is not a fully constituted self apart from God. This realization is, for Kierkegaard, the only preparation available for appropriation of the Gospel. Kierkegaard was consistent in his appeals to Scripture on this point and, in this writer's view, is absolved of culpability with regard to a lack of apologetic approach.

Third, the various hermeneutical models in S. K.'s work serve as a *reminder that there is indeed a variety of possible readings of the Bible*. One's life view includes basic presuppositions that will influence the reading and appropriation of the Scripture. In many respects, the various approaches to the Bible exhibited by the various Kierkegaardian pseudonyms are "ways" of appropriating Scripture. However, the majority of these are ultimately unsatisfactory. The Christian way of appropriation is, for Kierkegaard, realized through a passionate concern or inwardness that allows the message of the Gospel to confront the human heart.

Finally, Kierkegaard's approach to Scripture *offers a possible alternative to the polarities of the current "modernist-fundamentalist" controversy*. Kierkegaard rightly repudiated the kind of rationalism that sought to "go beyond" simple faith. The critical study of the Bible asked the wrong kinds of questions and in the wrong way, for Kierkegaard. These issues were, he warned, a diversion from hearing the biblical word.

He also condemned the rigid dogmatism of orthodoxy. He warned that Christian truth could not be reduced to propositional affirmations about God. Christianity was, for Kierkegaard, not a doctrine but a person—the God-man, the Lord Jesus Christ. In many ways, both the extreme right and left have succumbed to the seduction of the modern scientific mindset—as Kierkegaard warned.

Conclusion

Kierkegaard's ties to existential philosophy and neo-orthodox theology have been the basis for a general closed-mindedness to his thought by many in the American conservative evangelical community.[12] Recently, however, his work has become the focus of a new appreciation among evangelicals. Calling S. K. "an intellectual's intellectual," C. Stephen Evans observed:

> Kierkegaard, more than anyone I know, can help remind evangelicals that Christianity is a manner of being, a way of existing, not merely an affirmation of doctrine. But he can remind us of this in a way that will not precipitate a slide back into the contempt for reason and the life of the mind that has sometimes infected evangelicalism and fundamentalism.[13]

This writer has found a new depth of faith, a more profound appreciation of the Bible, a new fear and trembling at the demands of the Gospel, and a desire for consistent commitment to the demands of discipleship at the feet of Kierkegaard. As E. J. Carnell said of the Danish gadfly, "it is easy to follow the very one who wanted no followers."[14]

Appendix:
The Bible in Selected Kierkegaard Works

The following is a compendium of the various Scripture references noted in that portion of S. K.'s works examined for this study. Although based upon the work by Paul S. Minear and Paul S. Morimoto, *Kierkegaard and the Bible: An Index* (Princeton: Princeton Pamphlets, 1953), the following is unique in at least two ways. First, the following index lists references by consecutive page numbers in the given work in which they appear. Minear and Morimoto cataloged their references by consecutive page numbers in the given work in which they appear according to the books in the Bible. Second, more recent translations have generally been utilized. Therefore, in most cases, the actual page numbers are different from those cited in the *Index*.

There are four basic types of references noted. *Remote allusions* generally utilize a biblical phrase, character, or theme but do not suggest a theological interpretation of the passage. *Allusions* are more intentional uses of Scripture, but do not necessarily involve a larger biblical context. *References* and *quotes* generally provide a glimpse of biblical passages used in a larger interpretative context. *Texts* for discourses, articles, and other material generally provide the theme for a specific and extended exposition of a biblical idea. A brief quote or other explanation follows the classification of each reference. Passages not clearly falling into any of these categories are explained individually. Passages that are parallel or have a similar emphasis, listed as separate references in the *Index*, have been omitted. An asterisk indicates an entry not found in the *Index*.

Either/Or, Vol. I

Page	Passage	Type of Reference/Quote or Summary
22	Matt. 6:16	Misquote, remote allusion: "their reward taken away."
24	Job 15:11	Remote allusion: "like a whipped top."
26	Gen. 25:33	Remote allusion: "birthright for porridge."
39	Ex. 12:23-25	Remote allusion: "angel of death."
81	1 Sam. 16:16	Remote allusion: "David playing for Saul."
139	2 Sam. 24: 1-9	Remote allusion: "David's census."
140	Gal. 4:4	Allusion: "Christ came in the fulness of time."
140	John 1:29	Allusion: "Christ bore the sins of the world."
146	Heb. 10: 31	Allusion: "fall into the hands of living God."
148	Ex. 20: 5	Allusion: God "visits the sins of the fathers upon the children."

148	John 8:29	Allusion: Christ's "absolute obedience."
148	Job 20	Allusion: "Jehovah's curses."
149	Gen. 11:4	Remote allusion: "not our purpose to labor upon a Tower of Babel."
166	1 Kings 19:11	Allusion: "the divine voice is not heard in the rushing wind."
174	1 Sam. 28:7	Allusion: "Saul came in disguise before the battle to the Witch of Endor."
182	1 Pet. 3:4	Allusion: "her inner self is not the incorruptible essence of a quiet spirit."
183	Matt. 6:20	Remote allusion: "O you of little faith!"
192	Matt. 7:24	Remote allusion: "my thought stands like a house of God founded upon a rock."
225	Job	Creative use of biblical character.
226	Luke 15:11-24	Creative use of biblical character (Prodigal's father).
232	1 Cor. 1:23	Remote allusion: First love is a "stumbling block to the Jews."
282	Gen. 1:26	Creative use of biblical characters (Adam and Eve) and the theme of "boredom."
282	Gen. 2:18-24	Allusion: "humanity fell."
282	Gen. 11: 4-9	Allusion: "Tower of Babel" a reaction to boredom.
308	2 Sam. 12:1-7	Creative use of Nathan's charge to David: "There was a rich man."
330	Gen. 42:32	Creative use of Pharaoh's dream.
384	Gen. 31:34	Mistaken allusion to "Rebecca"[should be Rachel] stealing Laban's goods.
397	Mark 3:24	Allusion: "How can a kingdom stand which is at strife with itself?"
398	Gen. 30:31-36	Allusion: "Jacob had bargained with Laban."
412	Prov. 24:26*	Quote: "A good answer is like a sweet kiss, says Solomon."
432	Judg. 16:4-22	Remote allusion: "This is a secret, like Samson's hair, which no Delilah shall wrest from me."

Either/Or, Vol. II

Page	Passage	Type of Reference/Quote or Summary
5	2 Sam. 12:7	Quote: "Thou, O King, art the man."
13	Job 2:9	Remote allusion: "as Job's wife counselled him to curse God."
16	Phil. 4:7	Reference: "love [peace] surpasses understanding."
16	Phil. 2:6	Reference: "Christ did not count it robbery to be equal with God."
41	Phil. 2:6-8	Allusion: "God only once became flesh.."
41	Heb. 6:6	Quote: "sects in Christendom . . . impossibility of renewing again to repentance."
45	Gen. 24:1-67	Extended allusion: Isaac's marriage to Rebecca.
53	Gen. 3:6	Allusion: "it was Eve who seduced Adam."
69	1 Cor. 13:5-7	Quote: "love suffereth long."[power of love in marriage].
71	Gen. 1:28	Quote: "increase and multiply and replenish the earth". . . God blessed them."
71	Gen. 2:18	Quote: "Be fruitful and multiply."
71	1 Cor. 14:34	Quote: woman to "learn in quietness."
71	1 Tim. 2:11-15	Quote: "if they continue in faith and love."
82	Sirach 36:24	Quote: "a wife entereth upon a possession."
82	Gen. 21:9	Allusion: "wife not a bondswoman in Abraham's house."
83	Neh. 4:23	Remote allusion: "like Nehemiah, I am armed even in my sleep."
85	1 Pet. 2:11	Reference: "a stranger and pilgrim in the world."
89	Rom. 14:12	Allusion: "a blessed branch which bears such fruit."
90	2 Pet. 3:5*	Remote allusion: "married man ought always be ready to render an account."
93	Gen. 3:16	Reference: "woman shall bear children with pain and be subject unto her husband."
94	Gen. 2:24	Quote: woman as "helpmeet."

94	Gen. 2:18	Quote: "A man shall leave his father and mother and shall cleave unto his wife."
94	Gen. 3:17-19	Reference: "by the sweat of his brow."
100	1 Tim. 4:4	Misquote of "every good gift."
138	Luke 9:23	Allusion: "a cross bearer."
138	1 Cor. 15:31	Allusion: "not the business of dying daily."
139	Lev. 24:9	Allusion: "the offering I bring is not showbread."
153	Eccl.	General allusion: "the book of the Preacher."
164	Mark 5:9	Allusion: "like those unhappy demoniacs."
165	Josh. 6	Remote allusion: "march seven times around existence and blow the trumpet."
178	Rev. 14:13	Remote allusion: "works follow him" [them].
224	Matt. 16:26	Quote: "What would it profit a man if he were to gain the whole world."
236	Ex. 3:2	Remote allusion: "eternal Power the fire which pervades it without consuming it."
248	Deut. 6:5	Allusion: "Who shall deny that a man shall love God with all his heart."
248	1 Sam. 15:22	Quote: "To obey is better than sacrifice."
249	Romans 8:16	Reference: "let His Spirits witness along with his own spirit."
249	Matt. 10:37	Reference: "love God more dearly than father and mother."
254	John 17:3	Allusion: "to know God and become in love with Him."
260	Deut. 6:5	Quote: "Thou shalt love God with all thy heart."
262	Matt. 23:24	Remote allusion: "The life of such men is employed in straining at gnats."
297	Matt. 25:14f	Reference: "When the talent is not construed as a call."
317	1 Cor. 11:16	Reference: woman's "plentiful hair a token of her imperfection."
318	Gen. 2:24	Quote: "A man shall leave his father and mother and shall cleave to his wife."
320	Matt. 19:26	Allusion: "woman believes that with God all things are possible."
327	Heb. 9:27	Reference: "The Scripture teaches that every man must die."
343	Luke 19:41f	Extended quote: Jesus weeping over Jerusalem.
344	Gen. 19:29	Allusion: "righteous suffer with the unrighteous?"
344	Ex. 20:5	Quote: "the sins of the fathers upon the children unto the third and fourth generation."
345	Luke 13:2	Quote of Christ regarding the Tower of Siloam.
345	Matt. 5:45*	Allusion: "rain may fall upon the just and upon the unjust."
346	Gen. 32:26	Allusion: "but with God you will strive."
346	Job 40:2	Quote: "Thou shalt not contend with God."
346	Matt. 10:29	Allusion: "The sparrow falls to the ground."

Fear and Trembling

Page	Passage	Type of Reference/Quote or Summary
7	2 Tim. 4:7	Allusion: "oldster approached his end, had fought the good fight and kept the faith."
8	Luke 14:28-30*	Remote allusion: "it will hardly become a tower."
9	Gen. 21: 1-3	Background on Abraham: not alluded to directly.
9	Gen. 22	Actual story of Abraham offering Isaac.
9	2 Tim. 4:7	Allusion: "kept the faith."
9	Heb. 11:17-19	Allusion: Abraham "got a son a second time."
10f	Gen. 22:1-3	Quote: "God tempted Abraham."
10	Gen. 22:1-13	Allusion: Abraham offering Isaac.
10	Judith 10:11	Allusion: "Sarah watched them from the window as they went down the valley."
12	Gen. 12:1-3	Allusion: "her hope for all generations to come.

12	Gen. 17:2-21	Allusion: "her hope for all generations to come.
13	Gen. 16:6	Allusion: "he thought of Hagar and the son."
13	Gen. 21:9-21	Allusion: "he thought of Hagar and the son."
14	Gen. 15:2*	Allusion: "He took leave of Sarah, and Eliezer."
17	Heb. 11:8-9	Allusion: "by faith Abraham."
18	Gen. 17:17	Reference: "Sarah the object of mockery."
18	Gen. 18:18	Reference: "all the generations of the earth would be blessed."
18	Rom. 4:18-21	Allusion: "Abraham believed God and held to the promise."
18	Gal. 4:4	Allusion: "Fulness of time."
19	Ex. 17:6	Allusion: "Moses struck rock with his staff."
19	Gen. 22:1-13	Quote: "And God tempted Abraham."
19	Gen. 18:12	Reference: "Abraham did not laugh at it as Sarah did when the promise was announced."
19	Gen. 17:17	Reference: "Abraham did not laugh at it as Sarah did when the promise was announced."
20	Gen. 22:1	Allusion: Abraham "faithfully fulfilled the father's duty to love the son."
21	Gen. 18:22-23	Allusion: Abraham "did not pray for himself."
21	Gen. 22:3	Quote: "Abraham answered: Here am I."
21	Luke 23:30	Quote: "you did not say, . . . 'Hide me.'"
22	Gen. 8:4	Allusion: "not be mentioned in the way Ararat."
27	2 Thess. 3:10*	Quote: "Only one who works gets bread."
27	Matt. 5:45	Allusion: "Here it does not rain on the just and the unjust."
27	Matt. 3:9	Allusion: "not help to have Abraham as father."
27	Isa. 26:18	Allusion: "virgins of Israel, he gives birth to wind."
28	Matt. 19:16f	Allusion: "If the rich young man."
29	Gen. 3:24	Allusion: "A pastor is like a 'cherub with a flaming sword.'"
34	1 John 4:8	Reference: "God is love."
36	Matt. 18:21	Allusion: "I bow seven times to his name and seventy times to his deed."
37	John 2:1-10	Allusion: "miracle of faith, turning water into wine—it goes further and turns wine into water."
37	1 Cor. 10:12	Allusion: "remain standing in faith."
40	Gen. 25:29f	Allusion: "his appetite is keener than Esau's."
40	Col. 4:5	Allusion: "buys the opportune time."
46	Matt. 19:26	Allusion: "for God all things are possible."
47	Luke 23:7	Allusion: "she can just as well run to Herod as to Pilate."
49	Matt. 17:20	Allusion: "who has faith like a mustard seed."
49	Matt. 21:21	Allusion: "Can move mountains."
49	Matt. 19:16f	Allusion: "rich young man should have given away everything."
49	Jas. 1:17	Allusion: "look to heaven, from whence come all good gifts."
58	Judg. 11:30f	Allusion: "Jephthah binds God and himself."
61	Ex. 19:12	Allusion: "One approaches him . . . as Israel approached Mount Sinai."
61	Matt. 12:24	Allusion: A poet is not an apostle, he drives out devils only by the power of the devil."
63	Matt. 26: 15	Allusion: "not even Judas."
65	Matt. 1:18-25	Reference: "Mary bore the child wondrously."
65	Gen. 18:11*	Allusion: Mary "after the manner of women."
65	Luke 2	Extended reference to Christmas story.
65	Luke 1:38	Quote: "Behold, I am the handmaid of the Lord."
66	Luke 23:28	Allusion: "Do not weep for me, weep for yourself."
68	Matt. 22:37	Reference: "it is a duty to love one's neighbor."
68	Mark 12:30	Reference: "duty to love God."
72	Luke 14:26	Quote: "If anyone comes to me and does not hate his own father."
72	John 6:60*	Allusion: "This is a hard saying."
72f	Luke 14:28f	Discussion of the cost of discipleship.
74	Gen. 4:8	Allusion: "Cain and Abel are not identical."

77	Gen. 21:5	Reference: "It takes him seventy years to have a son of old age."
77	Gen. 16:1-6	Reference: "Sarah . . . got him to take Hagar."
78	Matt. 6:34*	Allusion: "let each day have its cares."
81	Luke 14	Reference: "one must interpret the passage."
87	Matt. 3:17	Allusion: "tragic hero is ethics' beloved son in whom it is well pleased."
87	Judg. 11:30f	Allusion: "as was Jephtha's daughter."
103	Tobit 8:4	Quote of Tobias' prayer.
104	Acts 20:35	Allusion: "better to give than to receive."
111	Matt. 6:16-18	Reference and quote: "irony . . . used to conceal the better part." "When you fast."
114	1 Cor. 14*	Allusion: "he speaks in tongues."
115	Gen. 22:8	Reference: "So Abraham did not speak."
120	Matt. 6:6*	Allusion: "God . . . sees in secret."

Philosophical Fragments

Page	Passage	Type of Reference/Quote or Summary
6	2 Sam. 6:16*	Allusion: "dancing in service of Thought."
6	1 Cor. 9:13	Allusion: "like the priest at the altar."
21	John 8:34	Allusion: "the slave of sin."
22	Luke 9:62	Allusion: "stand in a different relation."
22	Gal. 4:4	Reference: "let us call it the Fullness of Time."
23	2 Cor. 5:17	Reference: "or as we may call him: a new creature."
23	Phil. 3:13	Allusion: "quicken steps to that which lies before?"
23	John 3:3	Reference: "Let us call this transition the New Birth."
24	John 3:3	Reference: "not possible to be born anew en masse."
24	Rom. 13:8	Allusion: The disciple "in a deeper sense owes no man anything."
31	2 Cor. 11:1	Remote allusion: "waste our time while we might be coming to a decision."
35	Matt. 9:23	Allusion: "must be driven out . . . before gladness can enter in."
35	Pet. 3:8	Reference: "for a thousand years are as one day in his sight."
36	Matt. 6:28	Allusion: "arraying the lily in a garb more glorious than that of Solomon."
37	Ex. 33:20	Reference: "no man could see the God and live."
37	Luke 15:7*	Allusion: "they do not even dream that there is sorrow in heaven as well as joy."
38	John 3:8	Reference: "the man born anew."
38	John 8:32	Allusion: "truth makes him free."
39	Phil. 2:6-8	Allusion: "union . . . must be attempted by a descent."
39	Matt. 8:20	Allusion: "the God . . . has not a resting-place for his head."
40	Matt. 4:6	Allusion: "if angels guided them, not to prevent his foot from stumbling."
40	Mark 8:31	Allusion: "they are offended in him."
40	Matt. 9: 36*	Allusion: "his eye rests upon mankind with deep concern."
40	Isa. 42:3	Allusion: "for the shoots of an individual life may be crushed as easily as a blade of grass."
40	Heb. 1:3	Allusion: "sustain the heavens and the earth . . . by his omnipotent word."
40	Matt. 4:2*	Allusion: "hunger in the desert."
40	John 19:28	Allusion: "thirst in the time of his agony."
40	Mark 15:34	Allusion: "forsaken in death."
40	John 19:5	Reference: "behold the man!"
41	John 21:15	Reference: "Do you now really love me?"
41	Mark 14:34	Allusion: "For he knows where the danger threatens, and yet he also knows."

41	Luke 2:35	Remote allusion: "the learner might not understand it."
41	Luke 7:37*	Allusion: "tears than those of a repentant woman."
41	Luke 10:42	Allusion: "a woman whose heart's sole choice was the one thing needful."
41	John 2:4*	Allusion: "Man, what have I to do with thee?"
41	Mark 8:33	Allusion: "Get thee hence for thou art Satan."
41	Matt. 23:37*	Allusion: "see him weep also over me."
42	Luke 2:35*	Allusion: "heart is pierced by the sword."
42	Matt. 26:39*	Allusion: " O bitter cup!"
42	Luke 23:41	Allusion: "to suffer as one who is guilty."
43	Matt. 9:17	Allusion: "when new wine is poured in old leathern bottles, they burst."
43	Rom. 8:23	Allusion: "how convulsed with birth pangs!"
43	Luke 22:30	Allusion: "then to sit at table with Him."
44	Phil. 2:6-8	Allusion: "not to imagine that the God would make himself into the likeness of man."
48	Matt. 22:39	Allusion: "in order to command him to love his neighbor as himself."
54	Ps. 14:1	Reference: "fool says in his heart that there is no God."
54	Luke 5:5	Allusion: "At the word of God casts his net."
56	Matt. 6:26*	Reference: "to live like birds of the air."
59	Eccl. 9:11	Remote allusion: "success is to the accurate rather than to the swift."
68	Isa. 40:3	Allusion: "send someone before him."
69	Phil. 2:6-8	Extended allusion: "Aye in the humble form of a servant."
69	Matt. 3:3	Allusion: "doubtless give some sort of sign."
69	Luke 7:25*	Allusion: "not to be distinguished from the multitude of men neither by soft raiment."
69	Matt. 26:53*	Allusionn: "not yet by the innumerable legions of angels."
69	1 Cor. 7:31	Allusion: "he goes his way indifferent."
69	Matt. 6:24	Allusion: "like the birds of the air."
70	Matt. 8:19-22	Allusion: "who neither has nor seeks a shelter or a resting-place."
70	John 21:15	Allusion: "seeks one thing only, the love of the discipline."
71	Matt. 12:50	Allusion: "the learner is his brother and sister."
71	John 3:1,2	Allusion: "Some one of the authorized teachers of that city sought him out secretly."
71	Mark 1:15	Allusion: "The news of the day the beginning of eternity!"
71	Luke 2	Extended reference to "the God's appearance."
71	Luke 2:12	Allusion: "born in an inn, wrapped in swaddling clothes."
72	Luke 2:19	Allusion: "that the news of the day."
74	Matt. 27:24*	Allusion: "can wash his hands of the accusation, but that is all."
74	Matt. 4:4	Allusion: "If every word of instruction . . . more important to him than his daily bread."
74	Luke 23:39-43	Allusion: "when the teacher only had a day or two to live."
80	Mark 9:2-11	Remote allusion: "God gives the condition."
80	1 John 1:1	Allusion: "It is what he has seen and his hands have handled."
80	Luke 24:13	Allusion: "walked some distance with him on the way without realizing that it was he."
81	Matt. 13:17	Reference: "contemporary generation blessed, because it saw and heard."
81	Luke 10:23	Remote allusion: "this generation has doubtless also counted itself blessed."
82	1 John 1:1	Reference: "who saw and heard and grasped with their hands."
84	Luke 13:25	Reference: "I do not know you?"
84	1 Cor. 13:12	Reference: "knows him even as he is known."
101	Heb. 11:1	Allusion: "faith believes what it does not see."
116	Phil. 2:6	Allusion: "only in the form of a servant."
128	1 Cor. 1:23	Reference: "folly to the understanding."
130	Phil. 2:6	Allusion: "God has been in human form."

Concept of Anxiety

66	Gen. 3:16	Allusion: "woman's life culminates in procreation indicates that she is more sensuous."
67	Matt. 23:4	Allusion: "place upon men the heavy burden."
72	Ex. 20:5	Reference: "What Scripture teaches, that God avenges the iniquity of the fathers."
76	Gen. 3:7	Allusion: "eating of the fruit of the tree of knowledge."
79	Matt. 22:30	Reference: "A perfect spirit cannot be conceived as sexually qualified."
80	Heb. 4:15*	Reference: "it is said that Christ was tried in all human ordeals."
88	1 Cor. 15:52	Quote: "In the New Testament . . . Paul says that the world will pass away in a moment."
89	Mark 1:15	Remote allusion: "The moment is that ambiguity in which time and eternity touch."
90	2 Cor. 5:17	Allusion: "that which made all things new."
90	Gal. 4:4	Allusion: "fulness of time is the moment."
94	Eph. 4:19	Quote (Gk text): "those who are past feeling."
95	1 Cor. 2:4*	Reference: "There is only one proof of spirit and that is the spirit's proof within oneself."
95	Matt. 5:13	Reference: "If the salt becomes dumb."
97	1 Cor. 8:4	Reference: "what Paul said about the idol may be said of fate."
104	Heb. 7:27	Reference: "its sacrifice is not repeated."
104	Heb. 9:25f	Allusion: "the perfection of the sacrifice."
107	Matt. 25:21*	Allusion: "Well done, my son! Just keep on, for he who loses all, gains all."
112	2 Thess, 1:9	Quote (Gk): "it is said of those who do not know God and do not obey the gospel."
115	Matt. 7:18*	Allusion: "consequences of sin . . . perdition."
119	Matt. 8:28-34	Extended discussion of the demonic.
120	Mark 12:41-44	Remote allusion: "it will not be a question of a few conforting words, a mite."
124	Matt. 8:29	Variant on demons addressing Jesus (cf. Mk. 5:7)
124	Mark 5:7	Quote (Gk): demons to Jesus, "What have I to do with thee?"
124	Mark 5:17*	Reference: "implores Christ to go another way."
125	Matt. 12:24	Allusion: "constrain inclosing reserve to speak is either a higher demon . . . or the good."
128	John 8:44	Reference: "Therefore the devil is called the father of lies."
132	1 Thess. 5:1f	Allusion: "comes more suddenly than a thief in the night."
137	Mark 5:7	Quote (Gk): demons to Jesus, "What have I to do with thee?"
137	Matt. 8:29	Reference: "Leave me alone in my wretchedness."
138	Matt. 26:49	Allusion: "a Judas' kiss for the consequence."
138	John 8:32	Allusion: "the truth makes men free."
138	Jas. 3:15	Quote (Gk): "demonic wisdom."
138	Jas. 2:19	Quote (Gk): "even the demons believe."
140	Mark 5:7	Quote (Gk): demons to Jesus, "What have I to do with thee?"
145	Gen. 3:7	Allusion: "a fig leaf to cover what otherwise might have required a hypocritical cloak."
146	Eccl. 1:2	Quote: "all is vanity."
146	John 4:14	Reference: "inwardness is precisely the fountain springs up unto eternal life."
153	Matt. 12:36	Allusion: "Christianity teaches that a person must render an account."
155	Matt. 26:37f	Reference: Christ "was anxious unto death."
155	John 13:27	Reference: "What you are going to do, do quickly."
155	Matt. 27:46	Quote: "My God, my God why hast thou forsaken me?"
160	Luke 10:30	Allusion: "the man who traveled from Jericho."

Stages on Life's Way

Page	Passage	Type of Reference/Quote or Summary
27	Judg. 14:14	Allusion: quote of Sampson's riddle, "Out of the eater comes forth meat."
35	Ex. 19:23	Allusion: "as every beast was accursed which came near Sinai!"
39	Eccl. 1:8	Allusion: "the good Lord satisfies the stomach before the eye is satisfied."
43	2 Kings 20:1	Remote allusion: "set my house in order."
46	Gen. 43:34	Allusion: quote "they drank and they drank largely."
51	Gen. 2:22-23	Allusion: "Adam chose Eve, because there was no other."
102	Gen. 33:4	Reference: "In the book of Genesis where it is related that Esau kissed Jacob."
114	John 5:24	Quote: "He cometh not into judgement."
117	Matt. 25:30	Allusion: "perhaps in gnashing of teeth."
117	Matt. 25:36f*	Allusion: "cares for the sick, feeds the hungry, clothes the naked."
117	Luke 17:10	Allusion: "an unprofitable servant."
121	Eph. 1:10	Allusion: "fulness of time."
125	Ex. 33:20	Allusion: "he who beholds God must die."
125	Ex. 34:33f	Allusion: "veil hung before his eyes."
125	Gen. 1:1	Allusion: "God creates out of nothing."
132	Eccl. 1:13-14	Allusion: marriage saves from "vexation of spirit."
154	Prov. 18:22	Quote: "whoso findeth a wife findeth a good thing."
197	Luke 10:41	Quote: "Martha, one thing needful."
205	Gen. 25:20-24	Creative monologue: "Is this what it means to be a mother?"
208	Isa. 26:18	Allusion: "to sit and be with child and bring forth wind."
217	Gen. 1:27	Reference: "God created man in his own image."
218	Gen. 3:1	Allusion: "the devil never reveals himself."
218	John 16:4f	Quote: "These things have I not said unto you from the beginning."
220	Mark 14:3-9	Text for "Leper's Soliloquy."
220	Gen. 2:18	Allusion: "put the question to Him . . . said that it is not good for a man to be without society."
221	Luke 16:23	Allusion: "Father Abraham, . . . I shall awaken in thy bosom."
221	Mark 5:1-20	Allusion: "compassion has fled like me out among the graves."
221	Mark 12:41-42*	Remote allusion: "A little gift, a mite."
222	Luke 17:12	Allusion: "sermon is about the ten lepers."
224	Matt. 10:29	Quote: "not a sparrow falls to the ground."
224	Jer. 25:11-12*	Remote allusion: "seventy years is."
224	Ps. 90:4*	Allusion: "a thousand years are to Him."
225	Luke 18:12	Allusion: "I fast twice in the week."
236	Song of Sol.	Background for "Solomon's Dream."
237	Eccl.	Background for "Solomon's Dream."
237	Matt. 12:42	Allusion: "Queen of the South came to visit."
292	Job 38:1	Reference: "weak point in the structure of the Book of Job that God appears in the clouds."
307	Ps. 35:20	Allusion: "quiet of land."
322	Gen. 3:18	Allusion: "Did Adam dare to remind Eve . . . ?"
323	John 6:68	Quote: "To whom should I go but unto Thee."
325	Mark 16:9	Allusion: "Take Mary Magdalene."
330	Dan. 4:30-34	Creative monologue: "Nebuchadnezzar's Dream."
331	Acts 17:24	Allusion: "neither doth He dwell in His Temple."
410	Deut. 32:35	Reference: "to whom vengeance belongeth."
457	Heb. 12:14	Text for discourse: "What it means to seek God."

Concluding Unscientific Postscript

Page	Passage	Type of Reference/Quote or Summary
17	Matt. 22:21	Allusion: "to give unto Caesar his due."
19	Luke 14:26	Allusion: "individual hates father and."
19	Matt. 12:31*	Allusion: "unpardonable offense against the majesty of Christianity."
20	Matt. 25:1-13	Extended reference: "The foolish virgins had lost the infinite passion of expectation."
28	Matt. 5:18	Reference: "passionate interest . . . an iota is of importance."
32	Matt. 17:20	Reference: "faith which removes mountains."
33	Luke 18:8	Quote: "when Son of Man cometh shall he find faith on the earth?"
43	John 8:33-40	Allusion: "Jews appealed to circumcision."
46	Gen. 1:27	Allusion: "the God who created man in his own image!"
46	Dan. 5:25-28	Allusion: "weighed and found wanting."
46	Matt. 25:30	Allusion: "thrown into the outer darkness."
54	Matt. 21: 12f	Allusion: "moneychangers in the forecourt of the temple could be banished."
71	Matt. 20:1-6	Reference: "he found a few laborers."
83	Matt. 6:6f	Allusion: "to satisfy the inwardness of his prayer."
85	Ps. 90:4	Allusion: "ten thousand years are but trifle."
89	Gal. 3:28	Allusion: "more reprehensible than the one between Jews and Greeks."
95	1 Cor. 2:9	Allusion: "philosophical theorem which has entered the heart of man."
98	Luke 23:6-12	Allusion: "running between and forth between Herod and Pilate."
116	Luke 15:7	Allusion: "Greater joy in heaven over this one individual."
121	1 Cor. 3:6f	Remote allusion: "will not to know that his life had any other significance."
122	Luke 17:10	Allusion: "unprofitable servant."
122	Acts 1:16	Reference: "one of those for whom Judas became the guide."
124	2 Cor. 3:17	Allusion: "the spirit of Lord is the Lord."
124	Matt. 10:30	Reference: "as I have numbered the hairs of your head."
124	Rom. 11:35	Allusion: "Do you possess anything whereof you might give me?"
127	Gen. 3:7	Allusion: "sensuous mind it is his eyes delight . . . his fig leaf."
145	Luke 17:32	Allusion: "like Lot's wife."
145	Judg. 9:7-15	Allusion: "parable of the trees that want to make the cedar their king."
158	1 Thess. 5:18	Reference: "what does it mean that I am to thank God for the good he bestows upon me?"
159	1 Thess. 1:2	Allusion: "to give thanks always."
163	2 Cor. 12:1	Allusion: "appeal to visions and revelation."
164	Gal. 1:12	Reference: "Paul was converted by a miracle."
174	John 18:38	Allusion: "modernize the question of Pontius Pilate . . . what is madness?"
176	Rom. 8:9	Allusion: "expectation of the creature."
191	1 Cor. 1:23	Allusion: "Paradox . . . an offense to the Jews, and folly to the Greeks."
192	Luke 15:11-24	Allusion: "speculative philosopher is, not indeed the prodigal son."
192	Mark 12:1-12	Allusion: "speculative philospher were the restless tenant."
198	Gal. 4:4	Allusion: "fullness of time."
198	1 Pet. 1:8	Allusion: "the inexpressible joy."
201	Matt. 18:23-35	Allusion: "the paradox of the forgiveness of sins."
204	Matt. 9:1-8	Remote allusion: "But I cannot understand the divine mercy which is able to forgive sins."

354	Matt. 24:45-51	Allusion: "unfaithful servant may sometimes succeed in having his balances in order."
355	Matt. 25:1-13	Allusion: "sleepy as foolish virgin."
356	Mark 13:13	Allusion: "whole of time and existence should be a period of striving."
359	Acts 10:34	Allusion: "before God and the absolute *telos* we human beings are all equal."
361	Matt. 7:13-14	Reference: "The New Testament also speaks of two ways."
363	Rom. 2:4	Reference: "The Scriptures characterize God's patience in dealing with sinners."
364	Deut. 5:11	Allusion: "it is abhorrent to him as taking the name of God in vain."
366	Luke 16:26	Allusion: "for the absolute *telos* there is a yawning chasm fixed."
367	1 Cor. 7:30-31	Allusion: "the glory of his crown fades."
368	Matt. 10:29	Allusion: "man forfeits his eternal happiness or a sparrow falls to the ground."
380	Matt. 13:45-46	Allusion: "When I give all that I have for a pearl, it is not a venture."
385	Matt. 11:28-30	Allusion: "its yoke is easy and its burden light—for him who has thrown all burdens away."
392	Luke 6:24-26	Allusion: "favorites of fortune who do not suffer at all."
392	Matt. 11:28	Quote: "Come hither all ye who labor."
399	Isa. 57:15	Reference: "When the Scriptures say that God dwells in a contrite heart.."
399	1 Thess. 5:18	Allusion: "thanks God for all these blessings, the question is how."
404	Rom. 5:1-5	Allusion: "the reality of religious suffering as expressed."
404	Matt. 5:10-12	Allusion: "suffering has significance for an eternal happiness."
404	Jas. 1:3-4	Allusion: "but the rejoicing."
405	Acts 5:41	Reference: "But we read in the New Testament that the Apostles when they were scourged."
406	2 Cor. 12:7	Reference: "passage in the Epistle to the Corinthian about the thorn in flesh."
408	1 Cor. 7:29	Remote allusion: "Marriage is but a jest."
408	Gal. 3:28	Allusion: "whether one is Jew or Greek, free or slave."
416	1 Tim. 3:9	Reference: "lest the 'mystery of faith' . . . it should be kept."
417	John 5:19	Allusion: "for a human being can of himself do nothing."
420	John 5:19	Allusion: "that a man can do nothing of himself."
421	Eccl. 1:2	Allusion: "because everything is empty and vain?"
424	Matt. 6:1-18	Allusion: "true religiosity is the religiosity of the secret inwardness."
431	John 5:19	Allusion: "a man can do nothing of himself."
431	Matt. 21:13	Allusion: "then he transforms the temple, if not into a den of robbers."
433	Deut. 5:26	Reference: "what wonder then that the Jews assumed that to see God was to die."
434	Mark 13:13	Allusion: "he that never endured to the end the suffering."
435	1 Thess. 5:17	Allusion: "the inwardness of prayer . . . but by its persistence."
436	John 11:4	Allusion: "but this sickness is not unto death."
436	Eccl. 5:4	Reference: "But religiously one is very careful about making vows."
436	Jas. 4:8	Allusion: "the consent of a heart purified from all double-mindedness."
444	Eccl. 5:1	Allusion: "whoever is silent before God."
452	Rom. 8:28	Remote allusion: "transforms his outward activity into an inward matter."
452	2 Cor. 4:17-18	Remote allusion: "everything pleasing to God will prosper for the devout individual."
461	John 1:14	Reference: "Clergyman says: 'The word became pork' . . . that is comical."
472	Luke 18:9-14	Remote allusion: "humble before God."
481	Matt. 13:45-46	Allusion: "as a jewel which can be possessed as a whole."

510	2 Cor. 5:17	Allusion: "he must have become a new creature."
514	1 Cor. 2:9	Allusion: "confound Christianity with something which has indeed entered into the heart of man to believe."
516	Rom. 8:29	Allusion: "being God's elect."
517	Rom. 5:12-13	Allusion: "individual having come into the world is present . . . has become a sinner."
518	Matt. 7:13-14	Allusion: "the strait entrance to the narrow way is the offense."
519	Luke 14:26	Allusion: "is not this as though he hated them?"
521	Matt. 19:16-22	Reference: "young man who nevertheless could not make up his mind to give all his possessions."
522	Matt. 8:34	Reference: "people who besought Christ to depart from their country."
523	Gal. 4:4	Allusion: "in the fullness of time."
523	2 Cor. 12:9	Reference: "for Christianity makes man whose strength is in their weakness."
524	Matt. 19:12-15	Quote: "Suffer the little children to come."
524	Matt. 19:24-29	Quote: "forsaken houses, or brethren."
525	Matt. 18:1-5	Reference: "disciples rebuked the children."
525	Matt. 18:2	Quote: "Except ye turn and become as little children, ye shall in no wise enter the kingdom of heaven."
526	Luke 22:61	Reference: "like that look He gave to Peter."
526	Matt. 19*	Extended reference: "difficulty of entering into the kingdom of heaven."
527	John 3:4-11	Reference: "Forgetting the objection raised by Nicodemus and the reply to it."
527	Luke 2:12	Reference: "Christ at His birth was swaddled in rags and laid in a manger."
528	Phil. 2:5-11	Reference: "humiliation of coming in the lowly form of a servant."
529	Mark 10:45	Reference: "Christ came into the world in order to suffer."
530	1 Cor. 1:23	Allusion: "was to the Jews a stumblingblock and to the Greeks foolishness."
530	Matt. 2:1-12	Allusion: "the Three Kings of Orient."
530	John 3:31-33	Reference: "not John the Baptist even."
530	John 1:36-42	Reference: "the disciples until they were made to notice."
530	Isa. 53:2-4	Reference: "just as Isaiah had prophesied."
530	Phil. 2:5-11	Reference: "The form of a servant is the incognito."
533	Luke 17:32	Reference: "Lot's wife was turned to stone when she looked back."
533	Matt. 24:15	Allusion: "abomination of desolation."
535	1 Cor. 1:23	Allusion: "to the Jews a stumblingblock, to the Greeks foolishness."
539	Rom. 8:16	Allusion: "by the witness it bears together with his spirit."

Edifying Discourses, Vol. I

Page	Passage	Type of Reference/Quote or Summary
7	Gal. 3:23-29	Text for discourse, "Expectation of Faith"
9	Matt. 6:19-21	Allusion: Don't "trust in worldly treasures."
11	Matt. 22:37	Allusion: "Wish faith with all heart, might, and soul."
11	Mark 9:24	Remote allusion: "help thou my unbelief."
11	John 5:2-10	Allusion: "faith should come in such fortuitous fashion."
13	Gal. 3:25	Allusion: "Schoolmaster . . . yet must be educated by self."
14	Jas. 1:17	Allusion: "Giver of good gifts passed by."
20	Eccl. 1:14*	Allusion: "Nothing new under the sun."
22	Rom. 8:28	Quote: "all things work together for good . . . faith expects future victory."
24	Luke 10:42	Quote: "one thing needful."
28	Jas. 1:17	Reference: "faith rests in God in whom there is no variableness."

30	Matt. 22:37	Reference: "If a child (needing proof), could not love with soul and might."
35	Jas. 1:17-21	Text for discourse, "Every Good and Perfect Gift"
36	Jas. 1:13-14*	Allusion: "fearful error of believing that God would tempt a man."
36	Jas. 5:7	Reference: "heavens send the early and later rain."
38	1 John 5:7-8	Allusion: "spirit bears witness in heaven, but no spirit bears witness on earth."
38	Luke 15:7*	Allusion: "Joy in heaven."
40	1 Pet. 3:4	Allusion: "quiet spirit."
40	1 John 5:4	Allusion: "He [God] created the incorruptible essence of a quiet heart."
41	Rom. 3:5	Allusion: "speak with human wisdom."
42	Jas. 1:13	Quote: "you heard a voice which said, 'God does not tempt a man.'"
42	1 Pet. 5:6	Allusion: "when you humbled yourself under God's powerful hand."
43	Jas. 1:13	Quote: "but everyone is tempted when seduced and drawn away by his own desires."
44	Ps. 139:2	Quote: "so that He understands the thoughts of men from afar."
44	Heb. 1:14	Allusion: "ministering spirits."
45	Jas. 1:13	Allusion: "the error of believing that God would tempt man."
45	Heb. 13:8	Allusion: "He [God] remains the same while everything changes."
45	Luke 21:19	Allusion: "that we may win God in constancy, and save our souls with patience."
47	Eph. 6:12	Allusion: "spiritual hosts beneath heaven responsible . . . " for words of James?
47	1 Tim. 4:4	Quote: Paul says, "All of God's creation good."
47	1 Thess. 1:2	Allusion: "one ought always to thank God."
48	Rom. 8:28	Allusion: "always thank God . . . learn that all things serve for good."
49	1 Thess. 5:17	Allusion: "many promises are held out to the one who prays without ceasing."
49	2 Tim. 2:13	Allusion: "That you were faithless when God was faithful."
53	1 John 3:20	Allusion: "then would God not be greater than a man's troubled heart."
53	Jas. 1:13*	Quote: "God is tempted of no man."
54	2 Cor. 4:16	Allusion: "although the outward man perished, the inward man renewed."
54	Luke 23:43	Quote: "As the Lord himself says, Yet today."
54	Heb. 3:7f	Quote: "so the apostle of the Lord says, Yet today."
59	Matt. 13:4-8*	Allusion: These discourses "may be trodden upon, destroyed."
59	Prov. 25:13	Quote: "as the cooling snow on the day of harvest."
61	1 Pet. 4:7-12	Text for discourse, "Love Shall Cover a Multitude of Sins"
61	1 Cor. 13	Love chapter alluded to in a series of rhetorical questions.
62	Mark 12:42	Reference: Love "transforms the widow's mite."
63	Rom. 12:19	Allusion: Jewish love of childish mutability, ascribed "vengeance to God."
64	Col. 2:20	Allusion: Revenge one of the "rudiments of the world."
64	1 John 3:20	Allusion: "God is greater than the heart of man."
65	Matt. 20:1-16	Allusion: "forgiveness includes the enemy."
65	Rom. 2:5	Remote allusion: "day of wrath."
67	Matt. 15:18f	Reference: Internals more important than externals, "from within prodeedeth the evil eye."
67	Matt. 5:8	Allusion: "the pure always see God."
68	Matt. 6:22f	Quote: "eye is light of the body."
68	Prov. 10:10	Quote: "he who winketh with the eye."
68	Matt. 5:21f	Reference: "he who says Raca."
69	Gen. 4:7	Allusion: "when hate dwells in the heart, sin lies at a man's door."
69	Gal. 5:19-24	Reference: "works of flesh without love."

70	Gen. 1:1-31	Allusion: "happy . . . saw creation in its perfection . . . more happy . . . love that covers of sins."
71	Matt. 13:12	Reference: Sin as fruitful as "to him who hath shall be given."
71	Jas. 5:20	Quote: In contrast to preventing boredom, converted sinner "covers multitude of sins."
71	Matt. 12:20	Reference: "Love sees bruised reed, so covers sins, not broken."
71	Luke 15:20	Reference: "Love covers sins . . . prepares a feast like of the father of the Prodigal."
72	1 Cor. 13:7	Reference: "Love is never weary of believing, hoping, enduring all things."
72	1 Pet. 3:9	Allusion: Love "blesses and curses not."
72	1 Pet. 3:4*	Allusion: Love saves "like a woman 'without words.'"
72	Matt. 5:40f	Allusion: "Sin forces it to go first mile, but love goes two."
72	Matt. 18:22	Allusion: "Sin cannot forgive more than seven times, but love forgives seventy times seven."
73	Ps. 32:1	Quote: "blessed is the man whose sins are forgiven."
74	Acts 27:22	Reference: "Paul quieting the fears."
75	Matt. 24:22	Quote: "For the elect the days of distress will be shortened."
75	Heb. 4:12	Allusion: "God's thought is vivid and present."
75	Jas. 5:16	Reference: "prayer of a righteous man avails."
75	Gen. 18:22-23	Reference: "Abraham spoke to God . . . sought cover a multitude of sins."
76	1 Cor. 6:3	Allusion: "great is a man upright . . . judge angels . . . blessed to cover multitude of sins."
76	John 8:3-11	Extended treatment of "woman taken in adultery."
79	1 Pet. 4:7-12	Text for discourse, "Love Shall Cover . . . " II
79	1 Cor. 9:22	Allusion: "One who is all things to all men hasn't time for elaborate deliberation."
80	Rom. 13:12	Allusion: "night is far spent."
80	John 9:4	Allusion: "must work while it is day."
82	1 Cor. 9:27	Allusion: "become a castaway."
87	Luke 7:36-50	Extended comment on the "woman with alabaster box."
90	Luke 7:41-43	Quote: "The one forgiven five hundred p. will love more than one forgiven fifty p."
92	2 Cor. 4:16	Allusion: when our outward man has perished (prayer)
93	Eph. 3:13-21	Text for discourse, "Strengthened In The Inner Man."
95	1 Pet. 2:20	Allusion: no praise for one suffering for guilt.
95	1 Pet. 4:15f	Allusion: "virtue in suffering."
96	2 Cor. 6:10	Quote: Paul was apostle, "afflicted-joyful, poor-rich, . . . nothing-everything."
96	Mark 2:20	Allusion: Failure to give doctrine to men, "like bridegroom departed."
96	1 Cor. 9:26	Allusion: "does not run uncertainly."
99	Matt. 16:2-3	Reference: "one abandoned to worldly desires pays attention to weather."
99	Jas. 4:13	Quote: "Today or tomorrow . . . go to a city, buy."
99	Luke 12:16-21	Quote: "Worldly concern . . . tearing down for bigger barns."
104	Job 1:5	Allusion: "Job became old in the fear of God."
105	Matt. 4:8	Allusion: "Taken to the mountain and shown kingdoms of the world."
106	Luke 12:20	Quote: "This night thy soul is required of thee."
108	Luke 16:2	Quote: "Render an account."
109	Ex. 13:21-22	Allusion: "pillar of fire."
112	Rom. 5:4	Reference: "assurance gained through the endurance of adversity."
113	Gen. 23:17-20	Allusion: "Abraham possessed only a grave in Canaan."
114	I Cor. 2:9	Allusion: "God's comfort more blessed than anything which springs up in the human heart."
114	Phil. 4:7*	Allusion: God's comfort "passes all understanding."

115	2 Pet. 3:8	Allusion: "God can compensate for all trials . . . one thousand years are as a day."
116	Heb. 12:6	Allusion: "Whom God loves, he tests."
119	Rom. 8:38	Allusion: "things present . . . to come."

Edifying Discourses, Vol. II

Page	Passage	Type of Reference/Quote or Summary
7	Job 1:20-21	Text for discourse, "The Lord Gave . . . Blessed Be the Name of the Lord"
9	Job 7:11	Quote: "in bitterness of soul" Job cried to heaven.
9	1 Cor. 10:13	Allusion: "God makes every temptation . . . that we may be able to bear it."
11	1 Tim. 6:12*	Allusion: "one has fought the good fight."
13	1 Cor. 15:42	Allusion: "Reflection had been sown in corruption . . . incorruptible is a life of action."
13	Job 4:3-4	Quote: "his words had lifted upon the fallen."
13	Job 29:4-13	Allusion: "Job in his tent, old, with family about him."
13	Job 1*	The intital details of the story of Job.
14	Job 1:20-21	Quote: "Then Job stood up, rent his mantle . . . fell down . . . worshipped."
15	Gen. 41:30	Allusion: "Job did not forget the seven years of abundance in the seven years of famine."
16	Job 4:3-4	Quote: "whose weak hands had strengthened, whose feeble knees upheld."
16	Job 29:4-13	Reference: "Job remembered that he had not faltered."
19	Job 1:1	Quote: Job was "honest and upright before God."
19	Job 1:15-16	Allusion: "The Lord took . . . the reports of calamities didn't mention God."
21	Matt. 7:26	Allusion: "a house built on sand doesn't need adversity to overthrow it."
22	Ex. 33:22	Allusion: "One who sees God may also see him turn back as did Moses."
22	John 5:19	Allusion: God took all "you can do nothing."
22	Eph. 6:13*	Allusion: "Paul desired the striving . . . to stand."
23	1 Pet. 5:7	Quote: Job gathered his sorrows "cast them upon the Lord."
23	1 Cor. 13:1	Allusion: "faith and hope without love . . . tinkling cymbals, so gladness without suffering."
24	Job 2:9	Allusion: "Job's wife."
27	Jas. 1:17-21	Text for discourse, "Every Good and Every Perfect Gift . . . "
27	Gen. 2:17	Allusion: "knowledge brings tribulation into the world."
27	Gen. 1:31	Allusion: "If the prohibition had been obeyed all would have remained very good."
28	Gen. 2:22*	Allusion: "Adam's deep sleep . . . creation of Eve."
28	Isa. 11:6	Allusion: "creation had maintained the image of God, the lamb would lay down with the wolf."
28	Gen. 2:19	Reference: "Adam called everything by its right name."
28	Gen. 3:8f	Reference: "They heard God walking."
29	Gen. 3:13	Reference: "Serpent deceived Eve."
29	Gen. 3:23*	Reference: "The gate of the garden of Eden was closed."
30	Matt. 12:43f	Allusion: "Does doubt bind the strong man."
31	Matt. 12:29	Allusion: "Must first bind the strong man to enter his house."
31	Matt. 7:11	Quote: "If you who are evil know how to give good gifts."
32	Ps. 103:13*	Allusion: "a father pities his children."
32	1 Cor. 3:2	Allusion: "milk of the word for children, strong meat is for adults."
34	Luke 15:16	Allusion: "The Prodigal asked for bread . . . filled with husks."

34	Matt. 13:24f	Reference: "He who sowed, sowed good seed . . . not knowing what would happen to it."
36	Matt. 19:17	Reference: "No one is good except God."
37	143:10	Remote allusion: "God leads into the promised land."
38	Phil. 2:13	Reference: "God gives both to will and to do."
38	Acts 17:28	Reference: "doubt God's good gifts . . . in whom you still live, move, and have your being."
38	Job 28:1-11	Allusion: "knowledge of man is much, but doesn't know way to good."
39	Matt. 12:29	Allusion: "Word of faith would not fight doubt with own weapons."
42	John 8:9	Allusion: "when the crowds have separated and dispersed."
42	Ps. 141:1	Allusion: "Make haste O Lord to speak."
43	Prov. 14:29	Quote: "Slow to wrath."
43	Eph. 4:26	Allusion: "He will not let the sun go down on his anger."
43	1 Thess. 4:5	Allusion: "There is a curse upon the traces of bitterness."
43	Sirach 4:21	Allusion: "meekness discovers the hidden things."
44	Luke 11:13	Quote: "For if you being evil know how to give good gifts."
45	Jas. 1:17-22	Text for discourse, "Every Good Gift and Every Perfect Gift . . . " II
45	Jas. 2:1	Reference: "Having his faith in Christ."
46	Matt. 22:30	Allusion: "difference between man and woman, just as little as in the resurrection."
47	John 8:3-11	Reference: "when the woman finds forgiveness."
47	Matt. 5:28	Reference: "the man is judged whose eye only looked upon a woman to desire."
47	Jas. 2:8	Quote: "the divine law of equality that loves its neighbor as its self."
47	Ps. 23:4	Allusion: "the needy who must be content with having God as his rod."
47	Ex. 3:2	Allusion: "Divine equity burns like fire . . . without consuming."
48	Eph. 6:12	Reference: "fight good fight against flesh and blood, principalitiess and powers."
49	Job 1:20-21	Quote: "Naked I came into the world."
50	Matt. 15:5	Reference: "it is a gift."
51	Matt. 26:53	Allusion: "Providence does not need your gift, it has twelve legions of angels."
51	Luke 14:12	Allusion: "Equality . . . when the rich makes a feast for the rich."
52	Matt. 4:9	Quote: "All this will I give you if you will fall down and worship me."
52	Rom. 14:17	Allusion: "How much does a man need to live . . . life does not consist in meat."
52	Matt. 26:49	Allusion: "Would you thus betray your neighbor with a kiss?"
53	Matt. 16:26	Allusion: "Better and more blessed and more important to save a soul."
53	Matt. 6:3	Allusion: "all misgivings which the left hand finds when it consults with the right."
54	Prov. 13:12	Quote: "Hope deferred maketh the heart sick, but desire fulfilled is a tree of life."
54	1 Cor. 4:2	Reference: "Scripture says that no more is required of a steward."
54	Luke 18:1-8	Allusion: "Don't make the needy beg . . . the unrighteousnes in the judge."
56	Matt. 5:24	Reference: "to him who offers his gift . . . first see he has nothing against his brother."
59	1 John 4:20	Allusion: "If one thanks the benefactor he does see, how can he thank God."
60	John 9:1-38	Allusion: "We praise the man born blind."
61	Luke 16:21	Allusion: "Poor . . . one can even live on scraps . . . as if a dog."

62	Matt. 6:26f	Reference: "May wish you were . . . sparrow . . . lily of the field."
62	Luke 16:9	Allusion: "bought himself a friend with his doubtful mammon."
63	Matt. 10:24	Reference: "the disciple is not above the master, if the master loves."
64	Acts 20:35	Quote: "It is more blessed to give than to receive."
66	Rom. 13:8	Reference: "Paul says . . . [owe debt] of loving one another."
67	Luke 21:19	Text for discourse, "Acquire One's Soul in Patience."
67	1 Pet. 3:4	Allusion: "the incorruptible essence of a soul at peace."
69	Jas. 5:7	Allusion: "One who cultivates . . . waits upon the early and latter rain."
79	Luke 8:15	Allusion: "the good seed grows only in patience."
83	Jas. 4:14	Allusion: "What is a man's soul?"
84	1 John 3:1-3	Allusion: "we do not yet know."
84	Jas. 1:22-24	Reference: "the rightful hearer of the word is the doer of the word."
85	Jas. 2:19	Quote: "When the devil believes and trembles."

Edifying Discourses, Vol. III

Page	Passage	Type of Reference/Quote or Summary
5	Eccl. 7:2*	Quote: "going to a feast."
5	1 Thess. 2:1*	Quote: "entrance should be in vain."
7	Luke 21:19	Text for discourse: "To Preserve One's Soul in Patience."
9	1 Thess. 5:3	Allusion: "everyone saying peace and safety."
10	Phil. 2:12	Allusion: "working in fear and trembling."
13	1 Thess. 5:2	Allusion: "death . . . like a thief in the night."
16	Luke 14:28*	Allusion: "the tower cannot be too high."
18	Matt. 6:27	Reference: "No man can add a cubit to his stature."
20	Jas. 4:13-15	Allusion: "Patience . . . has discovered . . . today we shall do this."
20	Gen. 22:16	Reference: "God in heaven swears by Himself . . . for He can swear by no higher."
23	Jas. 1:23-24	Allusion: "the man loses his soul . . . the one who immediately forgot how he looked."
23	Matt. 20:1-16	Allusion: "lose soul who remained standing all day in the market place."
24	Heb. 6:4-6	Allusion: "enlightened . . . renounced the heavenly gift after having once tasted it."
24	Luke 16:3	Allusion: "Mockers and disgruntled . . . not able to dig . . . too proud to beg."
25	Matt. 4:5*	Allusion: "he stood at the pinnacle."
26	Luke 11:44-46	Allusion: "Happiness a hypocrite . . . more than those Pharisees, binds on heavy burdens."
27	Luke 10:29-37	Allusion: "Patience is in truth that Good Samaritan."
29	Rom. 15:5	Reference: "We call God the God of patience because He is Himself patient."
31	Ps. 95:7	Reference: "Patience has another word . . . yet today, says the Lord."
32	Matt. 19:3	Allusion: "Your thoughts . . . stood up like the Pharisees to tempt you with cunning words."
33	1 Cor. 10:13	Reference: "God will make the temptation and the escape . . . so that we may be able to bear it."
37	Luke 2:34-38	Text for discourse: "Patient in Expectation."
38	Gen. 8:22	Allusion: "Expectation . . . ceases just as little as day and night . . . as long as time."
40	John 8:56	Reference: "The chosen of the generations rejoiced in the vision."
40	Gal. 4:4*	Allusion: "Then came the fulness of time."

44	Gen. 29:20	Allusion: "only a steadfast lover serves seven years and seven years more."
47	1 John 2:17	Allusion: "for live and its desire perish . . . he who knows better perishes."
47	Matt. 25:1-13	Allusion: "[Did] the foolish bridesmaids fall asleep immediately . . . same time?"
48	Matt. 10:29	Allusion: "more forgotten than a sparrow that does not fall . . . except by will of God."
49	1 Thess. 5:19	Allusion: "quench not the spirit in unprofitable disputes."
49	1 Pet. 5:7	Reference: "cast once more your sorrow upon God."
50	2 Cor. 4:17	Allusion: "Expectation . . . makes the affliction light."
51	Acts 24:15	Allusion: "You expect the resurrection of the dead."
51	1 John 4:18	Allusion: "Patience, like love, drives out fear."
52	Luke 19:17	Allusion: "He who is faithful in little."
54	2 Tim. 1:7	Quote: "God . . . does not give the "spirit of cowardace, but . . . power."
56	Gen. 25:33	Allusion: "False expectation . . . in time of need . . . exchanges for a mess of pottage."
56	Prov. 25:11	Allusion: "Expectation in patience is like a good word . . . like an apple of gold."
58	Col. 1:11	Quote: "in all patience and long-suffering."
59	Matt. 17:21	Quote: "Impatience . . . 'only driven out by prayer and fasting.'"
60	Prov. 16:32	Allusion: "Praying sincerely is more difficult than taking a city."
64	Eccl. 1:9*	Allusion: "nothing new under the sun."
71	Eccl. 12:1	Text for discourse: "Remember Now Thy Creator In The Days Of Thy Youth."
74	Matt. 16:26	Allusion: "to compensate a man for the injury . . . upon his soul if he gave up of God."
76	Eccl. 1:14*	Quote: "'All is vanity and vexation of spirit,' says the Preacher."
76	Eccl. 11:9	Quote: "walk in the ways of the heart."
78	1 Cor. 15:2	Quote: "Sought to drive soul from security . . . prevented from 'believing in vain'."
78	Eccl. 12:4	Quote: "sound of the grinding is low and the daughters of music are brought low."
79	Matt. 16:26	Quote: "if the trumpet gives forth an uncertain sound."
80	Matt. 18:3	Allusion: "Holy Scripture makes as a condition for the Kingdom of Heaven . . . a man should become a child again."
82	Sirach 2:8*	Quote: "let youth 'wear the garlands of rosebuds before they be withered.'"
82	Sirach 2:6*	Allusion: "youth does it most naturally."
82	Gen. 45:10	Allusion: "[Proving God] busier than the Jews in Goshen."
84	Ex. 20:11	Quote: "[God] has created 'the heavens and the earth and all that in them is.'"
85	Acts 17:28	Allusion: "youth does not need to go far . . . to live and move and have his being in God."
85	Luke 15:8-10	Allusion: [if a thought is lost] like that woman, one lights a candle and goes and searches."
87	Matt. 18:10	Allusion: "let childhood keep angels who always behold God."
89	Rom. 13:8*	Allusion: "guidance of thought . . . in order not to owe anyone anything."
89	Num. 32:13*	Allusion: "wandered about in wilderness without refreshment."
90	Gen.	Reference: "as the first book of the Old Testament is called Birth."
90	Ex.	Reference: "the second book . . . Departure."
91	1 John 2:17	Quote: "the world and the lusts thereof perish."
92	Matt. 19:6*	Allusion: "woe to him who separates what God has joined together."
93	Prov. 31:30	Quote: "youth is only vanity . . . for 'beauty is deceitful and favor is vain.'"

95	2 Cor. 4:17-18	Text for discourse, "The Expectation of an Eternal Happiness."
96	Matt. 6:7	Allusion: "As heathen offer long and superfluous prayers."
97	1 Tim. 5:13	Quote: "learned to be idle and to wander about from house to house."
97	1 Tim. 1:4*	Allusion: "such people . . .only raise more questions."
98	2 Tim. 2:17	Quote: "whose idle speech eats as does a canker."
99	Matt. 6:19-21	Reference: "Therefore the man who owns treasure in heaven."
99	Luke 16:9	Allusion: "who here on earth acquired friends . . .able to welcome in next world."
101	Luke 16:23	Allusion: "picture the horror . . .[of] the rich man when he awakened in hell."
102	Gal. 6:7	Quote: "God is not mocked!"
102	Matt. 6:24-34	Quote: "no man can serve two masters."
102	Jas. 4:4	Quote: "love for the world is enmity toward God."
102	Matt. 6:28	Reference: "like the inactivity of the lillies which do not spin."
103	Matt. 6:33	Reference: "it seeks the kingdom of God and its righteousness."
104	1 Cor. 13:12	Allusion: "life in the temporal existence is seen only in part."
105	1 Thess. 4:13	Allusion: "in despair as one who has no hope."
106	2 Cor. 12:2	Reference: "Paul . . .carried up to the third heaven."
106	1 Cor. 1:23	Allusion: "Paul . . .a stumbling block to the Jews, to the Greeks foolishness."
107	1 Cor. 15:19	Quote: "experience declared Paul . . .'the most wretched of men.'"
108	Job 6:2	Quote: "all his calamities were laid in the balance."
108	1 Cor. 15:19*	Reference: "Paul 'had hope for the life only.'"
108	1 Cor. 2:9	Allusion: "a joy which did not originate in any human heart."
109	Matt. 19:21	Reference: "demanded of the rich young man . . .go away and sell all."
109	Matt. 8:21-22	Allusion: "first to go and bury the dead."
109	1 Cor. 9:9	Allusion: "mouth bound as not even the mouths of the oxen were bound."
110	Matt. 6:6	Allusion: "covenant of tears . . .heard by One who sees in secret."
112	Matt. 19:24	Allusion: "so that a camel can go through the eye of a needle."
112	Matt. 9:17	Allusion: "that is why the new wine bursts the old containers."
113	Ex. 26:33*	Allusion: "inwardness . . .holy of holies in the soul."
114	1 Sam. 5:3-4	Allusion: "statue of Dagon before the Ark."
114	Col. 2:8	Quote: "became a prey to worldly wisdom."
117	Matt. 6:2-4	Allusion: "the conscience of having done a good deed may cause one to lose his reward."
118	Luke 17:10	Allusion: "we are all unprofitable servants."
118	Matt. 20: 1-16	Reference: "if I were not called until the eleventh hour and our wage proved to be the same."
118	Luke 23:43	Allusion: "I were a robber who 'yet today'."
120	Matt. 14:29f	Allusion: "Peter stood more securely on the wave than one would in his own righteousness."
121	John 3:23-30	Text for discourse: "He Must Increase."
121	Josh. 2:1-6	Allusion: "woman of ill-repute concealed spies of Joshua."
122	Luke 11:20	Allusion: "finger of God."
123	Matt. 11:7-8	Allusion: "soft raiment . . .flexibility of a reed."
123	Matt. 3:3-15	Reference: "he [John the Baptist] was the voice of one crying in the wilderness."
123	John 1:15-36	Allusion: "not the Messiah, not one of the old prophets, not 'that prophet'."
123	John 1:27	Reference: "to prepare the way for the One who should come after him."
123	Matt. 11:11	Quote: "greatest born of women."
123	Luke 1:36	Reference: "his birth as marvelous."
124	Matt. 1:20	Reference: "that a pure virgin should give birth by the power of God."

124	Mark 1:3	Reference: "he remained the voice crying in the wilderness."
124	Matt. 11:11	Reference: "he also knew that it was destined to cease and be forgotten."
124	Matt. 2:1-12	Reference: "the One whose morning star had awakened wonder in the wise men."
124	Matt. 3:11	Reference: "baptism of water as against a baptism of fire and the Holy Ghost."
125	Gen. 17:20	Allusion: "the concubine's son was not without Abraham's blessing."
128	John 1:19	Reference: "when the commission sent by the Council almost caused John to be mistaken."
130	Matt. 24:25f	Reference: "parable of the unfaithful servant."
130	Matt. 20:28	Reference: "the one following . . .who came not to be ministered unto but to minister."
131	Acts 5:9	Allusion: "the feet of those who stand at the door who are to carry him out."
131	Jas. 4:5	Quote: "the Spirit that works within us . . .but gives greater grace."
131	Matt. 3:3-15	Reference: "Baptism of Jesus."
131	Mark 1:3	Reference: "voice of one crying."
132	Mark 1:3	Reference: "proclaimed in the wilderness."
132	Matt. 2:16	Allusion: "like Herod, he would command that all children under two years be slain."
133	Ex. 1:7-8	Allusion: "Perhaps a new Pharaoh ascended to the throne, who knew not Joseph."
133	Ps. 1:3	Allusion: "as if only that one increased who is planted by the water springs."
133	Mark 9:24	Allusion: "the worm of desire does not die."
134	Mark 1:6	Allusion: "under a camel's hair garment there can beat a heart so rich."
134	Eccl. 7:2	Allusion: "going to a feast."
134	Matt. 11:16-17	Allusion: "which even the children in the market place would not understand."
138	Jas. 5:9	Allusion: "Even in the moment of happiness, he 'groaned against' the stronger."

Edifying Discourses, Vol. IV

Page	Passage	Type of Reference/Quote or Summary
7	Jer. 17:9	Allusion: "the human heart is deceitful . . .too prone to take even high mindness in vain."
8	Job 6:15-18	Quote: "leads it into the desert."
9	1 Tim. 6:6	Reference: "But a little with contentment is great gain."
11	2 Cor. 12:9	Reference: "To let the grace of God suffice."
13	Luke 14:15-24	Allusion: "rest content . . .privilege setting at a table in the Kingdom of Heaven."
14	Heb. 13:9	Quote: "his heart is strengthened by grace and not by meat."
16	2 Cor. 5:17	Reference: "all things have become new, everything is changed."
17	Matt. 10:29	Remote allusion: "God nevertheless thinks of each individual separately."
19	2 Cor. 5:17*	Allusion: "his suffering is light."
19	Matt. 11:28	Allusion: "yoke of self-denial is easy."
20	John 2:10	Reference: "like the wonder at the wedding feast at Cana."
20	Matt. 26:39	Allusion: "he still has a bitter cup to drink."
21	Matt. 19:22	Allusion: "like the rich young man of many possessions."
22	John 5:19	Allusion: "What then . . .can he himself do nothing?"

25	Isa. 40:7	Reference: "O Lord . . .like a fading flower."
27	Ex. 10:22	Allusion: "level mountains . . .in comparison with letting a darkness fall upon Egypt."
27	Ex. 17:6	Allusion: "when the people are overcome by thirst in the desert."
32	John 11:4*	Allusion: "it knows that this sickness is not unto death but unto life."
36	Prov. 16:32	Allusion: "if by curbing his spirit he had become greater than one who conquers a city."
37	2 Cor. 11:30	Quote: "glories in his weakness."
39	Matt. 12:24	Allusion: "driving out devils with the help of the devil."
40	Matt. 8:28	Allusion: "asking to take up his habitation among the tombs like a leper."
41	Phil. 4:4	Quote: "Rejoice, and again I say rejoice."
43	Acts 7:48	Reference: "He does not live in a house built with hands."
43	Phil. 2:12	Allusion: "when he works out his salvation with fear and trembling."
46	Rom. 8:28	Allusion: "to know God as the power that makes all things work together for good."
49	2 Cor. 12:7	Text for discourse: "The Thorn in the Flesh."
55	Rom. 8:28	Allusion: [Satan's assault] "like everything else, must work for the good of the believer."
55	1 Cor. 10:13	Allusion: "there is no superhuman temptation."
56	Phil. 3:12-14	Allusion: "the eye cannot really fix itself on the one who is running because he is running."
56	2 Tim. 4:7	Reference: "learn . . . to run and finish the race."
56	2 Cor. 11:23f	Reference: "Mention now the tribulations."
58	Acts 7:56	Allusion: "the apostle sees Him, as did Stephen, standing at the right hand of God."
58	Rom. 8:38	Reference: "to separate him from the love to which God's testimony bears witness in his ear."
58	Rom. 15:24f	Allusion: "preaching of the word into Spain."
59	1 Cor. 9:22	Allusion: "apostle who seeks to be all things to all men."
60	Luke 16:20	Allusion: "more wretched than Lazarus."
60	Matt. 27:46	Allusion: "forsaken of God."
60	Deut. 4:24	Allusion: "wrath of God and its consuming fire."
62	Jas. 1:17	Allusion: "changeableness of God, a shadow of change . . .an angel of Satan."
63	Ps. 126:5	Allusion: "there must be sowing with tears."
63	Jas. 1:17*	Allusion: "there is no shadow of turning."
65	Matt. 7:3	Allusion: "sensual man . . .sees the mote in his brother's eye."
66	Acts 9:3-9	Reference: "kicked against the pricks."
67	1 Cor. 1:23	Reference: "he preached Christ and Him crucified."
67	Acts 7:58	Reference: "when Stephen was stoned, he . . .watched the garments."
67	Acts 9:1-2	Reference: "permission from the Sanhedrin."
68	Acts 26:24	Reference: "Thou art mad, Paul."
69	1 Cor. 15:9	Reference: "not worthy to be called an apostle . . .he had persecuted the church of God."
69	1 Thess. 5:3	Allusion: "peace and safety."
69	Phil. 3:14	Allusion: "grasp the treasure for all eternity."
72	Rom. 9:16	Quote: "it is not of him that willeth . . .but of God who showeth mercy."
75	2 Tim. 1:7	Text for discourse: "Against Cowardice."
75	Luke 7:11-16	Allusion: "feel like the son of the widow of Nain . . .awakened on his bier."
80	Josh. 10:12	Allusion: "It is a proud word that would halt the course of the sun."
80	Heb. 12:13	Allusion: "he who holds his foot steadfast on the way . . .[lacks] hero's stride."

90	Luke 17:10	Reference: "the right to call him an unprofitable servant."
92	Gen. 1:5*	Reference: "God . . .separated day and night."
93	Luke 14:28-30	Reference: "he who wishes to build a tower . . .makes an estimate."
93	Mark 12:41-44	Allusion: "did not the widow give infinitely more than the rich man . . .?"
100	Matt. 10:29-31	Reference: "in God's eyes not as important as the sparrow of the air."
102	Luke 10:38-42	Allusion: "thou didst not choose the better part."
102	1 Sam. 15:22	Reference: "for obedience is more pleasing to God than the fat of rams."
103	Matt. 6:17	Quote: "when thou fastest."
104	Matt. 6:16-18	Quote: "disfiguring his face."
107	Eccl. 4:10	Quote: "woe to him who is alone."
115	Matt. 13:45	Allusion: "How rewarding to meet in the Gospel or in life . . .a resolute man."
116	2 Tim. 4:7	Allusion: "The sensual man . . .refuses to understand what the good fight is."
128	Rev. 3:16	Allusion: "If he catches himself being lukewarm and thus apostate toward God."
137	John 14:3	Quote: "When I am gone away from you."
137	John 16:7	Quote: "and this is profitable for you."
140	Matt. 25:1f	Allusion: "buy new oil for the lamp of his expectation."

Christian Discourses

Page	Passages	Type of Reference/Quote or Summary
11	Luke 12:22-31	Extended references throughout the various discourses: "the lilies and the birds . . .return to the instruction of these teachers!"
12	Matt. 6:24-34	Text for returned to repeatedly in discourses on Anxiety.
13	Ex. 20:18	Reference: "summit of Sinai the law was given, amidst the thunders of heaven."
13	Matt. 5:1	Reference: "at the foot of the mountain the Sermon on the Mount is preached."
13	John 14:6	Reference: "He is 'the Teacher'—the Way and the Truth and the Life."
14	Mark 12:14	Quote: "the Teacher . . .careth not for any man."
17	Matt. 6:25	Text for discourse: "The Anxiety of Poverty."
17	John 9:25*	Quote: "this I know, that I am the blind man, see."
17	Ex. 16:4-30	Allusion: "'daily bread' . . .heavenly food which cannot be too long kept."
17	Luke 12:22-31	Reference: "birds and lilies."
18	Matt. 6:11	Allusion: "the daily bread."
20	Matt. 4:2*	Reference: "He 'was hungry in the desert . . .'"
20	John 19:28*	Reference: "and thirsted upon the cross."
20	John 4:34	Reference: "Christ's 'meat to do the Father's will.'"
22	Eph. 2:12	Quote: "without God in the world."
23	Matt. 17:27	Allusion: "pull a fish out of water . . .with which one pays the tax."
23	Luke 21:34	Reference: "a man can 'overcharge' his heart."
27	Matt. 6:25	Text for discourse: "The Anxiety of Abundance."
27	Matt. 7:15	Allusion: "riches and abundance become hypocritically clad in sheep's clothing."
27	Luke 12:22-31	Allusion: "The bird, however, has not this anxiety."
30	Luke 12:30	Allusion: "I may die . . .'this very night,' then I possess nothing."
36	Heb. 13:16	Quote: "To do good and to communicate forget not."

40	Matt. 6:25	Text for discourse: "The Anxiety of Lowliness."
40	Luke 12:22-31	Allusion: "Sparrows are divided into grey, yellow . . .golden."
51	Matt. 6:25	Text for discourse: "The Anxiety of Highness."
51	Luke 12:22-31	Allusion: "The bird . . .is always on high."
63	Matt. 6:27	Text for discourse: "The Anxiety of Presumption."
63	Luke 12:22-31	Reference: "The lily and the bird, however, have not this anxiety."
68	Ps. 59:10	Allusion: "His grace prevents the Christian."
69	Matt. 21:33ff	Quote: "Let us kill the son, and the vineyard will be ours."
70	Gen. 32:24	Reference: "If the God-fearing man 'halts upon his thigh' after having striven with God."
71	Matt. 4:5-6	Allusion: "presumptuous heathen . . .cast himself down from the pinnacle of the Temple."
71	Acts 8:18	Reference: "like that Simon . . .would purchase the Holy Ghost."
72	2 Thess. 1:9	Quote: "eternal destruction from the face of the Lord."
73	Matt. 6:34	Text for discourse, "the Anxiety of Self-Torment."
73	Luke 12:22-31	Reference: "This anxiety the bird has not."
77	Gen. 6:4	Reference: "Just as those demons of whom we read . . .begat children by earthly women."
77	Sirach 30:23	Quote: "Love thy soul, and comfort thy heart, and drive care from thee."
78	Matt. 6:13	Allusion: "For the Christian prays, 'Save me today from evil.'"
78	Matt. 21:1-9	Reference: "the people exultantly hailed him as King."
78	John 19:15	Referance: "they would cry, 'Crucify him!'"
79	Isa. 22:13	Quote: "Let us eat and drink, for tomorrow we shall die."
83	Matt. 6:24	Text for discourse, "The Anxiety of Irresolution."
83	Gen. 1:2	Allusion: "He makes use of the winds as His angels."
83	Luke 12:22-31	Allusion: "The lily and the bird have no occasion to become self-important."
83	Matt. 10:31	Allusion: [lily and bird] "are no less dear to God."
83	Luke 10:38-42	Allusion: "Mary did Christ more honour."
85	Matt. 23:8-10	Allusion: "only One who in suchwise is Master, is the Lord."
86	Mark 12:30	Reference: "he loves the Lord with all his heart and strength."
89	Sirach 2:12	Quote: "Woe unto the sinner that goeth two ways."
89	Matt. 12:25	Allusion: "Heathenism is a kingdom which is divided against itself."
89	1 Cor. 8:5	Allusion: "there have been many lords."
91	Luke 12:39	Allusion: "Then when irresoluteness has ruled . . .fickleness assumes the government."
96	Rom. 5:3-4	[Journal notes] Allusion: "tribulation, patience, hope."
96	Acts 12:14	[Journal notes] Allusion: "Rhoda . . .opened not the gate for joy"
96	Luke 24:41	[Journal notes] Allusion: said of his disciples that "for joy they disbelieved"
97	Ps. 49:4	Quote: [flyleaf] "I will incline mine ear."
103	Heb. 10:10	Reference: "He too suffered only once . . .but His whole life was suffering."
104	Job 38:11	Allusion: "And God said to the waters, 'Hitherto and no farther.'"
104	John 14:6	Allusion: "He made it true that He is the Truth."
105	Matt. 20:1-16	Reference: "labourers . . .called to work at different hours."
107	Rev. 7:17	Allusion: "every tear shall be wiped away from the eyes."
107	Dan. 6:16-24	Allusion: "unharmed did Daniel go from the lions' den."
107	Dan. 3:19-28	Allusion: "Three children going into the fiery furnace."
107	Matt. 6:19-21	Allusion: "As little as moth and rust can consume the treasure of eternity."
108	Luke 16: 19-31	Allusion: "the rich man in hell and Lazarus . . .yawning gulf fixed."
109	Matt. 26:39	Allusion: "to Christ the cup of suffering."
109	Luke 22:20	Reference: "He has drained it, this cup."
109	Matt. 20:22-23	Allusion: "man only suffers once."

109	Matt. 6:8-15	Reference: "In 'Our Father' the Christian prays for daily bread to-day."
110	Ps. 6:5	Remote allusion: "no remembrance more blessed."
110	Matt. 5:11	Quote: "When men shall reproach you."
112	Eph. 4:30	Allusion: "grief of the Holy Spirit within."
112	Ps. 57:8	Quote: "Awake psaltry and harp."
114	1 Kings 19:11f	Allusion: "God's voice . . .was in the gentle breeze, like a whisper."
119	2 Cor. 6:10	Allusion: "the poorer he becomes, the richer he can make others."
120	Luke 16:11	Allusion: "The unrighteous mammon . . .is itself unrighteous."
129	2 Cor. 12:9-10	Topic of Discourse: "The Weaker Thou Dost Become, the Stronger."
141	John 6:60	Quote: "a hard saying."
142	Acts 8:18	Reference: "in case one would buy the Holy Ghost with money, he is lost."
148	Prov. 7:23	Quote: "as a bird hasteth to the snare."
159	Matt. 6:33	Quote: "Seek ye first the kingdom of heaven."
162	Rom. 14:22	Quote: "the faith which thou hast, have thou to thyself before God."
166	Eccl. 5:1	[Journal notes] Quote: "Keep thy foot."
166	Matt. 19:27	[Journal notes] Reference: "What shall we have who have forsaken all?"
166	Rom. 8:28	[Journal notes] Reference: "All things work together for our good if we love God."
166	Acts 24:15	[Journal notes] Allusion: "Resurrection of the dead is at hand . . . just and unjust."
166	Matt. 5:10-12	[Journal notes] Allusion: "It is blessed to be mocked for a good cause."
166	Luke 6:26	[Journal notes] Quote: "Woe unto you if all men speak well of you."
166	Rom. 13:11*	[Journal notes] Allusion: "Now is our salvation nearer."
166	1 Tim. 3:16	[Journal notes] Reference: "Christ was believed in the world."
171	Eccl. 5:1	Text for discourse: "Keep Thy Foot . . ."
177	Eccl. 5:1-5	Allusion: "thou goest up to the house of the Lord to pay thy vows."
184	Matt. 19:27	Text for discourse: "Behold, We Have Forsaken All."
185	Job 1:20-21	Reference: "not a Job who says, 'The Lord hath taken away.'"
185	1 Cor. 13:1	Reference: "the Apostle uses a different expression, he says, we have 'forsaken all.'"
186	Gen. 22:1-2	Reference: "of Abraham he required expressly, as a test, only that he give up Isaac."
190	Matt. 4:20	Reference: "But as soon as Christ called him, he forsook all this."
197	Rom. 8:28	Text for discourse: "All Things Work Together."
202	Luke 19:8	Reference: "I will give half of my wealth to the poor."
205	Mark 9:50	Quote: "The Scripture says, 'Have salt in yourselves.'"
206	1 John 4:8	Reference: "the fact that God is love."
210	Acts 24:15	Text for discourse: "The Resurrection . . .at Hand."
211	Acts 23:7-8	Reference: "the Sadducees . . .were enraged when Paul talked of immortality."
213	Acts 24:25	Reference: "Felix was afraid when he heard Paul's discourse about immortality."
221	Rom.13:11	Text for discourse: "Now Are We Nearer Our Salvation."
228	Matt. 5:10-12	Text for discourse: "It Is Better . . .To Suffer."
235	Luke 6:26	Quote: "Woe unto you when all men shall speak well of you."
239	1 Tim. 3:16	Text for discourse: "He Was Believed in the World."
259	Luke 22:15	Text for discourse: "A Hearty Loning."
259	Luke 22:6	Allusion: "Judas was already bought to sell him."
261	John 3:8	Allusion: "The wind bloweth where it listeth."
262	John 12:32	Reference: "Him who was 'lifted up from the earth will draw all men unto Himself.'"

262	Eccl. 1:5-8	Allusion: "like that pious man . . .for all is vanity."
269	Matt. 11:28	Text for discourse: "Come Unto Me."
275	Heb. 3:7f	Allusion: "Thou art unchangeable . . .Thou sayest, 'yet today.'"
276	John 10:27	Text for discourse: "The Good Shepherd."
280	Matt. 5:23-24	Quote: "He Himself says, 'When thou art offering thy gift at the altar.'"
280	Gen. 4:3-5	Allusion: "Able sacrificed upon the altar, but Cain did not."
284	1 Cor. 11:23	Text for discourse: "The Night In Which He Was Betrayed."
284	Matt. 26:20ff	Exposition of the theme: the night Jesus was betrayed.
286	Matt. 27:24	Allusion: "we dare not wash our hands, at least we cannot do it, except as Pilate did."
286	Matt. 26:49	Allusion: "Judas indeed is the traitor, but at bottom all are traitors."
286	Matt. 26:56	Allusion: "for fear of man those disciples do the same who flee in the night."
286	Matt. 26:69f*	Allusion: "Peter, who denies Him in the court."
288	Matt. 26:6-13	Reference: "A woman anoints His head . . .she is remembered through all the centuries!"
288	Rom. 3:25	Allusion: "the cross is the sacrifice of propitiation for the sin of the world."
289	2 Tim. 2:12-13	Text for discourse: "He Abideth Faithful."
290	Matt. 7:6	Reference: "He who charged His disciples not to cast their pearl before swine."
292	Mark 6:56	Reference: "not even did a sick person touch the border of his garment without being healed."
294	Ps. 19:12	Quote: "cleanse thou me from secret faults."
297	1 John 3:20	Text for discourse: ""God Greater Than Our Heart."
297	John 8:3-11	Reference: "a woman apprehended openly in sin in order to accuse her."
299	Gen. 1	Reference: "When God created all things, He saw, and lo, 'it was very good'."
299	Matt. 11:6	Reference: "Blessed is he who is not offended."
301	John 3:16	Reference: "If God so loved the world."
301	Matt. 16:12f*	Allusion: "He died for someone in particular, not for the ninety and nine."
305	Luke 24:51	Text for discourse: "Christ's Blessing."
305	Acts 1:9-10	Quote: "a cloud received Him out of their sight."
305	Gen 32:26	Quote: "I will not let Thee go unless Thou bless me."
309	Ex.17:12	Allusion: "As another supported Moses when he prayed."
315	Luke 12:22-31	Allusion: [prayer] "that we again might learn it from the lilies and the birds."
317	Matt. 6:24-34	Quote: "No man can serve two masters."
322	Matt. 6:33	Quote: "Seek ye first the kingdom of God and his righteousness."
330	Matt. 6:9-13	Quote: "for the sake of praying in silence to God, 'Hallowed be Thy name!'."
333	Matt. 6:24	Text for discourse: "Obedience."
333	Luke 12:22-31	Extended reference: "But out there in the silence with the lilies and the birds."
336	Matt. 4:10	Quote: "Thou shalt love the Lord thy God, and him only shalt thou serve."
337	Matt. 6:13*	Allusion: "Here 'God's will is done, as in heaven, so on earth'."
337	Matt. 10:29	Quote: "it is true, as the Scripture says, 'not one sparrow falls to the ground.'"
344	Matt. 6:13	Quote: "when thou prayest to God, 'Lead us not into temptation.'"
344	Jas. 1:13	Quote: "there is no temptation, for 'God tempteth no man'."
347	Matt. 6:26	Text for discourse: "Joy."
347	Luke 12:22-31	Extended reference: "So then let us consider the lilies and the birds."
352	1 Pet. 5:7	Quote: take it absolutely with perfect literalness, "Cast all your cares upon God."

Works of Love

37	Luke 10:29	Reference: "Who then is one's neighbor?"
37	Matt. 5:46-47	Quote: "Do not the heathen do the same?"
38	Luke 10:36-37	Reference: "After having told the parable of the merciful Samaritan."
40	Jas. 2:8-9	Reference: "You shall love—this, then, is the word of the royal law."
40	Matt. 6:11	Reference: "almost made to forget that daily bread is a gift."
41	2 Cor. 5:17	Quote: "'All things are made new'—also fits this command of love."
42	1 Cor. 7:30	Reference: "According to the Bible, he who has earthly goods shall be like."
42	Rev. 3:16	Reference: "is neither cold nor hot, he can be certain that he does not have faith."
43	1 Cor. 2:9*	Allusion: "did not originate in any human heart."
43	Matt. 10:16-17	Quote: "When Christ says, 'Beware of men'.'Be shrewd as serpents'.'Be innocent as doves'."
43	2 Tim. 1:14	Allusion: "guarding yourself against men."
44	Mark 9:50*	Quote: "he also has, as the Scriptures say, 'salt in himself.'"
44	Matt. 9:20-22	Reference: "the woman with the hemorrhages."
45	Jer. 49:13	Allusion: "God in heaven is the only one who is truly in a position to swear by himself."
47	1 John 4:18	Allusion: "This security of the eternal casts out all anxiety."
48	Rom. 8:37	Quote: "in the same sense that faith 'more than conquers.'"
49	Jas. 3:10	Quote: "It is the same tongue with which we bless and curse."
50	1 Cor. 13:4	Reference: "love . . . by becoming duty does not know jealousy."
51	Matt. 25:10	Reference: "he does not know where he can go to buy new oil."
51	Rev. 21:4	Reference: "To what is said of eternal life, that there is no sighing and no tears."
52	Matt. 13:13	Reference: "through habit you have acquired the ear which hears and still does not hear."
53	1 Cor. 7:22-23	Allusion: "Duty, however, makes a man dependent and at the same moment eternally independent."
58	Matt. 22:37-39	Title of discourse: "You Shall Love Your Neighbor."
58	Matt. 22:37-39	Reference: "one ought to love God with his whole heart and his neighbor as himself."
58	Luke 10:29	Remote allusion: "One must rather take care to discern and divide rightly."
59	2 Cor. 10:5	Quote: "takes every thought captive to obey Christ."
60	1 Cor. 13:13	Allusion: "songs of faith and hope and love."
60	Luke 10:37	Reference: "go and do likewise."
64	Matt. 6:6	Reference: "shut your door and pray to God."
65	1 Cor. 7:9	Reference: "Does not Paul say it is better to marry than to burn!"
66	Matt. 5:46-47	Quote: "To love the beloved . . . 'Do not the pagans do likewise?'"
70	1 Cor. 1:23	Reference: "Christianity . . . to the natural man it is an offense."
71	Matt. 3:4*	Allusion: "if John, the rigorous judge, were to dress like a Beau Brummel."
71	Matt. 11:6	Reference: "Blessed is he who is not offended by it."
73	Matt. 22:39	Title of discourse: "You Shall Love Your Neighbor."
73	Jas. 2:8-9	Reference: "The royal lay."
74	Matt. 12:20	Allusion: "the teacher who never extinguished a single smoking candle."
74	1 John 4:7-8	Reference: "But God is love."
74	1 Cor. 3:9	Allusion: "God's co-workers—in love."
75	Rom. 2:11	Allusion: "before God there is no distinction."
75	Gen. 2:22*	Allusion: "Or perhaps God took from your side and gave you a beloved."
75	Rom. 12:15	Reference: "For heaven not only rejoices . . . with the joyful."
76	Matt. 5:4	Allusion: "Neither is Christian consolation a substitute compensation for lost joy."

76	1 Cor. 13:12	Allusion: "As the human eye cannot bear to look directly at the sun."
77	Matt. 5:46-47	Allusion: "As the human eye cannot bear to look directly at the sun."
79	Matt. 5:44	Reference: "Therefore he who in truth loves his neighbour loves also his enemy."
80	Matt. 6:6	Reference: "Shut your door and pray to God."
80	Jas. 2:1-7	Reference: "pay no attention to the differences, for they make no difference."
80	John 17:15	Reference: "pray God to take the disciples out of the world."
83	Jas. 2:1-7	Reference: "It teaches that everyone should lift himself above earthly distinctions."
84	Matt. 10:6	Allusion: "he easily becomes like a lost sheep among ravenous wolves."
84	Jas. 1:27	Reference: "to keep oneself pure and unspotted from the world is the task."
86	Ps. 1:1	Quote: "refrain from laughing with the 'council of the scornful'."
90	1 Cor. 13:13	Allusion: "as if this love to one's neighbour did not fit properly."
90	Luke 14:21	Allusion: "Imagine a man who gave a feast and invited to it the halt, blind, cripples, and beggars."
91	Luke 14:12-14	Quote: "When you give a dinner or a banquet, do not invite your friend."
92	Tobit 2:7-8	Quote: "his neighbors mocked him."
93	Deut. 5:21	Reference: "for one shall not covet what is his neighbour's."
98	Mark 12:31	Allusion: "You shall, you shall, you shall."
99	Rom. 13:10	Title for discourse: "Love is the Fulfilling of the Law."
100	Matt. 21:28-32	Extended reference: "There is found in Holy Scriptures a parable . . . a 'man had two sons.'"
104	John 18:38	Allusion: "How many have not asked, 'What is truth?'"
104	Luke 10:29	Quote: "When the Pharisee, 'desiring to justify himself,' asked, 'Who is my neighbour?'"
104	1 Cor. 3:19	Reference: "But God catches the wise in their foolishness."
106	Rom. 10:4	Quote: "Christ is the end of the law."
106	Rom. 3:20	Allusion: "Whereas the law with its demand thereby became the destruction of all."
106	Matt. 5:17-18	Reference: "so Christ came not to abolish the law, but to fulfill it."
106	John 8:46	Quote: "No one could convict him of any sin."
106	1 Pet. 2:22	Quote: "No guile was found in his lips."
106	John 4:34	Reference: "for his good was to do the Father's will."
106	John 10:30	Reference: "Thus he was one with the Father."
106	Luke 19:41-42	Reference: "Even when he wept."
107	John 11:38-44	Reference: "Lazarus's grave . . . he knew what he would do."
107	Luke 10:42	Quote: "Mary has chosen the good portion."
107	Luke 22:6	Reference: "and the same love which rebuked with a glance—or forgave—Peter."
107	Luke 10:17*	Reference: "he received the disciples who joyfully returned home."
107	Matt. 26:40-45	Reference: "the same love when he found them sleeping."
107	Matt. 12:49	Quote: "These are my mother."
107	John 9:4	Reference: "he did not rest before the night came when he could no longer work."
107	Luke 6:12	Reference: "for if he did not work, he watched in prayer."
108	1 John 4:19	Reference: "alas, God has nevertheless loved him first."
108	Matt. 6:33	Reference: "Let a man . . . seek first the Kingdom of God and his righteousness."
109	1 Cor. 1:23	Allusion: "in a certain sense it does not help to talk to man about the highest good."
110	Col. 2:17	Quote: "a shadow of things to come."
111	1 Tim. 1:5	Quote: "Love is the sum of the commandments."

111	Rom. 13:9	Reference: "the sum comprises all the single commandments, thou shalt not steal, etc."
111	Rom. 7:24	Reference: "Under the law man groans."
112	Matt. 5:17f	Reference: "Love is the fulfilling of the law."
113	1 Cor. 7:22-23	Allusion: "Every man is God's servant."
114	Matt. 5:44	Reference: "the Christian demand to love one's enemy any more."
114	Luke 14:26	Reference: "be capable of hating his father and mother and sister and beloved."
115	Matt. 16:23	Quote: "Get behind me, Satan."
116	John 17:14	Allusion: "in a world which for his sake might hate them."
116	Matt. 10:16-17	Allusion: "to toss them like lost sheep among ravenous wolves."
117	John 17:20-23	Reference: "he genuinely loved the disciples."
117	1 Cor. 7:33-35	Reference: "Love . . . by no means dares to be marital."
118	Matt. 10:22	Reference: "as a reward for his love he is hated by his beloved."
119	Eph. 2:12	Quote: "is without God in the world."
124	John 15:18-23	Reference: "Christian love is hated and detested and persecuted by the world."
124	1 Tim. 6:12	Reference: "Nevertheless he who fights the good fight to express that God is."
125	John 13:1	Reference: "has loved men and . . . continued to love them in spite of persecution and misjudgement."
126	Ps. 6:6*	Quote: "weary of sighing."
126	Tobit 3:11*	Quote: "so despondent that he wanted to hang himself."
130	Luke 6:26	Allusion: "give in to the suggestion of this false friendship, you will be loved and praised."
130	Jas. 4:4	Allusion: "the world by its upright friendship . . . will teach one to forget God."
136	1 Tim. 1:5	Text for discourse: "Love is a Matter of Conscience."
136	1 John 5:4	Reference: "the victory in which it has more than overcome the world."
137	1 Pet. 2:9	Reference: "Christians have been called a nation of priests."
139	Col. 3:18	Reference: "she shall be submissive to him."
139	John 18:36	Reference: "What Christ said about his kingdom that it is not of this world."
144	1 Tim. 3:9	Quote: "holds the mystery of faith."
145	2 Cor. 5:17	Allusion: "and thus make everything new."
145	Matt. 6:4	Allusion: "he sees in secret equally as well."
145	Matt. 26:53	Reference: "Christ . . . called the twelve legions of angels."
145	Luke 9:55	Reference: "he rebuked the apostles."
146	1 Cor. 8:4	Allusion: "that God is?—or that there is an idol—which nevertheless does not exist."
146	Rom. 12:20	Reference: "if someone loved his enemy—in order to heap coals of fire on his head."
148	Matt. 5:8	Allusion: "that heart must be bound to God."
153	1 John 4:20	Text for discourse: "Our Duty to Love Those We See." Returns to repeatedly throughout discourse.
153	Gen. 2:18	Quote: "God said that it is not good that the man be alone."
154	Matt. 14:14	Allusion: "He who loves the whole race."
154	Matt. 4:2	Reference: "he who had himself hungered in the wilderness."
154	John 21:15	Quote: "We read this in the Gospel of John: 'Jesus said to Simon Peter.'"
154	Matt. 3:14	Reference: "as when Christ would be baptized by John."
155	Matt. 26:34	Reference: "him who also denied three times."
155	Matt. 26:63	Reference: "He who did not have one word to answer the high priests."
155	Matt. 27:14	Reference: " . . . or to Pilate."
156	Jas. 5:9-10*	Quote: "one 'grumbles against' mankind."

207	Prov. 16:32	Allusion: "For it is more difficult to rule one's mind than to occupy a city."
207	Mark 4:27	Allusion: "While men sleep, the forces of nature do not sleep."
207	Luke 7:47	Allusion: "To him who loves much is much forgiven."
208	1 Cor. 13:4	Quote: "Love is patient."
208	Gal. 6:2	Reference: "does not bear the other person's burdens."
208	Gal. 6:5	Reference: "Each one bears his own burden."
209	1 Cor. 13:5-7	Quote: "Love does not insist on its own way."
209	Luke 15:22-24	Allusion: "Remember that the prodigal son's father was perhaps the only one."
210	1 Cor. 13:4*	Quote: "It is not jealous or boastful; it is not arrogant or rude."
213	1 Cor. 13:7	Text for discourse: "Love Believes All Things—and Yet Is Never Deceived."
213	1 Cor. 13:13	Quote: "So faith, hope, and love abide, these three; but the greatest of these is love."
220	Matt. 7:1	Quote: "lest you be judged."
220	Rom. 2:1	Allusion: "At the very moment you judge another person you judge yourself."
223	Luke 12:4	Reference: "One need not infinitely fear them who are able to kill the body."
223	Matt. 5:46-47	Allusion: "This view regards loving as a demand (reciprocated love is the demand)."
225	Luke 6:39	Allusion: "We are right in crying woe to one who leads the blind astray."
225	John 15:10	Reference: "the lover preserves himself in love, abides in love."
227	Matt. 5:42	Reference: "But someone who wishes to give away his money and does not demand it back."
228	2 Cor. 12:9	Reference: "the superior one also has the appearance of being the weaker?"
229	1 John 5:4	Reference: "for it overcomes the world!"
231	1 Cor. 13:7	Text for discourse: "Love Hopes All Things and Yet Is Never Put to Shame."
231	1 Cor. 15:58	Allusion: "an enlivening vision of a great expectation."
232	Luke 12:16-21	Allusion: "people gather stores full of what they reaped and rest upon earnings."
232	1 Cor. 15:42f	Reference: "parable of earthly life as sowing and eternity as the time of reaping."
232	1 Cor. 9:26	Allusion: "one who labors in vain and merely battles the air."
232	Matt. 25:31-46	Reference: "it shall be eternally decided who won the wreath of honour and who was put to shame."
233	John 16:33	Allusion: "Christianity's hope is the eternal and."
233	John 14:6	Reference: "Christ is the way."
233	Rom. 5:5	Allusion: "But love . . . takes hope upon itself as the work of hoping for others."
237	Mark 1:15	Allusion: "the eternal is continually near enough to be at hand."
240	Rom. 2:9	Allusion: "everything finally ends in wretchedness."
240	Matt. 5:21-22	Reference: "Even if one does not take murder upon his conscience."
245	Phil. 1:20*	Reference: "Scriptures speak of a hope which shall not be put to shame."
245	Luke 15:11-24	Reference: "If the prodigal son were dead in his sins."
247	1 Cor. 13:5	Text for discourse: "Love Seeks Not His Own."
247	Gen. 1:27	Reference: "he who created man in his image."
247	Matt. 5:48	Reference: "perfect as he is perfect and consequently attain unto the perfection which is God's own."
247	Matt. 19:17	Reference: "there is only one who is good, God, who gives all."
247	1 John 4:8	Reference: "since he is himself love."
250	1 Cor. 3:21	Quote: "As Paul says, 'All things are yours.'"
251	Matt. 10:39	Reference: "For he who loses his soul shall."

252	Matt. 6:28	Reference: "remember the beauty of the fields."
256	Matt. 6:2-4	Allusion: "benefaction is precisely the mode in which the only true benefaction is accomplished."
259	1 Cor. 3:9	Allusion: "If the lover in this respect has been God's co-labourer."
261	1 Pet. 4:8	Title for discourse: "Love Hides the Multiplicity of Sins."
261	1 John 4:18	Allusion: "people readily approach the lover, for he casts out fear."
262	1 John 4:18	Quote: "Love gives confidence in the day of judgement."
262	Judg. 14:14	Quote: "Out of the eater came forth meat."
263	Luke 7:47	Reference: "In Scriptures we read . . . many sins are forgiven one who loved much."
265	1 Cor. 14:20	Reference: "the apostolic injunction to be a babe in evil."
267	Matt. 27:12-14	Reference: "consider Christ in the moment when he was brought before the Sanhedrin."
268	Dan. 3:25	Reference: "the episode of the three men walking unscathed in the fiery furnace."
270	Matt. 6:13	Reference: "We pray in the Lord's Prayer that God will not lead into temptation."
273	2 Cor. 4:16f*	Reference: "faith always relates itself to what is not seen."
274	Isa. 38:17	Reference: "as Scriptures say of what God forgives, it is hidden behind his back."
275	Heb. 11:1-2	Reference: "Scriptures teach that faith is related to the unseen."
275	Gen. 4:10	Allusion: "a sin cries out for punishment."
276	Rom. 7:8	Reference: "Scriptures say that sin finds an opportunity in the commandment."
278	Matt. 18:7	Reference: "Woe unto the man by whom offence comes."
279	1 Cor. 13:13	Text for discourse: "Love Abides."
279	Rom. 8:38	Reference: "neither the present nor the future, neither angels nor devils."
280	1 John 4:16	Reference: "The lover abides; he abides in love, preserves himself in love."
292	Heb. 13:16	Quote: "Do not neglect to do good and to share."
292	Matt. 6:4	Allusion: "Christianity would last of all reward this mercilessness."
292	Jas. 5:9	Quote: "he must groan, in the Biblical sense, he must 'groan against'."
292	Matt. 23:14	Reference: "Woe unto him who devours the inheritance of widows and orphans."
293	1 Pet. 3:7	Quote: "'hinder our prayers,' as Scriptures."
293	Matt. 6:3	Reference: "whose left hand really does not know what the right hand is doing."
294	Luke 10:29-37	Reference: "If that man famous through eighteen hundred years, the merciful Samaritan."
294	Mark 12:41-44	Reference: "Take the story about the woman who placed the two pennies temple-treasury."
295	Luke 6:36	Allusion: "Because the world has understanding only for money—and Christ only for mercifulness."
296	Matt. 6:19-21	Reference: "nothing you can be so sure will never enter heaven as—money."
296	1 Thess. 2:9	Reference: "the Apostle Paul preferred to work with his own hands."
298	Eph. 5:2	Reference: "as Scripture says, a sweet scent in the nostrils of God."
299	Mark 12:41-44	Allusion: "For mercifulness works wonders; it makes two pennies into a great sum."
299	Luke 16:19-31	Reference: "It is told that Lazarus was laid full of sores."
300	Luke 10:29-37	Creative allusion: "Suppose that there was not one man who journeyed from Jericho."
304	Acts 3:1-8	Reference: "It is told of the apostle Peter that one day he went up to the temple."
306	Eph. 6:13	Quote: "And having overcome all, to stand."

307	Rom. 8:37	Reference: "Somewhere else Paul says that in faith we more than conquer."
308	Rom. 12:21	Allusion: "It is to triumph over evil with the good."
309	Matt. 5:23-24	Quote: "The words read, 'So if you are offering your gift . . . '"
310	Matt. 5:25	Quote: "Therefore the Scriptures say, 'Make friends quickly.'"
310	2 Cor. 5:20	Quote: "It is indeed God in heaven who through the apostle says, 'Be reconciled.'"
311	Luke 15:25-32	Creative allusion: "Let us suppose that the prodigal son's brothers had been willing."
315	Jas. 5:20	Allusion: "Certainly the lover desires to win this vanquished one."
315	2 Cor. 12:9	Allusion: "the strength must be in weakness."
317	Acts 17:26	Allusion: "That all men are blood-relatives."
319	Sirach 22:12	Quote: "Weep softly over one dead, for he has found rest."
320	Ps. 137:6	Quote: "If I forget thee, let my right hand forget its cunning."
320	Matt. 5:46-47	Reference: "the 'pagan' way, 'to love those who can make repayment.'"
323	Luke 18:1-8	Reference: "he does not besiege you as the widow did the Judge."
332	Matt. 10:39	Reference: "he must risk his life, a hazard which involves losing in order to win it."
333	John 5:19	Allusion: "you are able to do nothing at all."
333	Phil. 4:13	Reference: "if he is your support, you are able to do everything."
334	1 John 4:16	Reference: "for God is love."
335	John 5:19	Allusion: "he himself is capable of nothing."
336	Luke 17:7-10	Allusion: "makes himself nothing, an unprofitable servant."
337	2 Cor. 5:11	Quote: "Even an apostle says that he strives 'to win men.'"
337	1 Thess. 2:4-6	Quote: "So we speak, not to please men, but to please God."
338	Rom. 12:1	Reference: "Nothing is said any more of the highest, of being acceptable to God."
338	1 Cor. 4:10	Reference: "in our times all are the wise."
340	Jas. 4:4	Quote: "offended by the words, 'Love to God means hatred of the world.'"
343	Matt. 22:39	Reference: "true love is precisely love to one's neighbour."
344	Heb. 1:1	Quote: "we have tried 'in many times and in many ways' to praise love."
344	1 John 4:7	Quote: "John the apostle, saying: 'Beloved, let us love one another.'"
344	Matt. 22:39	Reference: "the commandment is that you shall love."
345	1 Cor. 1:23	Reference: "he was and is a stumbling block to the Jews, to the Greeks foolishness."
345	Ex. 21:24	Reference: "Christianity has abandoned . . . 'An eye for an eye, a tooth for a tooth'."
346	Matt. 8:5-13	Quote: "the centurion from Capernaum: 'Be it done for you, as you believed'."
348	Matt. 6:14	Quote: "It says, 'Forgive and you will also be forgiven.'"
349	Matt. 7:1-2	Reference: "Therefore to accuse another person before God is to accuse oneself."
350	Matt. 7:3	Quote: "Why do you see the speck that is in you brother's eye?"
352	Matt. 7:12	Reference: "what you do unto men you do unto God, and therefore what you do . . . God does unto you."
352	Jas. 1:17	Quote: "gratefully take wrongs from God's hand 'as a good and perfect gift,'."

Training in Christianity

Page	Passage	Type of Reference/Quote or Summary
9	Luke 19:10	Reference: "Saviour and Redeemer . . . out of love came to earth in order to seek the lost."
9	Acts 4:30	Reference: "to perform signs and wonders."
9	Matt. 11:16	Quote: "Blessed is he whosoever is not offended in Me."
10	Matt. 11:28-30	Quote: "Come hither to me, all ye that labor . . . I will give you rest."
13	John 1:1	Reference: "He is true to His word . . . He is the Word."
14	Matt. 20:15	Allusion: "O, man, why doth thine eye look only to its own?"
16	1 Cor. 14:8	Allusion: "Like the trumpet-call of the warrior which turns to all four quarters."
16	Luke 13:15	Allusion: "Ye who are . . . not even so much as for the beasts, which."
20	Matt. 12:20	Reference: "bruised reed He will not break."
20	Luke 15:11-24	Allusion: "When it is question of a sinner . . . as the father of the lost son waited."
20	Luke 15:3-7	Allusion: "as the shepherd sought the lost."
20	Luke 15:8-10	Allusion: "as the woman sought the lost coin."
21	Mark 9:17-27	Allusion: "Alas, that demoniac was not the only person possessed."
22	Matt. 6:17	Allusion: "come also with anointed head and a face newly washed."
26	Heb. 13:8	Reference: "Yes, He is the same yesterday and to-day."
26	Phil. 2:6-11	Reference: "humbled Himself and took the form of a servant."
31	John 8:42	Reference: "that He is who He said He was."
36	Matt. 20:28	Reference: "that He is who He said He was."
40	Matt. 11:6	Quote: "Blessed is he whosoever shall not be offended in me."
41	John 9:22	Allusion: "expulsion from the synogogue."
41	Matt. 11: 28-30	Quote: "Come hither . . . all ye that labour and are heavy laden."
42	Matt. 8:20	Quote: "has nowhere to lay his head."
42	John 19:5	Quote: "Behold the man!"
42	Matt. 9:3	Reference: "His whole generation was of the opinion that He 'blasphemed.'"
42	Luke 18:31-33	Reference: "They persecuted Him thus out of godly fear."
43	Matt. 26:67	Reference: "mocked and (as the Scripture adds) spat upon."
45	Matt. 20:28	Reference: "meant to be the servant of all."
46	Luke 3:23	Reference: "But He is already more than thirty years of age."
46	John 5:19	Reference: "And literally he is nothing."
47	Matt. 7:6	Reference: "He says not to cast your pearls before swine."
47	John 3:2	Reference: "If one could slyly visit Him by night and get that out of him."
49	Matt. 7:29	Reference: "The authority with which He is said to teach."
50	Matt. 9:16	Reference: "to what purpose His warning about putting a new piece of cloth upon an old garment?"
52	Matt. 14:16-21	Reference: "He continually repeats the miracle of the five small loaves."
55	John 3:2	Reference: "a man, who seriously sought Him out, and he came to Him by night."
57	John 7:6	Reference: "his time was not yet come."
57	Matt. 11:23-24	Reference: "had they been performed in Sodom and Gomorrah."
57	Luke 18:31-33	Allusion: "the Teacher is shunned, hated, despised."
58	John 9:22	Quote: "expelled from the synagogue."
58	Matt. 21:1-9	Allusion: "followed by such a train . . . surrounded by a shouting mob."
59	John 6:66	Allusion: "So the people fell away from Him."

66	1 Cor. 2:9	Quote: "to what has entered the heart of man."
67	Matt. 12:31*	Reference: "sin against the Holy Ghost."
69	Matt. 13:16	Quote: "Blessed are the eyes which see the things that ye see."
69	Phil. 2:6-11	Reference: "Christ humbled Himself and took upon Him the form of a servant."
69	Isa. 53:2	Quote: "there was 'nothing about Him for the eye, no glamour.'"
72	Matt. 7:13-14	Reference: "to enter by the narrow way, through the consciousness of sin, into Christianity."
79	John 6:68	Allusion: "blessed is the man who knows no other to go to."
80	1 John 5:4	Reference: "the victory that overcometh, for faith overcometh the world."
80	Matt. 10:28	Allusion: "fear not him who can kill the body, but fear thyself."
81	Acts 4:12	Reference: "no salvation for any but in Him."
82	John 14:6	Reference: "the Truth and the Life!"
82	Luke 19:41-48	Reference: "What suffering in His sorrow when He turned His eye."
82	Matt. 16:17	Quote: "'Blessed art thou, Simon'."
82	Luke 15:7	Allusion: "a conception of His joy over every believer."
82	John 21:15	Quote: "inquired of Peter, 'Lovest thou me?'"
86	Matt. 15:1-12	Quote of passage with extended exposition.
87	John 14:6	Reference: "believing for his own part that he is the truth."
93	Matt. 17:24-27	Quote of passage with extended exposition.
96	Matt. 11:2-10	Reference: "John the Baptist has sent from his prison messengers to Christ."
98	Luke 2:35	Allusion: "Christ came into the world that the thoughts of all hearts."
100	Heb. 12:2	Reference: "look at Jesus Christ, the author and finisher of faith."
100	John 6:51-68	Reference: "Christ says of Himself that He is the living bread."
102	John 6:33-62	Allusion: "only one who eats his body and drinks his blood."
103	Matt. 9:1-8	Quote: "Jesus says to the Pharisees, 'Wherefore think ye evil in you hearts?'"
103	Matt. 12:24	Quote: "This man doeth not cast out devils but by the prince."
103	Matt. 26:64-65	Quote: "Christ says, 'Hereafter shall ye see the Son of Man.'"
103	John 8:48-54	Reference: "the whole story about the man born blind."
103	John 10:20,30f	Reference (without comment).
105	Matt. 13:55	Quote: "Is not this the carpenter's son?"
105	John 7:27	Reference (without comment).
105	Matt. 26:31-33	Reference as illustrated the offense of the disciples at his lowliness.
106	Luke 22:31-34	Allusion: "When one talks of Peter's denial."
108	Matt. 10:24	Reference: "it appears that the disciple is not above the Master."
110	Matt. 13:21	Quote: "because of the word."
110	Matt. 5:10	Quote: "for righteousness' sake."
111	Matt. 19:27	Reference: "We read of the Apostles that they forsook all to follow Christ."
112	Matt. 18:8-9	Quote: "Wherefore, if thy hand or thy foot offend thee."
113	Matt. 19:12	Reference: "castrate thyself for the kingdom of heaven's sake."
113	Matt. 19:17-21	Quote: "To enter into life."
115	Matt. 13:20-21	Reference: "It is the parable about the different fate of the seeds."
117	Matt. 16:23-26	Reference: "Christ has spoken about what was in store for the Apostles."
120	Matt. 16:21-33	Quote: "Jesus began to show His disciples."
122	1 Cor. 4:13	Quote: "the refuse of the world."
124	Luke 2:34	Quote: "A 'sign of contradiction'."
126	Jas. 1:23-24	Allusion: "while one looks, one sees in a mirror, one gets to see one-self."
128	Matt. 16:17	Reference: "opposite of flesh and blood, which prompted Peter to recognize Him."
131	Phil. 2:6-11	Allusion: "that He became 'very man'."

134	John 10:30	Quote: "I am God, the Father and I are one."
134	1 Cor. 1:23	Reference: "He who to the Jews was a stumblingblock and to the Greeks foolishness."
135	John 3:16-18	Reference: "Christ said quite directly that He was the Only Begotten."
135	John 14:1	Quote: "Christ said, 'Believe in me'."
151	John 12:32*	Text for discourse, "And, I, if I be lifted up from the earth, will draw all men unto myself."
152	Jas. 1:17	Quote: "variableness or shadow of turning."
153	1 Cor. 11:24-25	Reference: "thou eatest bread and drinkest wine in remembrance of Him."
153	Phil. 2:6-11	Reference: "in the lowly form of a servant."
153	2 Cor. 8:9	Reference: "the poorest of all makes all men rich, both the rich and the poor."
154	1 Cor. 1:23	Reference: "to the Jews a stumblingblock."
154	John 14:6	Reference: "It is essential for 'the truth' to suffer in the world."
154	Ps. 34:12	Allusion: "Christendom's triumphant boast of 'seeing good days'."
155	John 5:17	Allusion: "but He works hitherto."
156	Luke 17:5	Quote: "Lord, increase my faith."
157	John 12:32	Text for discourse, "And I, if I be lifted."
160	John 14:6	Allusion: "Christ is the truth."
160	John 1:11	Reference: "in the strictest sense 'His own'."
161	Acts 1:9-10	Allusion: "His exaltation began with His ascension into heaven."
164	Matt. 17:17	Quote: "How long shall I suffer this generation?"
165	2 Pet. 3:8	Allusion: "the 1,800 years are as one day."
167	John 12:32	Text for discourse: "And I, if I be lifted."
167	John 1:1	Reference: "who from eternity was with God and was God."
167	John 17:5	Reference: "glorified with the glory which He had before the world."
167	Phil. 2:10-11	Reference: "whose name every knee shall bow."
167	Titus 2:13	Reference: "expecting His glorious appearing."
167	Matt. 1:19	Reference: "would have quietly deserted the despised virgin."
169	Matt. 26:6-13	Quote: "She hath kept this (i.e. the ointment) against the day of my burial."
169	John 6:15	Reference: "They would acclaim Him king."
169	Matt. 22:15-22	Quote: "Whose image is this that is stamped upon the coin?"
170	John 19:5	Quote: "Behold, what a man!"
175	Matt. 27:37	Quote: "written above His cross, 'The King of the Jews'."
177	Matt. 27:15-21	Quote: "as for the loving One, they cried, 'Crucify, crucify.'"
177	Matt. 26:53	Reference: "the Father would have sent Him legions of angels."
178	1 Cor. 2:2	Reference: "the Apostles . . . were resolved to know nothing save Christ and Him crucified."
180	John 12:47	Reference: "O Lord Jesus Christ, Thou who indeed did not come to judge."
180	John 12:32	Text for discourse: "And I, if I be lifted."
180	Matt. 22:14	Quote: "Many are called, but few are chosen."
180	Heb. 10:14	Reference: "He must Himself bring perfection."
180	Heb. 5:8	Reference: "by what He suffered—He learned obedience."
181	Phil. 2:8	Reference: "becoming obedient unto death, yes, the death of the cross."
181	Luke 2:7	Reference: "only in a stable was a place found for the tiny babe."
181	Heb. 12:2	Reference: "crucified like a malefactor—and then only did He ascend on high."
182	Phil. 2:9	Reference: "wherefore also God hath highly exalted Him."
184	John 16:12	Reference: "He had still much to say unto them, but did not say it because they were not able."
188	Mark 10:21	Reference: "Christ was well pleased with the rich young man."
189	1 Pet. 1:7	Reference: "heat the oven in which like gold he is to be tried."

189	1 Cor. 10:13	Reference: "and never tempts him beyond his capacity to bear."
190	Matt. 18: 3	Reference: "To enter the kingdom of heaven one must become again a little child."
192	Matt. 26:72	Quote: "I know him not!"
193	Mark 15:34	Reference: "but it had never occurred to Him that He might be deserted by God."
193	Heb. 10:37	Quote: "'Yet a little while'."
197	John 18:36-38	Reference: "Thy kingdom indeed was not of this world and is not."
197	John 12:32	Text for discourse: "And I, if I be lifted."
200	John 19:5	Quote: "Look, what a man!"
202	John 17:3	Quote: "This is life eternal, to know the only true God."
202	John 6:51	Reference: "Christ compares truth with food, and the appropriation of it with eating."
206	John 18:36-38	Reference: "What Christ said about His kingdom not being of this world."
208	Matt. 16:24	Reference: "There stands Christianity with its requirement of self-denial: 'Deny thyself.'"
213	Matt. 26:52	Reference: "Put up thy sword, therefore, into its sheath."
215	Luke 2:35	Allusion: "the thoughts of many hearts will be revealed."
217	Mark 13:10	Reference: "Christianity's will that it be preached before all."
218	Matt. 7:13-14	Allusion: "The way of life is no longer strait and narrow."
218	Matt. 16:18	Allusion: "the gates of hell have prevailed."
218	Jas. 4:4	Allusion: "the day when Christianity and the world become friends."
219	Matt. 10:24	Reference: "untreated as untruth the saying that the disciple is not above his master."
220	Matt. 7:13-14	Reference: "the gate of life, in spite of Christ's saying, is not narrow."
223	1 Cor. 3:18	Quote: "'becoming a fool in this world'."
225	Luke 23:34	Allusion: "They who defend Christianity know what they do."
227	Mark 10:45	Reference: "Thou didst not come to the world to be served."
227	John 14:6	Reference: "Thou wast the way and the truth."
227	John 12:32	Text for discourse: "And I, if I be lifted."
231	John 14:6	Reference: "declared Himself to be, namely, the way, the truth."
235	Deut. 5:21	Reference: "for, as the Scripture says, thou shalt not covet."
240	John 3:1-5	Reference: "it was Nicodemus."
242	Matt. 19:22	Allusion: "the rich young man might have been eligible."
242	Matt. 8:21-22	Allusion: "that man might be eligible who merely wanted first to bury his father."
244	Matt. 26:33	Allusion: "in case all were to fall away."
244	Matt. 23:29-33	Allusion: "the men who built the tombs of the Prophets."
248	Matt. 27:5	Allusion: "as Judas did the thirty pieces of silver, casting them far, far away from him."
249	Rev. 3:15	Allusion: "if one cannot say of him that he is lukewarm."
251	John 12:32	Text for discourse, "And I, if I be lifted."
251	John 12:33	Quote: "This He said . . . signifying what death He should die."
252	1 Thess. 4:11	Quote: "'seek for honour by living quietly'."
261	Luke 7: 36-50	Text for discourse: "The Woman That Was A Sinner."
261	Luke 1:38	Quote: "'Behold the handmaid of the Lord'."
261	Luke 2:35	Reference: "for it is true that the sword pierced through her heart."
261	Luke 10:38-42	Allusion: "From a woman thou doest learn concern for the one thing needful."
264	John 11:4	Allusion: "a mortal sickness which yet is very far from being unto death."
267	Matt. 6:16-18	Quote: "When thou fastest, anoint thy head."
267	Mark 14:3-9	Reference: "she takes with her an alabaster cruise of ointment."
269	Prov. 16:32	Reference: "Verily he that subdueth himself is greater than he that taketh a city."

271   John 15:13   Allusion: "No love is greater than this."

Attack upon *"Christendom"*

Page	Passage	Type of Reference/Quote or Summary
5	Acts 1:8	Allusion: "witness to the truth."
7	1 Cor. 4:13	Reference: "the 'filth' (which the Apostle says he was)."
17	Matt. 10:34	Quote: "I came not to bring peace but dissension."
18f	Matt.8:20	Allusion: "Jesus Christ (the poor . . .)"
18f	Matt. 27:29	Allusion: Jesus Christ "(. . . mocked and spat upon)"
20	Matt. 4:29	Quote: "Follow me."
20	John 18:36	Quote: "my kingdom is not of this world."
20	2 Cor. 11:23f	Reference: "suffering for the doctrine, suffering hunger and thirst and cold and."
21	Acts 24:15	Reference: "So the 'way' has now become a different one."
21	Heb. 13:7	Quote: "Remember those who had the rule over you."
21	Luke 16:15	Quote: "What is exalted among men is an abomination in the sight of God."
24	Acts 7:59	Reference: "the feast of the martyr Stephen."
24	Mark 13:2	Text for article: "Seest thou these great buildings?"
27	1 Cor. 9:26	Quote: "not to run uncertainly."
27	Mark 12:38	Quote: "Beware of those who go about in long robes."
27	Matt. 10:32	Quote: "Confess me before the world."
27	Matt. 8:21-23	Quote: "Follow me."
27	Matt. 11:28	Quote: "Come unto me."
33	Mark 9:47-50	Text for article: "Salt."
34	Matt. 8:21-23	Reference: "Christ required 'followers'."
34	Matt. 16:24	Reference: "Christ talks about: cross and agony and suffering."
35	John 14:3	Reference: "but predicted his coming again."
35	Luke 18:8	Quote: "When the Son of Man cometh, will He find faith on earth?"
36	Matt. 27:6	Reference: "For it was blood-money Judas received for Christ's blood."
41	Luke 12:49	Quote: "I am come to set fire on the earth."
46	Luke 18:8	Quote: "When the Son of Man cometh, shall He find faith on the earth?"
58	Matt. 25:6	Quote: "But at midnight there is a cry."
100	Matt. 7:14	Quote: "Narrow is the gate and strait."
105	Matt. 7:13-14	Reference: "The way that leadeth unto life is straitened."
106	Gen. 30:37-45	Allusion: "in order to get speckled lambs he laid speckled rods."
106	Luke 18:8	Quote: "When I come again, shall I find faith on the earth?"
108	Matt. 6:2-4	Reference: "we are warned against hypocrisy."
108	Eph. 2:9	Reference: "against presumptuous reliance upon good works."
120	Matt. 23:29-33	Text for article: "Christ's Judgement."
123	Matt. 23:29-33	Reference: "better than those who killed the prophets."
123	Matt. 12:34	Quote: "them who 'walk in long robes'."
123	Matt. 21:13*	Reference: "whip of small cords and drive them out of the temple."
123	Matt. 3:7	Quote: "Ye hypocrites, ye serpents, ye generation of vipers."
123	Matt. 22:33	Allusion: "prepared for thee to be shocked at me."
123	Mark 12:38	Reference: "putting words into His mouth: serpents, generation of vipers."
158	1 John 4:8	Reference: "the declaration that God is love."
174	Mark 12:38	Text for pamphlet: "Beware of they that walk in long robes."
181	1 Cor. 1:28	Quote: "God hath elected the base things of the world."
182	Matt. 19:21	Quote: "Sell all that thou hast, and give it to the poor."
188	Matt. 10:28	Reference: "not to fear those who are able to kill the body."
192	Mark 16:17-18	Quote: "In my name they shall cast out devils."

203	Matt. 4:19	Text for article: "Fishers of Men."
208	Matt. 6:33	Reference: "it is the kingdom of God, which indeed one must seek first!"
208	Luke 23:6-12*	Allusion: "he runs from Herod to Pilate."
219	1 Cor. 7:1-8	Reference: "Such an important step as marriage . . . God advises against."
219	Ex. 20:13	Quote: "Thou shalt not kill."
220	1 Cor. 7:9	Quote: "it is better to marry than to burn."
222	Matt. 23:13	Quote: "'Woe unto you,' says Christ to the 'lawyers'."
222	Luke 11:52	Quote: "them that were entering ye hindered."
229	1 Pet. 2:11	Quote: "We are strangers and pilgrims in this world."
239	Matt. 10:41-42	Text for article: "Contemporaneousness."
245	1 John 4:8	Quote: "God is love."
250	1 Cor. 15:19	Quote: "If in this life only we have hope, we are of all men most pitiable."
260	Gal. 6:7	Quote: "Be not deceived, God will not suffer Himself to be mocked."
277	John 5:44	Text for article: "How can ye believe who receive honor?"

Notes

Chapter 1

1. Jarslaov Pelikan, *From Luther to Kierkegaard: A Study in the History of Theology* (St. Louis: Concordia, 1967), 114.

2. Karl Barth, "A Thank You and a Bow: Kierkegaard's Reveille," *Canadian Journal of Theology 11* (1965), 5. Barth also praised the theologians who "read Kierkegaard and went through his school . . . . to attend schools other than that of Kierkegaard." Cf. Barth, "Kierkegaard and the Theologians," *Canadian Journal of Theology 13* (1967), 65.

3. Emil Brunner, *Truth as Encounter* (Philadelphia: Westminster, 1964), 112.

4. Brita K. Stendahl, *Søren Kierkegaard* (Boston: Twayne Publishers, 1976), 19.

5. Hannay reflects on some of the conflicting assessments of Kierkegaard. On the one hand, he cites William Heinesen, "Kierkegaard is the dire sufferer of his own satanism. He is, one might say, the tragic satan." On the other hand, Hannay cites Wittgenstein, "Kierkegaard was by far the most profound thinker of the last century. Kierkegaard was a saint." Alastair Hannay, *Kierkegaard* (London: Routledge, Kegan and Paul, 1983), ix. Some critics reject any claim that Kierkegaard was a philosopher. Analytical philosophy routinely dismisses Kierkegaard and existentialism as "little more than a literary movement." J. C. A. Gaskin, *The Quest for Eternity* (New York: Penguin Books, 1984), 13.

6. *On Authority*, 5.

7. Cf. *Training* and *Attack*.

8. For example, contrast the idealized, almost worshipful work by Walter Lowrie, *Kierkegaard* (New York: Harper, 1962) and the critical and creative interpretation by Josiah Thompson, *Kierkegaard* (London: Victor Gollancz, 1974).

9. John William Angell, "The Theological Methodology of Søren Kierkegaard" (Th. D. dissertation, The Southern Baptist Theological Seminary, 1949), 3.

10. Stendahl, *Kierkegaard*, 48.

11. Ibid., 17.

12. S. K. said, "Every time a witness for the truth makes the truth a heart-felt matter of inwardness . . . the established order will be offended in him." *Training*, 88.

13. *Journals and Papers*, V, 310, no. 5874.

14. Ibid., 243, no. 5690.

15. As cited by E. Skjoldager, "The Family," BK (1983), XII, p. 13. Cf. *Journals and Papers*, V, 472, no. 109.

16. Stendahl, *Kierkegaard*, 48. There is some psychoanalytic support for the theory that S. K.'s expressed love for his father was in reality a repressed hatred and that he suffered from an Oedipus complex complicated his relationship to Regina. See Henning Fenger, Kierkegaard, *The Myths and Their Origins*, trans. G. C. Schoolfield (New Haven: Yale University Press, 1980), 69.

17. *Point of View*, 76.

18. *Training*, 190.

19. Thompson, *Kierkegaard*, 204.

20. *Journals and Papers*, VI, 145-146, no. 6389.

21. Thompson, *Kierkegaard*, 40.

22. As cited by Stendahl, *Kierkegaard*, 51.

23. *Journals and Papers*, V, 334, no. 5913.

24. Ibid., VI, 84, no. 6298.

25. Ibid., V, 120, no. 5328.

26. Ibid., 140-141, no. 5430. Lowrie saw "Quidam's Diary," incorporated in *Stages*, as autobiographical, particularly the section entitled "Solomon's Dream." Cf. Lowrie, *Kierkegaard*, 69f.

27. *Journals and Papers*, 122, no. 5335.

28. *Point of View*, 82.

29. Ibid., 83f.

30. *Journals and Papers*, VI, 191-92, no. 6472.

31. Ibid., 193.   32. Ibid., 194.   33. Ibid., 194-95.

34. Thompson, *Kierkegaard*, 105.

35. Stendahl, *Kierkegaard*, 55.

36. Alexander Dru, ed. and trans. *The Journals of Søren Kierkegaard*, a Selection (London: Oxford University Press, 1938), xxxviii.

37. Stendahl, *Kierkegaard*, 59.

38. *Point of View*, 79.

39. Cf. Miss Hanna Mourier's letter to Regina Schlegel indicating her recollection of Regina's conversation with her. As cited in "Regina," BK (1983), XII, 38.

40. *Either/Or*, February 20, 1843; *Two Edifying Discourses*, May 16, 1843, *Repetition, Fear and Trembling*, and *Three Edifying Discourses*, October 16, 1843; *Four Edifying Discourses*, December 6, 1843; *Two Edifying Discourses*, March 5, 1844; *Three Edifying Discourses*, June 8, 1844; *Philosophical Fragments*, June 13, 1844; *The Concept of Anxiety*, and *Prefaces*, June 17, 1844; *Four Edifying Discourses*, August 31, 1844; *Three Edifying Discourses on Imagined Occasions*, April 29, 1845; *Stages on Life's Way*, April 30, 1845; *Concluding Scientific Postscript*, February 27, 1846; *A Literary Review*, March 30, 1846; *Edifying Discourses in Various Spirits*, March 13, 1847; *Works of Love*, September 29, 1847; *Christian Discourses*, April 26, 1848; *The Crisis and a Crisis in the Life of an Actress*, July 24-27, 1848.

41. S. K. stated that "'The Seducer's Diary' was intended to repulse." *Journals and Papers*, VI, 196, no. 6472.

42. Sent to her husband to be forwarded to Regina, a request he gave a "polite, but decided refusal." "Regina," 38.

43. Ibid.

44. Stendahl, *Kierkegaard*, 61.

45. *Journals and Papers*, VI, 203, no. 6473.

46. Ibid., V, p. 310, no. 5873.

47. *Stendahl*, n. 17, 217.

48. Elias Bredsdorff, "The Corsair," BK (1983), XII, 129.

49. *Journals and Papers*, VI, 316, no. 6621.

50. Lowrie, *Kierkegaard*, 91.

51. *Journal and Papers*, I, 343, no. 737.

52. *Journals and Papers*, V, 300, no. 5860-5862.

53. As cited by Bredsdorff, "The Corsair," 138.

54. *Journals and Papers*, V, 316, no. 5887.

55. Ibid., 301, no. 5863.   56. Ibid.   57. Ibid., VI, 386, no. 6013.

58. As cited by Bredsdorff, "The Corsair," 139.

59. As cited in *Journals and Papers*, V, 544, no. 1529. Bredsdorff pointed out that Goldschmidt's recollections were written years after the fact (1877) and that he probably was attempting some self-justification with the then recent publication of Kierkegaard's papers. See Bredsdorff, "The Corsair," 142.

60. Thompson, *Kierkegaard*, 192.

61. *Journals and Papers*, VI, 125, no. 6356.

62. Ibid.

63. Stendahl, *Kierkegaard*, 66.

64. *Point of View*, 58.

65. Hakom Stangerup, "His Polemic with the Press," BK (1983), XII, 125.

66. *Journals and Papers*, V, 443, no. 6131-6132.

67. Dru, *Journals*, 11; Lowrie, *Kierkegaard*, 392f. However, Thompson was more skeptical of the significance of this event.

68. *Journals and Papers*, V, 445, no. 6133.

69. *The Lilies of the Fields* and the *Birds of the Air*, May 14, 1849; *Two Minor Ethico-Religious Treatises*, May 19, 1849; *The Sickness Unto Death*, July 30, 1849; *Three Discourses at Communion on Fridays*, November 13, 1849; *Training in Christianity*, September 27, 1850; *Two Edifying Discourses at the Communion on Fridays*, 1851; *For Self-Examination*, September 10, 1851; and *Judge for Yourself*, 1851-52, (published posthumously).

70. *Self-Examination*, 39f.

71. Ibid., 56.

72. *Journals and Papers*, VI, 491, no. 6853.

73. David F. Swenson, *Something About Kierkegaard* (Minneapolis: Augsburg, 1945), 23.

74. Thompson, *Kierkegaard*, 222. Thompson contends that Kierkegaard may also have waited until the fall of the conservative government in order to avoid a trial under Danish laws prohibiting the ridicule of established religion. Although S. K. did publish after a more lenient regime was in power, part of his reason for delay was the collection of a memorial fund in honor of Mynster.

75. Cf. *Attack*.

76. Ibid., 32.   77. Ibid., 37-38.   78. Ibid., 287-88.

79. Cf. Thompson, *Kierkegaard*, xiii. For various theories surrounding the cause of Kierkegaard's death see "His Death" by R. J. Widenmann and C. Jorgensen, BK (1983), XII, 176-187, and "Kierkegaard in the Doctor's Office," chapter 3 of *Kierkegaard, The Myths and Their Origins*, 62-80.

Chapter 2

1. Immanuel Kant, *Critique of Pure Reason*, trans. N. K. Smith (London: Macmillan, 1923), 7f.

2. Kant was convinced that a priori-synthetic knowledge, based on the categories of the understanding, provides a thorough and final answer to the problems raised by Hume. Cf. David Hume, "On Causation," in *An Enquiry Concerning Human Understanding*, ed. L. A. Selby-Bigge (Oxford: Clarendon Press, 1894).

3. Immanuel Kant, *Critique of Practical Reason*, trans. L. W. Beck (Indianapolis: Bobbs-Merrill, 1956), 126f.

4. Ibid., 43.

5. Ibid., 127.

6. Immanuel Kant, *Religion Within the Bounds of Reason Alone*, trans. T. M. Greene and H. H. Hudson (Chicago: Open Court, 1934), 5.

7. Allen W. Wood, *Kant's Moral Religion* (Ithaca, N. Y.: Cornell University Press, 1970), 14. Cf. also, R. E. Friedman, "Kant and Kierkegaard: The Limits of Reason and the Cunning of Faith," *International Journal of the Philosophy of Religion*, 19 (1986), 3-22.

8. *Journals and Papers*, II, 515, no. 2236. Although it is true that S. K. "showed no overwhelming interest in Kant" and drew more from "Socrates, Hamann, and Lessing," his epistemology is clearly neo-Kantian. Niels Thulstrup, "Theological and Philosophical Studies," *BK* (1978), I, 56. Cf. Robert L. Perkins, "Kierkegaard's Epistemological Preferences," *International Journal of Philosophy of Religion* 4 (1973), 197-217.

9. Jerry Gill, "Kantianism," BK (1981), VI, 223.

10. Hong and Hong refer to Kierkegaard's "critical observations on Kant's thought at three points" and refer to epistemology, radical evil, and ethics as

points of disagreement. However, for the present discussion, "radical evil" is not a major issue. Cf. *Journals and Papers*, II, 611. Kant's concept of the beautiful as "disinterested satisfaction" is also in agreement with S. K.'s own conception of the aesthetic; however, this is not significant for the present discussion.

11. Gill, "Kantianism," 228.

12. *Irony*, 138-39.

13. *Journals and Papers*, II, 515, no. 2235. Hegel's mistake was, according to S. K., greater. Kant's skepticism regarding thought is answered (in Hegel) by "thinking through." Cf. *Postscript*, 292.

14. Gill suggested that "it can be argued that SK himself did not affirm an irrationalist posture," noting that the "leap" is advocated by Johannes de Silentio and Johannes Climacus, the ironic persona in Kierkegaard's "indirect communication." Gill, "Kantianism," 228. Gill presses this interpretation of S. K.'s pseudonyms to argue that Kierkegaard is really a mediating position between objectivity and irrationalism, an ally of what Gill describes as "post-critical philosophy." Cf. Gill, *On Knowing God* (Philadelphia: Westminster, 1981), 106-09.

15. George Schrader, "Kant and Kierkegaard On Duty and Inclination," *Kierkegaard: A Collection of Critical Essays*, ed. J. Thompson (New York: Doubleday, 1972), 324f.

16. Cf. *Either/Or*, II.

17. Cf. *Purity*.

18. Thus, duty to God supersedes duty to others, as illustrated by Abraham being called of God to kill his son Isaac. *Fear*, 77.

19. *Postscript*, Book Two, Part One, 59-114.

20. *Fragments*, title page. S. K. actually misquoted Lessing's dictum substituting "eternal" for "necessary." Cf. *Postscript*, 86. See Claus v. Bormann, "Lessing," *BK* (1982), X, 137. S. K. dealt with Lessing's thought in broad outline and appears to have been based upon the writings of D. F. Strauss, according to Bormann.

21. *Concluding Unscientific Postscript*, 540.

22. Henry Chadwick, "Lessing, Gotthold Ephraim" *Encyclopedia of Philosophy* (Reprint ed.), III & IV, 445.

23. Ibid.

24. *Postscript*, 31.

25. Ibid., 55.

26. Bormann, "Lessing," 142f.

27. See Chapter Three and Four of this study. An excellent study of the significance of "paradox" in Kierkegaard's thought is found in Leroy Kay Seat, "The Meaning of 'Paradox': A Study of the Use of the Word 'Paradox' in Contemporary Theological and Philosophical Writings with Special Reference to Søren Kierkegaard" (Th.D. dissertation, The Southern Baptist Theological Seminary, 1966).

28. Bormann, "Lessing," 156.

29. G. W. F. Hegel, *Science of Logic*, trans. W. H. Johnston and L. G. Struthers (New York: MacMillan, 1929), 55. Hegel's *Science of Logic* is generally acknowledged to be the cornerstone of his idealistic thought. Hereafter referred to simply as *Logic*. A shorter and more understandable version of the *Logic* is found in his *Encyclopedia of Philosophy*.

30. Ibid, 33. Hegel sought to move beyond a narrow view of understand (*Verstand*) that is content to expose theoretical opposites. Reason (*Vernunft*) is more inclusive and incorporates speculative thought and intuition.

31. Ibid, 94. The *Logic* moves from the Doctrine of Being to the Doctrine of Essence to the Doctrine of Notion or Concept (*Begriff*).

32. Ibid.

33. G. W. F. Hegel, *Encyclopedia of Philosophy*, trans. by G. E. Mueller (New York: Philosophical Library, 1959), 87. Hereafter referred to as *Encyclopedia*.

34. Ibid.

35. Ibid.

36. Ibid., 117.

37. Ibid., 133. "Concept," said Hegel, is "the essence of personality."

38. Quentin Lauer, *Hegel's Concept of God* (Albany, N.Y.: SUNY, 1982), 81.

39· Quentin Lauer, *Hegel's Idea of Philosophy* (New York: Fordham University Press, 1971), 3.

40. G. W. F. Hegel, *The Phenomenology of the Mind*, Rev. ed. trans. by J.B. Ballie (New York: MacMillan, 1931), 81. Hereafter referred to as *Phenomenology*.

41. Ibid., 89.

42. Cf. Walter Kaufmann, *Hegel: A Reinterpretation* (Notre Dame: University of Notre Dame Press, 1978), 236f.

43. Ibid., 298.

44. Ibid.

45. G. W. F. Hegel, *Reason in History*, trans. by R. S. Hartman (New York: Liberal Arts Press, 1953), 20. Much has been made of Hegel's doctrine of the state, especially by Marxists and Nietzsche, and others. However, he appears to argue for "states" and not a unified world order. Hegel's philosophy of history has been virtually ignored by most historians. Cf. W. H. Walsh, *An Introduction to Philosophy of History* (London: Hutcheson, 1951).

46. Kaufmann noted that Hegel did not start from the *Critique of Pure Reason* but with Kant's *Religion Within the Bounds of Mere Reason Alone* (1793). See W. Kaufmann, *Discovering the Mind* (New York: McGraw-Hill, 1980), I, 204.

47. As cited by Raymond K. Williamson, *Introduction to Hegel's Philosophy of Religion* (Albany, N.Y.: SUNY Press, 1984, 21.

48. Cf. George S. Hendry, "Theological Evaluation of Hegel," *Scottish Journal of Theology*, 34 (1982), 344.

49. As translated by Robert L. Perkins, "Hegel and the Secularization of Religion," *The International Journal for Philosophy of Religion* 1 (1970), 137.

50. G. W. F. Hegel, *Lectures in the Philosophy of Religion*, trans. E. B. Spears and J. Burdon (London: Routledge & Keagan Paul, 1962), III, 2f.

51. Ibid., 3.   52. Ibid.

53. Thulstrup has provided the definitive work tracing the extent to which S. K.'s knowledge is dependent on the Danish Hegelians and to what extent S. K. had studied the system for himself. He argues that S. K. and Hegel had completely different purposes, therefore S. K.'s authorship is the "radical cure" for speculation, and that he has an accurate knowledge of Hegel on points he was interested in attacking. Cf. Niels Thulstrup, *Kierkegaard's Relation to Hegel*, trans. G. L. Stengren (Princeton: Princeton University Press, 1980), 12-13. Also see N. Thulstrup's two-part article on "Kierkegaard and Hegel," *BK* (1979), IV, 52-113. Hannay focuses on the "unhappy consciousness" as a common ground between S. K. and Hegel with the former only differing with the latter as to the nature of the dialectic. See Alastair Hannay, *Kierkegaard* (London: Routledge, Kegan and Paul, 1983), 19f.

54. *Journals and Papers*, II, 221, no. 1608.

55. *Postscript*, 55.

56. Ibid., 70-71.

57. *Journals and Papers*, II, 210, no. 1578.

58. *Fear*, 121-122.

59. *Journals and Papers*, II, 222, no. 1611.

60. *Postscripts*, 119. Hegel, said Kierkegaard, made "the state the court of last resort." Ibid., 450.

61. Ibid., 521.

62. Ibid., 308.

63. Neils Thulstrup, "Kierkegaard's Approach to Existence versus Hegelian Speculation," Part II of "Kierkegaard and Hegel," *BK* (1979), IV, 112.

64. Lowrie divides Kierkegaard's polemic against the Church into an attack upon the State Church of Denmark and upon what Kierkegaard called "dei *Bestaaende*" or the "existing Church, Christianity in its all too established form." See Walter Lowrie, *Kierkegaard* (New York: Harper, 1962), 427.

65. Niels Thulstrup, "Theological and Philosophical Studies," *BK* (1978), I, 42.

66. *Journals and Papers*, III, 64, no. 2463.

67. Ibid., V, 21, no. 5092. This is a reference to the moderate rationalism represented by H. N. Clausen.

68. G. Tolderlund-Hansen, "History of the Danish Church," *The Danish Church*, ed. Poul Hartling and trans. S. Mammen (Copenhagen: J. Jorgensen & Co., 1964), 53-55. Hereafter referred to as "History."

69. John A. Bain, *Søren Kierkegaard: His Life and Religious Teaching* (London: SAM, 1935), 15-21.

70. Tolderlund-Hansen, "History," 60.

71. Ibid.

72. Bain, *Kierkegaard*, 16.

73. Neils Thulstrup, "H. N. Clausen," *BK* (1982), X, 161.

74. Ibid.   75. Ibid., 166.

76. Tolderlund-Hansen, "History," 64.

77. Ibid.

78. Bain, *Kierkegaard*, 21.

79. *Journals and Papers*, V, 440, no. 6122.

80. Ibid., VI, 384, no. 6733.

81. Ibid.

82. Cf. Chapter 1, 26f.

83. Tolderlund-Hansen, "History," 62. Thulstrup states that "Mynster arrived in the summer of 1803 at a decisive turning-point in his spiritual development. First of all he gained a firm conviction of the unconditional validity of conscience, from which flowed a resignation towards all desires for earthly happiness and honour, and secondly, he attained faith in the truth of the Gospel accounts and hence a belief in Christ as the redeemer of each individual person." Neils Thulstrup, "Mynster," *BK* (1982), X, 21.

84. Ibid., 29.   85. Ibid., 30.   86. Ibid., 32.

87. Jarslaov Pelikan, *From Luther to Kierkegaard: A Study in the History of Theology* (St. Louis: Concordia, 1967), 114.

88. J. H. Schjorring, "Martensen," *BK* (1982), X, 185.

89. Ibid.

90. Hannay, *Kierkegaard*, 94.

91. *Journals and Papers*, V, 81, no. 5181.

92. *Postscript*, 262.

93. *Fragments*, 137-38.

94. *Journals and Papers*, I, 329, no. 705.

95. *Fragments*, 139.

96. *Journals and Papers*, II, 226-27, no. 1619.

97. K. Grobel, "Biblical Criticism," *The Interpreter's Dictionary of the Bible*, ed. G. A. Buttrick (Nashville: Abingdon Press, 1962), I, 408-10.

98. Ibid., 411-412.

99. F. F. Bruce, "The History of New Testament Study," *New Testament Interpretation*, ed. I. H. Marshall (Grand Rapids: Eerdmans, 1977), 39.

100. Ibid., 40.

101. Schweitzer divides the nineteenth-century quest into "before Strauss . . . after Strauss." See Albert Schweitzer, *The Quest of the Historical Jesus*, trans. W. Montgomery (New York: Macmillan, 1961), 10.

102. *Journals and Papers*, II, 234, nos. 1641 & 1642.

103. Schweitzer, *Quest*, 309.

104. Herbert C. Wolf, "Kierkegaard and the Quest for the Historical Jesus" *The Lutheran Quarterly* 16 (1964), 3. Wolf has suggested that this is because S. K. was not discovered as a biblical exegete until the twentieth century. Yet, more recent historical summaries also exclude mention of S. K. Cf. F. F. Bruce, "The History of New Testament Study," while clearly unsympathetic to the negative conclusions of the early "quest" Bruce ignored the ready ally biblical scholarship has in the work of S. K.

105. A. Richardson and W. Schweitzer, *Biblical Authority for Today* (London: SCM, 1951), 149. For a recent discussion of S. K.'s significance for biblical scholarship see Janet Forsythe Fishburn, "Søren Kierkegaard, Exegete," *Interpretation*, 39 (1985), 229-245.

106. *Stages*, 218.

107. J. Pedersen, "Kierkegaard's View of Scripture," *BK* (1978), II, 27.

108. Paul S. Minear and Paul S. Morimoto, *Kierkegaard and the Bible—An Index* (Princeton: Princeton Theological Seminary, 1953), 3.

109. *Journals and Papers*, I, 87, no. 216.

110. Endel Kallas, "Kierkegaard's Understanding of the Bible with Respect to His 'Age'," *Dialogue* 26 (1987), 30.

111. *Postscript*, 24f.

112. Ibid., 27.

113. Ibid., 28.

114. *Journals and Papers*, III, 275, no. 2877.

115. *Postscript*, 26.

116. *Journals and Papers*, I, 83, no. 202.

117. Ibid., 85, no. 210.

118. Fishburn, "Søren Kierkegaard, Exegete," 232. Lowrie refers to J. P. Ruckett whose commentaries on Ephesians and Philippians were published in 1833 and 1834 and urged that the exegete should stand with Paul in order to understand his message as having an influence on S. K. See Walter Lowrie, *Kierkegaard*, 53.

119. J. Pedersen, "Kierkegaard's View of Scripture," 41-42.

120. *Journals and Papers*, I, 83-84, no. 205.

121. Ibid, 86, no. 213.

122. *Crucial Situations*, 38.

123. *On Authority*, 167.

124. Ibid., 166.

125. "Second Preface," Ibid., xvi.

126. Ibid., p. xv. Cavell has suggested that this is not an apologetic effort but an effort at "re-providing . . . meaning." See Stanley Cavell, "Kierkegaard's On Authority and Revelation," in *Kierkegaard: A Collection of Critical Essays*, ed. J. Thompson (New York: Anchor Books, 1972), 377.

127. *On Authority*, (Doubleday), xviii.

128. Ibid., 15. 129. Ibid., 20-21. 130. Ibid., 24-26. 131. Ibid., 26. 132. Ibid. 133. Ibid. 134. Ibid., 27. 135. Ibid., 104. 136. Ibid., 44. 137. Ibid., 67.

138. Ibid., 103f. Published as an essay "The Difference Between a Genius and an Apostle."

139. *On Authority*, 105.

140. Ibid., 108-09.

141. Ibid., 58.

142. Ibid., 59.

143. Ibid., 113.

144. Joe R. Jones, "Some Remarks on Authority and Revelation in Kierkegaard," *The Journal of Religion* (July, 1977), 245.

145. Ibid., 246.

146. Josiah Thompson, *Kierkegaard* (London: Victor Gollanez, 1974), 121.

147. Lowrie, *Kierkegaard*, 284-90.

148. Brita K. Stendahl, *Søren Kierkegaard* (Boston: Twayne Publishers, 1976), 20.

149. Reidar Thomte, *Kierkegaard's Philosophy of Religion* (Westport, Conn.: Greenwood Press, 1948), 15.

150. Paul Sponheim, *Kierkegaard On Christ and Christian Coherence* (London: SCM, 1968), 42.

151. James Collins, *The Mind of Kierkegaard* (Princeton: Princeton University Press, 1983 edition), 35.

152. Ibid, 35-41.

153. *Postscript*, 551.

154. *Point of View*, 5.

155. Ibid.

156. Ibid., 6.

157. Ibid., 12.

158. Ibid.

159. Stephen Crities, "Pseudonymous Authorship as Art and As Act," in *Kierkegaard: A Collection of Critical Essays*, ed. J. Thompson (New York: Doubleday, 1972), 184.

160. *Postscript*, 261.

161. Collins, *Mind*, 43.

162. *Point of View*, 31.

163. These works are discussed more fully in Chapter Three.

164. Thomte, *Kierkegaard's Philosophy of Religion*, 36.

165. *Postscript*, 261f.

166. *Point of View*, 31.

167. Ibid., 35.

168. Ibid., 39.

169. Ibid., 40-41.

170. The autobiographical "Guilty/Not Guilty," especially the section "Quidman's Diary" in *Stages*, parallels numerous *Journal* entries and illustrates S. K.'s struggle with guilt.

171. *Point of View*, 49.

172. Ibid., 43.

173. Fr.-Eb. Wilde, "Category," *BK* (1980), III, 12.

174. *Journals and Papers*, III, 706, no. 3684.

175. Ibid., II, 401f, no. 2004.

176. *Journals and Papers*, I, 75, no. 187.

177. Ibid., 74, no. 186.

178. Ibid., VI, 186, no. 6461.

179. David F. Swenson, *Something About Kierkegaard* (Minneapolis: Augusburg, 1945), 123.

180. *Point of View*, 67-68.

181. Ibid., 155.

182. Thomte, *Kierkegaard's Philosophy of Religion*, 209.

183. *Postscript*, 292.

Chapter 3

1. Alastair Hannay, *Kierkegaard* (London: Routledge, Kegan and Paul, 1983), 90. Cf. Reidar Thomte, *Kierkegaard's Philosophy of Religion* (Westport, Conn.: Greenwood Press, 1969), 16-37.

2. J. Leslie Dunstan, "The Bible in *Either/Or*," *Interpretation*, 6 (1952) 310.

3. *Point of View*, 5-6.

4. See Jane Duran, "Kierkegaard Christian Reflectivity: Its Precursors in the Aesthetic of *Either/Or*," *International Journal for Philosophy of Religion*, 17 (1985) 131-137.

5. There are at least ninety unique references to the Bible in *Either/Or* according to Paul S. Minear and Paul S. Morimoto, *Kierkegaard and the Bible: An Index* (Princeton: Princeton Pamphlets, 1953), hereafter referred to as *Index*. Parallel passages, listed as separate references in the *Index*, have not been counted. Three other references were located in the course of this study. Dunstan pointed out that only thirty references were noted in the 1944 Princeton edition of *Either/Or* but he calculated that over one hundred and fifty could be found in the two volumes. "The Bible in *Either/Or*," 311.

6. *On Authority and Revelation*, 166.

7. *Either/Or*, I, 39-40.

8. Ibid., 81 (1 Sam. 16:16).   9. Ibid., 139 (2 Sam. 24:1-9).   10. Ibid., 174 (1 Sam. 28:7-25).   11. Ibid., 225.   12. Ibid., 282 (Gen. 1:26; 2:18-24).   13. Ibid., 308 (2 Sam. 12:1-7).   14. Ibid., 330 (Gen. 41:32).   15. Ibid., 384 (Gen. 31:34).   16. Dunstan, "The Bible in *Either/Or*," 313.   17. *Either/Or*, II, 94, 318.   18. Ibid., 100.   19. Ibid., 317 (1 Cor. 11:5).   20. Ibid., I, 103.   21. Ibid., 220.   22. Ibid., 432.   23. Ibid., 282.   24. Ibid., 27.   25. Ibid., II, 71.

26. Dunstan, "The Bible in *Either/Or*," 317.

27. For example, the explanation of "woman being saved through child bearing." *Either/Or*, II, 71.

28. Herbert C. Wolf, "Kierkegaard and the Quest for the Historical Jesus," *The Lutheran Quarterly, 16 (1964)*, 6.

29. Dunstan, "The Bible in *Either/Or*," 316.

30. The *Index* listed sixty unique references to the Scripture. There are at least fourteen other references in the critical notes to the text and/or located in the course of this study.

31. Edmund Perry, "Was Kierkegaard a Biblical Existentialist?" *The Journal of Religion*, 36 (1956) 17.

32. *Fear*, 7 (2 Tim. 4:7).

33. Janet Fishburn, "Søren Kierkegaard, Exegete," *Interpretation*, (July, 1985), 237.

34. *Fear*, 10.

35. Ibid.

36. David A. Pailin, "Abraham and Isaac: A Hermeneutical Problem Before Kierkegaard," *Kierkegaard's "Fear and Trembling"*: *Critical Appraisals*, ed. R. L. Perkins (University of Alabama: University of Alabama Press, 1981), 28.

37. *Fear*, 28 (Matt. 19:16-22).

38. Ibid., 66.   39. Ibid., 48-49 (Matthew 17:20).   40. Ibid., 59.

41. Ibid.   42. Ibid., 66.   43. Ibid., 68.   44. Ibid., 72.   45. Ibid., 73.   46. Ibid.

47. *Fear*, 81.

48. Ibid., 82.   49. Ibid., 117f.   50. Ibid., 120.   51. Ibid., 121-22.

52. Walter Lowrie, *A Short Life of Kierkegaard* (Princeton: Princeton University Press, 1942), 157.

53. Gregor Malantschuk, *Kierkegaard's Thought*, ed. and trans. H. V. and E. H. Hong (Princeton: Princeton University Press, 1971), 237.

54. Fishburn, "Søren Kierkegaard, Exegete," 240.

55. *Fear*, 10.

56. Fishburn, "Søren Kierkegaard, Exegete," 245.

57. The *Index* listed sixty-six different references. There are at least fourteen other references in the critical notes to the text and/or located in the course of this study.

58. *Fragments*, 11.

59. Rorty has suggested that "a theory of representation" or epistemology is a modern concern. S. K.'s point is that idealism's epistemic assumptions must be examined before they are accepted as a basis for Christian theology. Richard Rorty, *Philosophy and the Mirror of Nature* (Princeton: Princeton University Press, 1979), 12.

60. *Fragments*, p. 13.

61. Ibid., 15. 62. Ibid., 16. 63. Ibid. 64. Ibid., 17. 65. Ibid. 66. Ibid., 19. 67. Ibid., 21. 68. Ibid. 69. Ibid., 21-22. 70. Ibid., 22. 71. Ibid. 72. Ibid. 73. Ibid., 23. 74. Ibid. 75. Ibid. 76. Ibid., 24. 77. Ibid., 32-34.

78. *Fragments*, 35.

79. Ibid., 39. 80. Ibid. 81. Ibid., 41.

82. In contrast, only a couple of obscure allusions have been noted in the "Preface" and eight in Chapter I, "A Project of Thought." The largest number of references in any portion of the book, thirty-seven, occur in Chapter II, "The God as Teacher and Saviour: An Essay of the Imagination."

83. *Fragments*, 40.

84. Ibid. 85. Ibid. 86. Ibid. 87. Ibid. 88. Ibid., 41. 89. Ibid. 90. Ibid., 46-67. 91. Ibid., 52. 92. Ibid., 54 (cf. Ps. 14:1; 53:1). 93. Ibid., 61. 94. Ibid., 66. 95. Ibid., 68. 96. Ibid., 68 (cf. Isa. 40:3; Matt. 3:3-15). 97. Ibid., 73. 98. Ibid.

99. *Fragments*, 74-75.

100. Ibid., 76. 101. Ibid., 101. 102. Ibid., 103. 103. Ibid., 93. 104. Ibid., 95. 105. Ibid., 93. 106. Ibid., 103. 107. Ibid. 108. Ibid., 106. 109. Ibid., 108. 110. Ibid., 116. 111. Ibid., 130. 112. Ibid., 120. 113. Ibid., 132 (cf. John 16:7). 114. Ibid., 133. 115. Ibid., 138 (cf. 1 Cor. 2:9). 116. *Fragments*, 139.

117. *Either/Or*, I, 45-134.

118. Stephen N. Dunning, "Kierkegaard's Systematic Analysis of Anxiety" *International Kierkegaard Commentary: The Concept of Anxiety*, ed. R. L. Perkins (Macon, Ga.: Mercer University Press, 1985), 10.

119. Lee Barrett, "Kierkegaard's 'Anxiety' and the Augustinian Doctrine of Original Sin," *International Kierkegaard Commentary: The Concept of Anxiety* (Macon, Ga.: Mercer University Press, 1985), 60. S. K. sought to overcome the artificial distinction between "state" and "act" of traditional theology.

120. *Anxiety*, 16.

121. Ibid., 10. 122. Ibid., 19. 123. Ibid., 18.

124. The *Index* listed eighty-two different references. There are at least nine other references in either the critical notes to the text and/or located in the course of this study.

125. *Anxiety*, 25.

126. Ibid., 28. 127. Ibid., 33. 128. Ibid., 29. 129. Ibid., 32. 130. Ibid.

131. Dunning, 32.

132. *Anxiety*, 40.

133. Ibid., 41. S. K. said that this view is in "full accord with that of the Bible, which by denying that man in his innocence has knowledge of the difference between good and evil denounces all the phatasmagoria of Catholic meritoriousness."

134. Ibid., 37. 135. Ibid., 38. 136. Ibid., 48. 137. Ibid. 138. Ibid., 49. 139. Ibid., 54. 140. Ibid., 60. 141. Ibid., 81f. 142. Ibid., 85. 143. Ibid., 81.

144. *Anxiety*, 89.

145. Ibid., 90.

146. Dunning, "Kierkegaard's Systematic Analysis of Anxiety," 19-20.

147. Ibid., 90. 148. Ibid, 93f. 149. Ibid, 96f. 150. Ibid, 103f. 151. Ibid., 111. 152. Ibid., 114. 153. Ibid., 119. 154. Ibid., 111, 119. 155. Ibid., 119 (Mk. 5:17). 156. Ibid., 136-37. 157. Ibid., 137-154. 158. Ibid., 137. 159. Ibid., 151. 160. Ibid., 155. 161. Ibid., 117. 162. Ibid., 161. 163. Ibid., 162.

164. Dunning, "Kierkegaard's Systematic Analysis of Anxiety," 32.
165. Reinhold Niebuhr, *The Nature and Destiny of Man* (New York: Charles Scribner's Sons, 1947), I, 182.
166. Brita K. Stendahl, *Søren Kierkegaard* (Boston: Twayne Publishers, 1976), 148.
167. There are forty-five unique references to Scripture listed in the *Index*. At least five other references were located in the course of this study.
168. *Stages,* 22.
169. Ibid., 27 (Judg. 14:14). 170. Ibid., 39 (Ecc. 1:8). 171. Ibid., 43 (2 Kgs. 20:1). 172. Ibid., 46 (Gen. 43:34). 173. Ibid., 46. 174. Ibid., 48. 175. Ibid., 51 (Gen. 2:22-23). 176. Ibid. 177. Ibid., 61. 178. Ibid., 67. 179. Ibid., 74. 180. Ibid., 76. 181. *Stages,* 80. 182. Ibid., 81. 183. Ibid., 87. 184. Ibid., 103. 185. Ibid.,106. 186.Ibid.,120-122. 187.Ibid., 114. 188.Ibid., 117 (Matt. 25:30). 189. Ibid.,117 (Lk. 17:10; Matt. 25:36-40). 190. Ibid., 121 (Gal. 4:4). 191. Ibid., 132 (Ecc. 1:13-14). 192. Ibid., 154 (Prov. 18:22). 193. Ibid., 125 (Ex. 33:20; Ex. 34:33f; Gen. 1:1). 194. Ibid., 173-177.
195. *Stages,* 192.
196. Ibid., 197. 197. Ibid., 205 (Gen. 25:20-24). 198. Ibid., 208 (Isa. 26:18). 199. Ibid., 217 (Gen. 1:27). 200. Ibid., 237. 201. Ibid., 322 (Gen. 3:18). 202. Ibid., 330 (Dan. 4:30-34). 203. Ibid., 455.
204. Ibid., 458. The Index listed this verse as the only biblical passage in *Stage* receiving a "conscious and explicit exposition," *Index,* 15, 32.
205. *Stages,* 461.
206. *Postscript,* "Editor's Introduction," xvi.
207. Ibid., 225-266.
208. Cf. Chapter 1, 13f.
209. The *Index* listed one hundred and fifty-two unique references to Scripture. Only a couple of other clear references were located in the course of this study.
210. *Postscript,* 25-35, 312-322, 330-340, and 520-537.
211. Ibid., 23. 212. Ibid., 25. 213. Ibid. 214. Ibid., 26. 215. Ibid., 29. 216. Ibid., 31. 217. Ibid., 30. 218. Ibid., 31. 219. Ibid. 220. Ibid., 32 (Matt. 17:20). 221. Ibid. (Matt.5:18). 222. Ibid., 33. 223. Ibid. 224. Ibid., 55. 225. Ibid., 59f. 226. Ibid., 71. 227. Ibid., 83. 228. Ibid., 89. 229. Ibid., 95. 230. Ibid., 98. 231. Ibid., 116 (Luke 15:7). 232. Ibid., 122 (Acts 1:16). 233. Ibid., 141 (Judges 9:7-15). 234. Ibid., 206 (Rev. 3:15). 235. Ibid., 195. 236. Ibid., 205 (1 Thess. 5:18). 237. Ibid., (Matt. 5:13). 238. Ibid., 206 (Rev. 3:15). 239. Ibid., 308. 240. Ibid., 304 (Luke 10: 29-37). 241. Ibid., 316. 242. Ibid.,321. 243.Ibid. 244.*Postscript,*333. 245.Ibid.,334. 246.Ibid.,339. 247. Ibid., 362. 248. Ibid., 366 (Luke 16:26). 249. Ibid., 380. 250. Ibid., 494 251. Ibid., 512. 252. Ibid., 518 (Matt. 7: 13-14). 253. Cf. Ibid., 260 (Matt.18:3), 361 (Matt.7:13-14), 417, 419 (John 5:19), and 461 (John 1:14). 254. Ibid., 521. 255. Ibid. 256. Ibid., 523 (Gal. 4:4). 257. Ibid. 258. Ibid., 523 (2 Cor. 12:9) 259. Ibid., 524. 260. Ibid. 261. Ibid. (Matt. 19).
262· *Postscript,* 525.
263. Ibid., 527 (John 3:4-11). 264. Ibid., 528, 530 (The kenosis passage of Phil. 2). 265. Ibid., 540.

Chapter Four

1. *Sickness unto Death* and *Training in Christianity* were published under the pseudonym of Anti-Climacus, who stands as a superior Christian in contrast to Johannes Climacus. Glenn observed that "[I]t is generally recognized that Kierkegaard 'stands behind' the ideas expressed in The *Sickness Unto Death* in a sense that is not true of all the pseudonymous writings" Cf. John D. Glenn, Jr., "The

Definition of the Self and the Structure of Kierkegaard's Work," *International Kierkegaard Commentary: Sickness unto Death*, ed. R. L. Perkins (Macon, Ga.: Mercer University Press, 1987), 5. S. K. saw himself as "above Job [of Repetition], Climacus and below Anti-Climacus." Cf. Brita K. Stendahl, *Søren Kierkegaard* (Boston: Twayne Publishers, 1976), 194.

2. The term "second literature" is generally attributed to Robert L. Perkins, editor of the *International Kierkegaard Commentary*.

3. Søren Kierkegaard, *The Point of View of My Work as an Author and My Activity as an Author* (New York: Harper and Row, 1962), 12.

4. Søren Kierkegaard, *Edifying Discourses I* (Minneapolis: Augsburg Publishing House, 1943-46), 5. A total of eighty-two discourses were penned by S. K., twenty of which were dedicated to the memory of his father. "Note by the Translator," *Training*, 260.

5. *Edifying Discourses*, I, 5.

6. "Introduction," Ibid., vii.

7. Ibid., IV, 7-47.

8. As cited by Hong, "Translator's Introduction," *Works of Love*, 11.

9. Paul S. Minear and Paul S. Morimoto, *Kierkegaard and the Bible: an Index* (Princeton: Theological Seminary, 1953), hereafter referred to as *Index*, listed three hundred and sixty-five unique references to the Scripture. There are at least thirty-two other references in the critical notes to the text and/or located in the course of this study.

10. *Edifying Discourses*, I, 9.

11. Ibid. 12. Ibid., 18. 13. Ibid., 19. 14. Ibid. 15. Ibid., 21. 16. Ibid., 22. 17. Ibid., 26. 18. Ibid., 27. 19. Ibid. 20. Ibid., 33. 21. *Edifying Discourses*, I, 66. 22. Ibid., 67. 23. Ibid. 24. Ibid., 68. 25. Ibid., 77. 26. Ibid. 27. Ibid., 97. 28. Ibid.

29. Ibid., 101. 30. Ibid., 103. 31. Ibid. 32. Ibid., 117.

33. *Edifying Discourses*, II, 7.

34. Ibid., 15. 35. Ibid., 22.

36. John D. Caputo, *Radical Hermeneutics: Repetition, Deconstruction, and the Hermeneutic Project* (Bloomington, Ind.: Indiana University Press, 1987), 32.

37. *Edifying Discourses*, II, 32.

38. Ibid., III, 49. 39. Ibid., 51. 40. Ibid., 63. 41. Ibid., 82. 42. Ibid., 97. 43. Ibid., 103. 44. Ibid. 45. Ibid., 114. 46. Ibid., 118. 47. Ibid., 130.

48. "Introduction," *Edifying Discourses*, IV, vi.

49. Ibid., 10. 50. Ibid., 11-12. 51. Ibid., 16. 52. Ibid. 53. Ibid., 19. 54. Ibid., 20.

55. Ibid., 24f. S. K. cited Moses as an example of the inability to do anything apart from God. Ibid., 27-28.

56. Ibid., 41. 57. Ibid., 46. 58. Ibid., 49. 59. Ibid. 60. Ibid.

61. *Crucial Situations*, "Introduction," i. The references to Scripture in this brief volume are not included in the earlier total for the *Edifying Discourses*.

62. Ibid., 2 63. Ibid., 9. 64. Ibid. 65. Ibid., 10. 66. Ibid., 12-13. 67. Ibid. 68. Ibid., 13. 69. Ibid., 14. 70. Ibid. 71. Ibid., 16. 72. Ibid. 73. Ibid. 74. Ibid., 19.

75. *Crucial Situations*, 21.

76. Ibid., 22. 77. Ibid., 24. 78. Ibid., 24-25. 79. Ibid., 30. 80. Ibid., 38. 81. Ibid.

82. "Introduction," *Christian Discourses*, xv.

83. "Preface," Ibid., v. Lowrie claimed these discourses were published after S. K.'s metamorphosis because that experience made direct communication possible for S. K. "Introduction," Ibid., xvii.

84. The *Index* listed one hundred and forty-seven references. There are at least thirty-seven other references in the critical notes.

85. *Christian Discourses*, 16.
86. Ibid., 13.   87. Ibid., 15.   88. Ibid., 17.   89. Ibid.   90. Ibid., 20.   91. Ibid., 27.   92. Ibid., 30.   93. Ibid., 33.   94. Ibid., 36 (Heb. 13:16).   95. Ibid.   96. Ibid., 40, 51.   97. Ibid., 40.   98. Ibid., 43.
99. *Christian Discourses*, 45.
100. Ibid., 46.   101. Ibid., 53.   102. Ibid., 57.   103. Ibid.   104. Ibid., 57.   105. Ibid.   106. Ibid., 63, 73.   107. Ibid., 83.   108. Ibid., 86.
109. The seven discourses in this section are: "The Joy of it—that we suffer only once but triumph eternally," Ibid., 101f, "The Joy of it—that affliction does not bereave of hope, but recruits hope," 111f, "The Joy of it—that the poorer thou dost become, the richer thou canst make others," 119, "The Joy of it—that the weaker thou dost become, the stronger dost God become in thee," 129, "The Joy of it—that what thou dost lose temporally thou dost gain eternally," 139, "The Joy of it—that when I 'gain all I lose nothing at all," 149, "The Joy of it—that Misfortune is Good Fortune."
110. Ibid., 101.   111. Ibid., 103.   112. Ibid., 148.   113. Ibid., 110.   114. Ibid., 127.   115. Ibid., 130.
116. Ibid., 132. In an extended note in a later discourse, S.K. argued that "God's omnipotence is His goodness" not simply the power to do anything. Lutheran theology stressed that God's power is always used consistent with the attributes of his nature—which includes goodness. *Christian Discourses*, 187.
117. Ibid., 118, 128, 138, 148, 153, 163.
118. As cited by Hong, "Translator's Introduction," *Works of Love*, 12.
119. A small number of dissertations and a few articles are referred to in Sylvia I. Walsh's chapter, "Forming the Heart: The Role of Love in Kierkegaard's Thought," *The Grammar of the Heart*, ed. R. H. Bell (New York: Harper and Row, 1988), endnote 2. Indeed, with a few notable exceptions, love has not been a major interest of either modern philosophy or theology. Walsh has provided one of the best summary introductions available to *Works of Love*. Hong lists several modern theological discussions of love which S. K.'s work anticipated. Cf. Hong, "Translator's Introduction," *Works of Love*, 15.
120. The *Index* listed two hundred and ninety-six unique references to the Scripture. There are at least twenty-one other references in the critical notes and/or located in the course of this study.
121. *Works of Love*, 23 (Lk. 6:44).
122. There are at least twenty extended treatments of part or all of 1 Corinthians 13, commonly referred to as the "love" chapter of the New Testament. There are also at least seventeen extended treatments of 1 John, an epistle emphasizing "God is love" and love for fellow believers. Finally, at least thirteen references to the Epistle of James focus on practical application of faith through works.
123. *Works of Love*, 74.
124. Matt. 22:39 "You shall love your neighbor as yourself" is the text for two discourses. Ibid., 34f, 73f.
125. Ibid, 136 (1 Tim. 1:5), 153f (1 John 4:10), and 171 (Rom. 13:8).
126. Ibid., 199 (Cf. 1 Cor. 8:1).
127. Ibid., 213f, 231f (1 Cor. 13:7), 247f (1 Cor. 13:5), 279f (1 Cor. 13:13).
128. "The Work of Love in Remembering One Dead" is the lone exception, containing the fewest explicit biblical references. *Works of Love*, 317f.
129. Ibid., 344f.
130. Buber says that S. K. "contradicts his master" with his emphasis on the single individual before God. Yet *Works of Love* demonstrates S. K.'s concern for loving God and neighbor in precisely the way Buber suggests this love should exist. See Martin Buber, "The Question to the Single One," *Between Man and Man*, trans. R. S. Smith (London: Kegan Paul, 1947), 51f.

131. *Works of Love*, 31.   132. Ibid., 59, 70.   133. Ibid., 146.   134. Ibid., 27.   135. Ibid., 199.   136. Ibid., 113.   137. Ibid., 60.   138. Ibid., 113.   139. Ibid., 68.   140. Ibid., 40.   141. Ibid., 37 (cf. Luke 10:29).   142. Ibid.   143. *Works of Love*, 37, 66.   144. Ibid., 320.   145. Ibid., 145.   146. Ibid.   147. Ibid., 139. 148. Ibid., 108.   149. Ibid., 99 (cf. Rom 13:10).

150. George E. Arbaugh and George B. Arbaugh, *Kierkegaard's Authorship: A Guide to the Writings of Kierkegaard* (Rock Island, Ill.: Augustana College Library, 1967), 260.

151. Ibid.

152. *Works of Love*, 100-101.

153. Ibid., 101.   154. Ibid., 141.

155. Cf. *Two Ages.*

156. Gal. 5:22-23; *Works of Love*, 199-212.

157. Ibid., 202.   158. Ibid., 204 (cf. 1 Cor. 13:4).   159. Ibid., 206.   160. Ibid., 209 (Lk. 15:22-24).

161. The first portion of the title, "love believes all things," is taken from 1 Cor. 13:7. Ibid., 213-230.

162. Ibid., 221.   163. Ibid., 222.   164. Ibid., 223   165. Ibid., 228 (cf. 2 Cor. 12:9).   166. Ibid., 229 (cf. 1 John 5:4).   167. Ibid., 231-246.   168. Ibid., 233.   169. Ibid., 237.   170. Ibid., 245.

171. *Works of Love*, 246.

172. Ibid., 247-260.   173. Ibid., 247.   174. Ibid., 248.   175. Ibid., 250.   176. Ibid., 251.   177. Ibid., 259.   178. Ibid., 260.

179. Ibid., 261-278. Cf. "Love Shall Cover A Multitude Of Sins," *Edifying Discourses*, I, 66f.

180. *Works of Love*, 279-291.

181. Ibid., 282.   182. Ibid., 283.   183. Ibid. 290.   184. Ibid., 292-305.   185. Ibid., 300.   186. Ibid., 301.   187. Ibid., 306-316.   188. Ibid., 311.   189. Ibid., 316.

190. Ibid., 317-329. There are only five references to the Scripture in this discourse, though the theme of love without reciprocity is repeatedly emphasized, with ample biblical citations, throughout the *Works of Love.*

191. Ibid., 321.   192. Ibid., 328.   193. Ibid., 330-343.   194. Ibid., 331, 336.   195. Ibid., 343.   196. Ibid., 344.   197. Ibid.

198. *Works of Love*, 344.

199. Ibid., 353.   200. Ibid.

201. Cf. Chapter 1, 23f.

202. S. K. even toyed with, before finally rejecting, the subtitle of "An Endeavour to Introduce Christianity into Christendom." Cf. Lowrie, "Introduction," *Training*, xviii. S. K. also said it would not have been pseudonymous, if published later. "With Regard to the new edition of *Training in Christianity*," *Attack*, 54.

203. *Training*, 9.

204. T. H. Croxall, *Glimpses and Impressions of Kierkegaard* (Welwym, Herts: Nisbet, 1959), 35.

205. The *Index* lists one hundred and seventy-six unique references to the Scripture. In addition, there are nine references to Scripture in discourse, "The Woman Who Was a Sinner," which is included at the end of the book by the editor. Only two other references were located in the course of this study.

206. *Training*, 11-72.

207. Ibid, 79-144   208. Ibid, 145-254.   209. Ibid., 9.   210. Ibid. (cf. Lk. 19:10).   211. Ibid.   212. Ibid., 10.   213. Ibid., 13.   214. Ibid., 16.   215. Ibid., 18.   216. Ibid., 20.   217. Ibid., 22.

218. Ibid., 27-28. This may have been a subtle slap at the various "lives of Jesus."

219. Ibid., 28.   220. Ibid., 29.   221. Ibid., 32.

222. *Training*, 34.
223. Ibid. 224. Ibid., 37. 225. Ibid. 226. Ibid., 38. 227. Ibid., 39. 228. Ibid., 45f. 229. Ibid., 49f. 230. Ibid., 52. 231. Ibid., 52f. 232. Ibid., 54. 233. Ibid., 54f. 234. Ibid., 55 (John 3:2). 235. Ibid., 59 (John 6:66). 236. Ibid., 63. 237. Ibid., 66. 238. Ibid., 67. 239. Ibid., 69. 240. Ibid. (cf. Phil. 2:6-11). 241. Ibid. (Isa. 53:2). 242. Ibid., 71. 243. Ibid. (cf. *Anxiety*, 117f) 244. *Training*, 72. 245. Ibid., 79. 246. Ibid., 81. 247. Ibid., 82. 248. Ibid., 87. 249. Ibid., 92. 250. Ibid., 85. 251. Ibid., 93-94. 252. Ibid., 96 253. Ibid., (Matt. 11:6). 254. Ibid., 98. 255. Ibid., 99. 256. Ibid., 101. 257. Ibid., 105 (Matt. 13:55). 258. Ibid., 106. 259. Ibid., 107. 260. Ibid., 112. 261. Ibid., 108. 262. Ibid., 109. 263. Ibid. 264. Ibid., 115 (Matt. 13:21).
265. *Training*, 117 (John 16:23).
266. Ibid., 120. 267. Ibid., 122. 268. Ibid., 124. 269. Ibid., 125. 270. Ibid., 127. 271. Ibid., 132f, 136f, and 140f. 272. Ibid., 151.
273. Cf. Num. 21:9.
274. *Training*, 156.
275. Ibid., 160. 276. Ibid., 167. 277. Ibid., 168. 278. Ibid., 178. 279. Ibid., 179. 280. Ibid., 180. 281. Ibid., 184. 282. Ibid., 201. 283. Ibid., 207. 284. Ibid.,209. 285. Ibid.,218. 286. Ibid. 287. Ibid.,226. 288. Ibid. 251, 254. 289. Ibid., 262. 290. Ibid., 266. 291. Ibid., 269. 292. Ibid., 270.
293. Chapter 1, 25f.
294. The *Index* lists only sixty unique references to the Bible.
295. *Attack*, 29ff, 127, 167, 191, 277.
296. Ibid., 108. 297. Ibid., 210, 20 (2 Cor. 11:23-28). 298. Ibid., 197. 299. Ibid., 111. 300. Ibid., 119. 301. Ibid., 3-55, 67-72. 302. Ibid., 7. 303. Ibid., 5. 304. Ibid., 13.
305. *Attack*, 12.
306. Ibid., 37. 307. Ibid., 38. 308. Ibid. 309. Ibid., 59-60.
310. *Fragments*, 22. Cf. "When is 'the Instant'?", *Attack*, 280-281.
311. *Attack*, 144-146.
312. Ibid., 145. 313. Ibid., 209. 314. Ibid., 268-270. 315. Ibid., 181. 316. Ibid., 160. 317. Ibid. 318. Ibid. 319. Ibid., 120-124.
320. Cf. Howard A. Johnson, "Kierkegaard and the Church: A Supplement to the Translator's Introduction," *Attack*. Johnson points out that while S. K.'s attack was focused on the Danish Lutheran Church, he was also critical of both Roman Catholicism and the Free Church tradition.
321. *Attack*, 283.
322. Ibid., 287.
323. Croxall, *Glimpses and Impressions of Kierkegaard*, 106.

Chapter Five

1. Patrick Bigelow, "Kierkegaard and the Hermeneutical Circle," *Man and World*, 15 (1982), 67.
2. John D. Caputo, *Radical Hermeneutics: Repetition, Deconstruction and the Hermeneutic Project* (Bloomington, Ind.: Indiana University Press, 1987), 1.
3. Janet Forsythe Fishburn, "Søren Kierkegaard, Exegete" *Interpretation* (July, 1985), 229.
4. David H. Kelsey, *The Uses of Scripture in Recent Theology* (Philadelphia: Fortress, 1975), 15 (Cf. Chapter 1, 27 of this study).
5. *Journals and Papers*, I, 84, no. 208.
6. Robert Merrihew Adams, "Kierkegaard's Arguments Against Objective Reasoning in Religion," *Contemporary Philosophy of Religion*, eds. S. N. Cahn and D. Shatz (New York: Oxford University Press, 1982), 227.

7. Jerry H. Gill, *On Knowing God: New Directions for the Future of Theology* (Philadelphia: Westminster, 1981), 108-109.

8. Cf. W. Lowrie, "Introduction by the Translator" and H. A. Johnson, "Kierkegaard and the Church: A Supplement to the Translator's Introduction," *Attack*, xi-xxxiii.

9. Ray Stedman, *Expository Studies in John 13-17: Secrets of the Spirit* (Waco, Texas: Word Books, 1975), 88-89.

10. S. K. apparently never dealt with this verse anywhere in his major writings. Cf. Paul S. Minear and Paul S. Morimoto, *Kierkegaard and the Bible: An Index* (Princeton: Princeton Pamphlets, 1953) has no listing for this verse.

11. J. K. S. Reid, *Christian Apologetics* (London: Hodder and Stoughton, 1969), 9-10.

12. Vernon C. Grounds and E. J. Carnell were notable exceptions to this trend. Cf. Vernon C. Grounds, "Take Another Look at S. K.," rev. of Carnell's *The Burden of Søren Kierkegaard* (Eerdmans), *Christianity Today*, February 18, 1966, 33.

13. C. Stephen Evans, "A Misunderstood Reformer," *Christianity Today*, September 21, 1984, 29.

14. E. J. Carnell, *Christian Commitment: An Apologetic* (New York: Macmillan, 1957), 73.

Bibliography

Primary Sources

Drachman, A. B., J. L. Heiberg, and H. O. Lang, eds. *Søren Kierkegaard's Samlede Vaerker.* Copenhagen: Gyldendalske Boghandel Nordisk Forlag, 1901.

Dru, Alexander, trans. and ed. *The Journals of Søren Kierkegaard, a Selection.* London: Oxford University Press, 1938.

Heiberg, P. A., Victor Kuhr, and Einer Torsting, eds. *Søren Kierkegaard's Papirer.* 20 vols. Copenhagen: Gyldendalske Boghandel Nordisk Forlag, 1909.

Hong, Howard and Edna, trans. and eds. *Søren Kierkegaard's Journals and Papers.* 7 vols. Bloomington: Indiana University Press, 1967-78.

Kierkegaard, Søren. *Attack upon "Christendom" 1854-55.* Trans. Walter Lowrie. Princeton: Princeton University Press, 1968.

_____. *Christian Discourses.* Trans. Walter Lowrie. London: Oxford University Press, 1949.

_____. *The Concept of Anxiety: A Simple Psychologically Orienting Deliberation on the Dogmatic Issue of Hereditary Sin.* Trans. Reider Thomte. Princeton: Princeton University Press, 1980.

_____. *The Concept of Irony.* Trans. Lee M. Chapel. New York: Harper and Row, 1966.

_____. *Concluding Unscientific Postscript.* Trans. David Swenson and Walter Lowrie. Princeton: Princeton University Press, 1959.

_____. *Either/Or.* Trans. of vol. I. David Swenson and Lillian Marvin Swenson; vol. II, Walter Lowrie; 2nd ed. rev. Howard A. Johnson. Princeton: Princeton University Press, 1959.

_____. *Edifying Discourses, I-IV.* Trans. David Swenson and Lillian Swenson. Minneapolis: Augsburg Publishing House, 1943-46.

_____. *Fear and Trembling* and *Repetition: An Essay in Experimental Psychology.* Ed. and tr. Howard and Edna Hong. Princeton: Princeton University Press, 1969.

_____. *For Self-Examination and Judge for Yourself.* Trans. Walter Lowrie. London: Oxford University Press, 1941.

_____. *Johannes Climacus, or De omnibus dubitandum est, and A Sermon.* Trans. T. H. Croxall. London: Adam and Charles Black, 1958.

_____. *On Authority and Revelation: The Book on Adler, or, a Cycle of Ethico-Religious Essay.* Trans. Walter Lowrie. Princeton: Princeton University Press, l955.

_____. *Philosophical Fragments.* Trans. David Swenson. 2nd ed. Princeton: Princeton University Press, 1962.

_____. *The Point of View for My Work as an Author and My Activity as an Author.* Trans. Walter Lowrie. New York: Harper and Row, 1962.

_____. *Purity of Heart.* Trans. Douglas Steere. 2nd ed. New York: Harper and Row, 1962.

_____. *The Sickness Unto Death: A Christian Psychological Exposition for Upbuilding and Awakening.* Trans. Howard and Edna Hong. Princeton: Princeton University Press, 1980.

_____. *Stages on Life's Way.* Trans. Walter Lowrie. Princeton: Princeton University Press, 1940.

_____. *Thoughts on Crucial Situations.* Trans. D. F. Swenson. Minneapolis: Augsburg, 1941.

_____. *Training in Christianity.* Trans. Walter Lowrie. Princeton: Princeton University Press, 1978.

_____. *Two Ages: The Age of Revolution and the Present Age.* Trans. Howard and Edna Hong. Princeton: Princeton University Press, 1978.

_____. *Works of Love.* Trans. Howard and Edna Hong. New York: Harper and Row, 1962.

LeFevere, Perry D., trans. and ed. *Prayers of Kierkegaard.* Chicago: University of Chicago Press, 1956.

Oden, Thomas C., trans. and ed. *Parables of Kierkegaard.* Princeton: Princeton University Press, 1978.

Secondary Sources

Books

Allen, W. Wood. *Kant's Moral Religion.* Ithaca, N.Y.: Cornell University Press, 1970.

Arbaugh, George E. and George B. Arbaugh. *Kierkegaard's Authorship: A Guide to the Writings of Kierkegaard.* Rock Island, Ill.: Augustana College Library, 1968.

Bain, John A. *Søren Kierkegaard: His Life and Religious Teaching.* London: SCM, 1935.

Brunner, Emil. *Truth as Encounter.* Philadelphia: Westminster, 1964.

Buber, Martin. *Between Man and Man.* Trans. R. S. Smith. London: Kegan Paul, 1947.

Caputo, John D. *Radical Hermeneutics: Repetition, Deconstruction, and the Hermeneutic Project.* Bloomington: Indiana University Press, 1987.

Carnell, Edward J. *The Burden of Søren Kierkegaard.* Grand Rapids, Mich.: Eerdmans, 1965.

Collins, James. *The Mind of Kierkegaard.* Princeton: Princeton University Press, 1983.

Connell, George. *To Be One Thing: Personal Unity in Kierkegaard's Thought.* Macon, Ga: Mercer University Press, 1985.

Croxall, Thomas H. *Glimpses and Impressions of Kierkegaard.* Welwym, Herts: Nisbet, 1959.

_____. *Kierkegaard Commentary.* New York: Harper, 1956.

_____. *Kierkegaard Studies.* Lutterworth, 1948.

Diem, Hermann. *Kierkegaard's Dialectic of Existence.* Trans. Harold Knight. Edinburgh: Oliver and Boyd, 1959.

Dunning, Stephen. *Søren Kierkegaard's Dialectic of Inwardness.* Princeton: Princeton University Press, 1985.

Dupre, Louis K. *Kierkegaard as Theologian.* London: Sheed and Ward, 1963.

Elrod, John W. *Kierkegaard and Christendom.* Princeton: Princeton University Press, 1981.

_____. *Being and Existence in Kierkegaard's Pseudonymous Works.* Princeton: Princeton University Press, 1975.

Evans, C. Stephen. *Kierkegaard's "Fragments" and "Postscript": The Religious Philosophy of Johannes Climacus.* Atlantic Highlands, N.J.: Humanities Press, 1983.

_____. *Subjectivity and Religious Belief.* Grand Rapids, Mich: Eerdmans, 1978.

Fenger, Henning. *Kierkegaard, The Myths and Their Origins.* Trans. G. C. Schoolfield. New Haven, Conn: Yale University Press, 1980

Garelick, H. M. *The Anti-Christianity of Kierkegaard.* The Hague: Martinus Nijhoff, 1965.

Gaskin, J. C. A. *The Quest for Eternity.* New York: Penguin Books, 1984.
Gill, J. H., editor. *Essays on Kierkegaard.* Minneapolis: Burgess, 1969.
_____. *On Knowing God.* Philadelphia: Westminster, 1981.
Haecker, Theodor. *Kierkegaard the Cripple.* Trans. C. Van O. Bruyn. New York: Philosophical Library, 1950.
Hannay, Alastair. *Kierkegaard.* London: Routledge, Kegan and Paul, 1983.
_____. "Kierkegaard: Philosophy of Mind" in *Contemporary Philosophy: Philosophy of Mind,* ed. G. Floistad. The Hague: Martinus Nijhoff, 1984.
Hegel, G. W. F. *Encyclopedia of Philosophy.* Trans. G. E. Mueller. New York: Philosophical Library, 1959.
_____. *Lectures in the Philosophy of Religion.* Trans. E. B. Spears and J. Burdon. London: Routledge & Kegan Paul, 1962.
_____. *The Phenomenology of Mind.* Rev. ed. Trans. J. B. Ballie. New York: Macmillan, 1931.
_____. *Reason in History.* Trans. R. S. Hartman. New York: Liberal Arts Press, 1953.
_____. *Science of Logic.* Trans. W. H. Johnston and L. G. Struthers. New York: Macmillan, 1929.
Heinecken, Martin J. *The Moment Before God.* Philadelphia: Mulenberg, 1956.
Hume, David. *An Enquiry Concerning Human Understanding.* Ed. L. A. Selby-Bigge. Oxford: Clarendon Press, 1894.
Jaspers, Karl. *Reason and Existence.* New York: Noonday Press, 1955.
Johnson, H. A. and Nels Thulstrup, eds. *A Kierkegaard Critique.* New York: Harper, 1962.
Kant, Immanuel. *Critique of Practical Reason.* Trans. L. W. Beck. Indianapolis: Bobbs-Merrill, 1956.
_____. *Critique of Pure Reason.* Trans. N. K. Smith. London: Macmillan, 1923.
_____. *Religion Within the Bounds of Reason Alone.* Trans. T. M. Greene and H. H. Hudson. Chicago: Open Court, 1934.
Kaufmann, Walter. *Discovering the Mind.* New York: McGraw-Hill, 1980.
_____. *Hegel: A Reinterpretation.* Notre Dame: University of Notre Dame Press, 1978.
Kelsey, David. *The Uses of Scripture in Recent Theology.* Philadelphia: Fortress, 1975.
Lauer, Quentin. *Hegel's Concept of God.* Albany, N.Y.: SUNY, 1982.
_____. *Hegel's Idea of Philosophy.* New York: Fordham University Press, 1971.
Lowrie, Walter. *Kierkegaard.* 2 vols. New York: Harper, 1962.
_____. *A Short Life of Kierkegaard.* Princeton: Princeton University Press, 1951.
Mackey, Louis. *Kierkegaard: A Kind of Poet.* Philadelphia: University of Pennsylvania Press, 1971.
Macquarrie, John. *Existentialism.* New York: Penguin, 1972.
Malantschuk, Gregor. *Kierkegaard's Thought.* Ed. and trans. H. V. and E. Hong. Princeton: Princeton Pamphlets, 1953.
Minear, Paul S., and Paul S. Morimoto. *Kierkegaard and the Bible: An Index.* Princeton: Theological Seminary, 1953.
Niebuhr, Reinhold. *The Nature and Destiny of Man.* New York: Charles Scribner's Sons, 1947.
Pelikan, Jarslaov. *From Luther to Kierkegaard: A Study in the History of Theology.* St. Louis: Concordia, 1967.
Reid, J. K. S. *Christian Apologetics.* London: Hodder and Stoughton, 1969.
Richardson, A. and W. Schweitzer. *Biblical Authority for Today.* London: SCM, 1951.

Rohde, Peter P. *Søren Kierkegaard: An Introduction to His Life and Philosophy.* Trans. Alan M. Williams. London: Allen Unwin, 1963.

Rorty, Richard. *Philosophy and the Mirror of Nature.* Princeton: Princeton University Press, 1979.

Schweitzer, Albert. *The Quest of the Historical Jesus.* Trans. W. Montgomery. New York: Macmillan, 1961.

Sontag, Frederick. *A Kierkegaard Handbook.* Philadelphia: John Knox, 1980.

Sponheim, Paul R. *Kierkegaard on Christ and Christian Coherence.* London: SCM, 1968.

Stedman, Ray. *Expository Studies in John 13-17: Secrets of the Spirit.* Waco, Tex.: Word Books, 1975.

Stendahl, Brita K. *Søren Kierkegaard.* Boston: Twayne Publishers, 1976.

Swenson, David F. *Something About Kierkegaard.* Minneapolis: Augsburg, 1945.

Taylor, Mark C. *Kierkegaard's Pseudonymous Authorship.* Princeton: Princeton University Press, 1975.

_____. *Journeys to Selfhood: Hegel and Kierkegaard.* Berkeley: University of California Press, 1981.

Thomas, John Heywood. *Subjectivity and Paradox.* New York: Macmillan, 1957.

Thompson, Josiah. *Kierkegaard.* London: Victor Gollancz, 1974.

_____, ed. *Kierkegaard: A Collection of Critical Essays.* Garden City, N.Y.: Doubleday, 1972.

Thomte, Reidar. *Kierkegaard's Philosophy of Religion.* Westport, Conn.: Greenwood Press, 1969.

Thulstrup, Niels, and M. M. Thulstrup, eds. *Bibliotheca Kierkegaardiana.* 14 vols. Copenhagen: C. A. Reitzels Forlag, 1978-1985.

Thulstrup, Niels. *Kierkegaard's Relation to Hegel.* Trans. George L. Stengern. Princeton: Princeton University Press, 1980.

Walsh, W. H. *An Introduction to Philosophy of History.* London: Hutcheson, 1951.

Williamson, Raymond K. *Introduction to Hegel's Philosophy of Religion.* Albany, N.Y.: SUNY Press, 1984.

Wyschogrod, Michael. *Kierkegaard and Heidegger: The Ontology of Existence.* New York: Humanities Press, 1954.

Articles in Books

Adams, Robert Merrihew. "Kierkegaard's Arguments against Objective Reasoning in Religion." *Contemporary Philosophy of Religion.* Eds. Stephen N. Cahn and David Shatz. New York: Oxford University Press, 1982.

Barrett, Lee. "Kierkegaard's 'Anxiety' and the Augustinian Doctrine of Original Sin." *International Kierkegaard Commentary: The Concept of Anxiety.* Ed. Robert L. Perkins. Macon, Ga: Mercer University Press, 1985.

Bormann, Claus v. "Lessing." *Bibliotheca Kierkegaardiana,* Vol. X. Eds. Niels Thulstrup and Marie M. Thulstrup. Copenhagen: C. A. Reitzels Forlag, 1983.

Bredsdorff, Elias. "The Corsair." *Bibliotheca Kierkegaardiana,* XII. Eds. Niels Thulstrup and Marie M. Thulstrup. Copenhagen: C. A. Reitzels Forlag, 1983.

Bruce, F. F. "The History of New Testament Study." *New Testament Interpretation.* Ed. I. H. Marshall. Grand Rapids, Mich: Eerdmans, 1977.

Cavell, Stanley. "Kierkegaard's On Authority and Revelation." *Kierkegaard: A Collection of Critical Essays.* Ed. J. Thompson. New York: Doubleday, 1972.

Chadwick, Henry. "Lessing, Gotthold Ephraim." *Encyclopedia of Philosophy.* Reprint ed., III-IV, 443-446.

Crities, Stephen. "Pseudonymous Authorship as Art and As Act." *Kierkegaard: A Collection of Critical Essays.* Ed. J. Thompson. New York: Doubleday, 1972.

Dunning, Stephen N. "Kierkegaard's Systematic Analysis of Anxiety." *International Kierkegaard Commentary: The Concept of Anxiety.* Ed. Robert L. Perkins. Macon, Ga: Mercer University Press, 1985.

Gill, Jerry. "Kantianism." *Bibliotheca Kierkegaardiana,* Vol. VI. Eds. Niels Thulstrup and Marie M. Thulstrup. Copenhagen: C.A. Reitzels Forlag, 1981.

Glenn, John D., Jr. "The Definition of the Self and the Structure of Kierkegaard's Work." *International Kierkegaard Commentary: Sickness Unto Death.* Ed. Robert L. Perkins. Macon, Ga: Mercer University Press, 1987.

Pailin, David A. "Abraham and Isaac: A Hermeneutical Problem Before Kierkegaard." *Kierkegaard's Fear and Trembling: Critical Appraisals.* Ed. Robert L. Perkins. University of Alabama: University of Alabama Press, 1981.

Pedersen, J. "Kierkegaard's View of Scripture." *Bibliotheca Kierkegaardiana,* Vol II. Eds. Niels Thulstrup and Marie M. Thulstrup. Copenhagen: C. A. Reitzels Forlag, 1978.

"Regina." *Bibliotheca Kierkegaardiana,* Vol. XII. Eds. Niels Thulstrup and Marie M. Thulstrup. Copenhagen: C. A. Reitzels Forlag, 1978.

Schrader, George. "Kant and Kierkegaard On Duty and Inclination." *Kierkegaard: A Collection of Critical Essays.* Ed. J. Thompson. New York: Doubleday, 1972.

Schiorring, J. H. "Martensen." *Bibliotheca Kierkegaardiana,* Vol. X. Eds. Niels Thulstrup and Marie M. Thulstrup. Copenhagen: C. A. Reitzels Forlag, 1983.

Stangerup, Hakom. "His Polemic with the Press." *Bibliotheca Kierkegaardiana,* Vol. XII. Eds. Niels Thulstrup and Marie M. Thulstrup. Copenhagen: C. A. Reitzels Forlag, 1983.

Thulstrup, N. "H. N. Clausen." *Bibliotheca Kierkegaardiana,* Vol. X. Eds. Niels Thulstrup and Marie M. Thulstrup. Copenhagen: C. A. Reitzels Forlag, 1982.

_____. "Mynster." *Bibliotheca Kierkegaardiana,* Vol. IV. Eds. Niels Thulstrup and Marie M. Thulstrup. Copenhagen: C. A. Reitzels Forlag, 1979.

_____. "Theological and Philosophical Studies." *Bibliotheca Kierkegaardiana,* Vol. I. Eds. Niels Thulstrup and Marie M. Thulstrup. Copenhagen: C. A. Reitzels Forlag, 1978.

Tolderlund-Hansen, G. "History of the Danish Church." *The Danish Church.* Ed. Poul Hartling. Trans. S. Mammen. Copenhagen: J. Jorgensen and Co., 1964.

Walsh, Sylvia I. "Forming the Heart: The Role of Love in Kierkegaard's Thought." *The Grammar of the Heart.* Ed. R. H. Bell. New York: Harper and Row, 1988.

Widenmann, R. J., and C. Jorgensen. "His Death." *Bibliotheca Kierkegaardiana,* Vol. XII. Eds. Niels Thulstrup and Marie M. Thulstrup. Copenhagen: C. A. Reitzels Forlag, 1983.

Wilde, Fr.-Eb. "Category." *Bibliotheca Kierkegaardiana,* Vol. III. Eds. Niels Thulstrup and Marie M. Thulstrup. Copenhagen: C. A. Reitzels Forlag, 1980.

Periodicals

Barth, Karl. "A Thank You and a Bow: Kierkegaard's Reveille." *Canadian Journal of Theology,* 11 (1965), 3-7.

_____. "Kierkegaard and the Theologians." *Canadian Journal of Theology,* 13 (1967), 64-67.

Bigelow, Patrick. "Kierkegaard and the Hermeneutical Circle." *Man and World,* 15 (1982), 67-82.

Brookfield, C. M. "What Was Kierkegaard's Task? A Frontier to Be Explored." *Union Seminary Quarterly Review,* 18 (1962), 23-35.

Campbell, Richard. "Lessing's Problem and Kierkegaard's Answer." *Scottish Journal of Philosophy,* 19 (1966), 35-54.

Dunstan, J. Leslie. "The Bible in *Either/Or.*" *Interpretation*, 6 (1952), 310-320.

Duran, Jane. "Kierkegaard's Christian Reflectivity: Its Precursors in the Aesthetic of *Either/Or.*" *International Journal for Philosophy of Religion*, 17 (1985), 131-137.

Edwards, Paul. "Kierkegaard and 'The Truth of Christianity.'" *Philosophy*, 46 (1971), 89-108.

Evans, C. Stephen. "Kierkegaard on Subjective Truth: Is God an Ethical Fiction?" *International Journal for Philosophy of Religion*, 7 (1976), 288-199.

_____. "A Misunderstood Reformer." *Christianity Today* (September 21, 1984), 26-29.

Fishburn, Janet Forsythe. "Søren Kierkegaard, Exegete." *Interpretation*, 39 (1985), 229-245.

Friedman, R. E. "Kant and Kierkegaard: The Limits of Reason and the Cunning of Faith." *International Journal of the Philosophy of Religion*, 19 (1986), 3-22.

Jones, Joe R. "Some Remarks on Authority and Revelation in Kierkegaard." *The Journal of Religion*, July 1977, 232-251.

Gordis, Robert. "Faith of Abraham: A Note on Kierkegaard's Teleological Suspension of the Ethical." *Judaism*, 25 (1976), 414-419.

Green, Ronald M. "Abraham, Isaac, and the Jewish Tradition: An Ethical Reappraisal." *Journal of Religious Ethics*, 10 (1982), 1-21.

Grounds, Vernon C. "Take Another Look at S. K." Review *The Burden of Søren Kierkegaard*, by E. J. Carnell, *Christianity Today* (February 18, 1966), 33.

Hendry, George S. "Theological Evaluation of Hegel." *Scottish Journal of Theology*, 34 (1982), 339-356.

Hustwit, Ronald. "Adler and the Ethical: A Study of Kierkegaard's *On Authority and Revelation.*" *Journal of Religious Studies*, 21 (1985), 331-348.

_____. "More Notes on Kierkegaard's 'Ideal Interpretation,'" *Journal of Religious Studies*, 8 (1980), 12-18.

Kallas, Endel. "Kierkegaard's Understanding of the Bible with Respect to His 'Age'" *Dialogue* 26 (1987), 30-34.

Kellenberger, James. "Kierkegaard, Indirect Communication, and Religious Truth." *International Journal of the Philosophy of Religion*, 8 (1984), 153-160.

McLane, Earl. "Kierkegaard and Subjectivity." *International Journal for Philosophy of Religion*, 8 (1977), 211-232.

Perkins, Robert L. "Hegel and the Secularization of Religion," *The International Journal for Philosophy of Religion*, 1 (1970), 130-146.

_____. "Kierkegaard's Epistemological Preferences," *The Journal of Philosophy of Religion*, 4 (1973), 197-217.

Perry, Edmund. "Was Kierkegaard a Biblical Existentialist?" *The Journal of Philosophy of Religion*, 36 (1956), 17-23.

Poijman, Louis. "Kierkegaard on the Justification of Belief." *International Journal for Philosophy of Religion*, 8 (1977), 75-93.

_____. "The Logic of Subjectivity." *Southern Journal of Philosophy*, 19 (1981), 73-84.

_____. "Kierkegaard on Subjectivity: Two Concepts." *Proceedings of the Southwestern Philosophical Society*, (October, 1982).

Roberts, Robert. "Thinking Subjectively." *International Journal of Philosophy of Religion*, 11 (1980), 71-92.

_____. "Kierkegaard on Becoming an Individual." *Scottish Journal of Theology*, 31 (1978), 133-152.

Schmitt, R. "The Paradox in Kierkegaard's Religiousness A." *Inquiry*, 8 (1965).

Solomon, Robert, "Kierkegaard and Subjective Truth." *Philosophy Today*, 21 (1977), 202-215.

Wolf, Herbert C. "Kierkegaard and the Quest for the Historical Jesus." *Lutheran Quarterly*, 16 (1964). 3-40.

Unpublished Material

Anderson, Raymond Eugene. "Kierkegaard's Theory of Communication." Ph.D. dissertation, University of Minnesota, 1959.

Angell, John. "The Theological Methodology of Søren Kierkegaard." Th.D. dissertation, The Southern Baptist Theological Seminary, 1949.

Boyd, Terrance Malcolm. "Truth and Its Expression: A Study of Søren Kierkegaard's Existence-Communication." Ph.D. dissertation, New York University, 1982.

Buessem, George Everhardt. "Subjectivity and Solopsism in Kierkegaard." Ph.D. dissertation, DePaul University, 1982.

Campbell, Charles Ray. "The Attack from Behind: Irony and Søren Kierkegaard's Dialectic of Communication." Ph.D. dissertation, Syracuse University, 1973.

Campbell-Nelson, John Stanley. "Kierkegaard's Christian Rhetoric." Ph.D. dissertation, School of Theology at Claremont, 1982.

Christopherson, Myrvin Frederick. "Søren Kierkegaard's Dialectic of Communication: An Approach to the Communication of Existential Knowledge." Ph.D. dissertation, Purdue University, 1965.

Early, Fieman Anderson. "The Problem of Religious Knowledge in the Writings of Søren Kierkegaard." Th.D. dissertation, The Southern Baptist Theological Seminary, 1944.

Goold, Patrick Allen. "The Faith of Hidden Inwardness: Theses Possible or Actually Attibutable to Kierkegaard." Ph.D. dissertation, Brown University, 1985.

Gouwens, David Jay. "Kierkegaard's Dialectic of the Imagination." Ph.D. dissertation, Yale University, 1982.

Madden, Myron C. "The Contribution of Søren Kierkegaard to a Christian Psychology." Th.D. dissertation, The Southern Baptist Theological Seminary, 1956.

McKinnon, Alastar. Letter to author. Jan. 27, 1987.

Perkins, Robert L. Letter to author. May 29, 1985.

Salladay, Susan. "A Study of the Nature and Function of Religious Language in Relation to Kierkegaard's Theories of Subjective Truth and Indirect Communication." Ph.D. dissertation, Boston College, 1974.

Seat, Leroy Kay. "The Meaning of 'Paradox': A Study of the Use of the Word 'Paradox' in Contemporary Theological and Philosophical Writings with Special Reference to Søren Kierkegaard." Th.D. dissertation, The Southern Baptist Theological Seminary, 1966.

Twine, Horace Edgar. "Existentialism and Evangelism: A Study of the Thought of Blaise Pascal, Søren Kierkegaard, and Denzil Patrick." Th.M. thesis, The Southern Baptist Theological Seminary, 1955.

Van Roekel, Joseph Gilbert. "Decisive Authorship is the Authorship of Søren Kierkegaard." Th.D. dissertation, The Southern Baptist Theological Seminary, 1953.

Viesland, Jorgen Steen. "Kierkegaard and the Dialectic of Modernism." Ph.D. dissertation, University of Washington, 1982.